**WITHDRAWN
UTSA LIBRARIES**

**UTSA DT LIBRARY RENEWALS 458-2440**
**DATE DUE**

# COMPARATIVE GOVERNANCE REFORM IN ASIA: DEMOCRACY, CORRUPTION, AND GOVERNMENT TRUST

# RESEARCH IN PUBLIC POLICY ANALYSIS AND MANAGEMENT

Series Editor: Lawrence R. Jones

Recent Volumes:

| | |
|---|---|
| Volumes 1–9: | Research in Public Policy Analysis and Management |
| Volume 10: | Public Management: Institutional Renewal for the Twenty-First Century – Edited by Lawrence R. Jones and Fred Thompson |
| Volume 11A & B: | Learning from International Public Management Reform – Edited by Lawrence R Jones, James Guthrie and Peter Steane |
| Volume 12: | The Transformative Power of Dialogue – Edited by Nancy C. Roberts |
| Volume 13: | Strategies for Public Management Reform – Edited by Lawrence R. Jones, Kuno Schedler and Riccardo Mussari |
| Volume 14: | Public Ethics and Governance: Standards and Practices in Comparative Perspective – Edited by Denis Saint-Martin and Fred Thompson |
| Volume 15: | Comparative Public Administration: The Essential Readings – Edited by Eric E. Otenyo and Nancy S. Lind |
| Volume 16: | Cultural Aspects of Public Management Reform – Edited by Kuno Schedler and Isabella Proeller |

RESEARCH IN PUBLIC POLICY ANALYSIS AND
MANAGEMENT   VOLUME 17

# COMPARATIVE GOVERNANCE REFORM IN ASIA: DEMOCRACY, CORRUPTION, AND GOVERNMENT TRUST

EDITED BY

**BIDHYA BOWORNWATHANA**
*Chulalongkorn University, Thailand*

**CLAY WESCOTT**
*Asia Pacific Governance Institute,
Washington, DC, USA*

JAI

United Kingdom – North America – Japan
India – Malaysia – China

JAI Press is an imprint of Emerald Group Publishing Limited
Howard House, Wagon Lane, Bingley BD16 1WA, UK

First edition 2008

Copyright © 2008 Emerald Group Publishing Limited

**Reprints and permission service**
Contact: booksandseries@emeraldinsight.com

No part of this book may be reproduced, stored in a retrieval system, transmitted in any form or by any means electronic, mechanical, photocopying, recording or otherwise without either the prior written permission of the publisher or a licence permitting restricted copying issued in the UK by The Copyright Licensing Agency and in the USA by The Copyright Clearance Center. No responsibility is accepted for the accuracy of information contained in the text, illustrations or advertisements. The opinions expressed in these chapters are not necessarily those of the Editor or the publisher.

**British Library Cataloguing in Publication Data**
A catalogue record for this book is available from the British Library

ISBN: 978-1-84663-996-8
ISSN: 0723-1318 (Series)

Printed and bound in UK by MPG Books Ltd, Bodmin, Cornwall

Awarded in recognition of Emerald's production department's adherence to quality systems and processes when preparing scholarly journals for print

INVESTOR IN PEOPLE

Library
University of Texas
at San Antonio

# CONTENTS

INTRODUCTION
   *Bidhya Bowornwathana and Clay G. Wescott*     *1*

IMPORTING GOVERNANCE INTO THE THAI POLITY: COMPETING HYBRIDS AND REFORM CONSEQUENCES
   *Bidhya Bowornwathana*     *5*

ADMINISTRATIVE REFORM IN HONG KONG: AN INSTITUTIONAL ANALYSIS OF FOOD SAFETY
   *John P. Burns*     *21*

CIVIL SERVICE REFORM IN INDONESIA
   *Prijono Tjiptoherijanto*     *39*

COMBATING CORRUPTION AS A POLITICAL STRATEGY TO REBUILD TRUST AND LEGITIMACY: CAN CHINA LEARN FROM HONG KONG?
   *Anthony B. L. Cheung*     *55*

ANTI-CORRUPTION AGENCIES IN FOUR ASIAN COUNTRIES: A COMPARATIVE ANALYSIS
   *Jon S. T. Quah*     *85*

REGULATORY REFORM AND BUREAUCRACY IN SOUTHEAST ASIA: VARIATIONS AND CONSEQUENCES
   *David S. Jones*     *111*

A PRELIMINARY ASSESSMENT OF PUBLIC
MANAGEMENT REFORM IN TAIWAN'S
LOCAL GOVERNMENT
    *Milan Tung-Wen Sun*      *135*

BUILDING NATIONAL INTEGRITY THROUGH
CORRUPTION ERADICATION IN SOUTH KOREA
    *Pan Suk Kim*      *155*

CORRUPTION AND GOVERNMENT TRUST: A
SURVEY OF URBAN AND RURAL INHABITANTS IN
THE NORTH AND NORTHEAST OF THAILAND
    *Suchitra Punyaratabandhu*      *179*

ASSESSING GOVERNMENT EFFORTS TO (RE)BUILD
TRUST IN GOVERNMENT: CHALLENGES AND
LESSONS LEARNED FROM JAPANESE
EXPERIENCES
    *Masao Kikuchi*      *201*

LINKING ACCOUNTABILITY, CORRUPTION, AND
GOVERNMENT EFFECTIVENESS IN ASIA:
AN EXAMINATION OF WORLD BANK
GOVERNANCE INDICATORS
    *Gene A. Brewer, Yujin Choi and Richard M. Walker*      *227*

ABOUT THE AUTHORS      *247*

# INTRODUCTION

## Bidhya Bowornwathana and Clay G. Wescott

As the 21st century moves ahead, it is increasingly evident that globalization and democratization are strong forces playing crucial roles in shaping public sector transformation around the world. For Asian countries, the key questions are, how should selected reform ideas from other countries be diffused, and which parts of one's traditional government and culture should be retained? A common choice among Asian countries is to replace government with governance. Transforming bureaucracies from government to governance involves the acceptance of certain democratic principles such as accountability, openness, transparency, integrity, corruption-free, and high performance standards (Bowornwathana, 2006, pp. 667–680).

Since Asian countries are highly diverse in terms of wealth, culture, and historical experience, reform tools should be used selectively, and adapted to local conditions (Cheung, 2005, pp. 274–275). Batley and Larbi (2004, pp. 5–6, 29–30) point out some key differences in context between developed and developing countries. First, the pace and nature of reforms in developed countries are designed and carried out by the respective governments, and with the democratic support of their electorates. By contrast, reforms in developing countries are often designed by international agencies, and not fully understood or supported by citizens. In some cases, these reforms may be carried out by bureaucratic and political elites with the intent of preserving their existing interests, although the eventual outcome could be different (Cheung, 2005, pp. 276–277). Secondly, common reform packages designed to address governance challenges in developed countries are being transferred to a highly diverse set of countries, including transition economies, weak capacity and post-conflict states, post-authoritarian democracies, and Confucian meritocracies. Many of these developing countries have much deeper fiscal crises and sharper declines in public service than developed countries, yet programs often used Organization for Economic Co-operation and Development (OECD) country designs as models. Where programs vary, the reason is often more failure to meet negotiated conditions, rather than differences in design. Thirdly, implementation of reforms in developing countries is uneven, with stroke-of-the-pen reforms often moving quickly, while necessary structural changes move slowly or not at all. In addition, chronic institutional weaknesses in many developing countries hinder reform effectiveness.

Successful reformers take these differences in context fully into account in crafting policy, institutional and regulatory changes for their countries.

The chapters in this issue are intended to be of interest to both academics and practitioners. The diversity of the Asian region is well reflected in the 11 chapters which cover a wide range of topics, methodologies, and findings. They were first presented at the Sixth Asian Forum on Public Management on "Comparative Governance Reform in Asia: Democracy, Corruption, and Government Trust" organized by the Department of Public Administration, Chulalongkorn University in Bangkok, Thailand, January 12–13, 2007.

To start with, Bidhya Bowornwathana analyzes how governance is being imported into the Thai polity, resulting in competing hybrids and reform consequences. The next chapter on Hong Kong by John P. Burns traces the evolution of Hong Kong's political and administrative systems from one dominated by its bureaucracy to one dominated by the political executive. He illustrates the impact of the change on the institutional arrangements in one policy domain, food safety. From Indonesia, Prijono Tjiptoherijanto sets out the basics of pay and employment in the Indonesian civil service, the imperative for reform, and some of the challenges being faced. Anthony B. L. Cheung notes that certain aspects of the experience of controlling corruption in colonial Hong Kong may have lessons for China's leadership today, and suggests that if a politically motivated strategy for controlling corruption could be aligned with public expectations for effective action, progress may be possible. Another scholar from Singapore, Jon S. T. Quah, concludes that if political will and the policy context are favorable, the best method for curbing corruption is to establish an independent anti-corruption agency and equip it with adequate powers, personnel, and funding; however, where these conditions are not present, alternative modalities should be considered, and great care should be taken if it is decided to set up such agencies. The next chapter by Professor David S. Jones considers the burdens on business caused by regulatory procedures imposed by bureaucracy in the countries of Southeast Asia, and how the reform of such procedures has varied across region, with a particular focus on certain key business functions. From Taiwan, Milan Tung-Wen Sun attempts to evaluate the results of government reform in Taiwan's local government by focusing on one major question: Have local governments in Taiwan become "smaller and better"? The chapter by Pan Suk Kim reviews the efforts of the South Korean government to develop major anti-corruption infrastructure such as the anti-corruption legislation and the anti-corruption agency. He also discusses the role of civil society in curbing corruption and the international evaluation of the South Korean government's efforts to eradicate corruption. Suchitra Punyaratabandhu investigates citizen attitudes toward control of corruption, their trust in government, and the relationship between trust and corruption in order to determine whether these factors are conducive to governance reform. From Japan, Masao Kikuchi attempts to show the current level of trust in the Japanese government. Government reform efforts to rebuild government trust at the central and local governments are assessed. Lastly, Gene A. Brewer, Yujin Choi, and Richard Walker use World Bank Governance Indicators to investigate government effectiveness in Asia. The key factors considered are: accountability and voice, control of corruption, wealth and income, and the presence of a democratic form of government.

# REFERENCES

Batley, R., & Larbi, G. A. (2004). *Changing role of government the reform of public services in developing countries*. Basingstoke Hampshire, UK: Palgrave Macmillan.

Bowornwathana, B. (2006). Transforming bureaucracies for the 21st century: The new democratic governance paradigm. In: E. E. Otenyo & N. S. Lind (Eds), *Comparative public administration: The essential readings*. Oxford: Elsevier.

Cheung, A. B. L. (2005). The politics of administrative reforms in Asia: Paradigms and legacies, paths and diversities. *Governance, 18*(2), 257–282.

# IMPORTING GOVERNANCE INTO THE THAI POLITY: COMPETING HYBRIDS AND REFORM CONSEQUENCES

Bidhya Bowornwathana

## ABSTRACT

*The import of the idea of "governance" into the Thai polity has resulted in several competing interpretations. The body of knowledge on governance in Thailand is not yet well developed. Chaos and contradictions are characteristics of the field of study. First, the author explains the six interpretations of governance: the new democracy or democratic governance, good governance, the efficiency perspective, the Ten Guiding Principles for the King, the Thaksin system, and the ethical issue interpretation. Second, the author discusses the four reform consequences arisen from the import of governance: the difficulty in determining which is the correct prototype of governance, the problem from cloning deformed hybrids, the confrontation among competing hybrids, and the appropriate level of analysis for the concept of governance.*

## INTRODUCTION

The central argument is that the import of governance paradigms into the Thai polity has generated various competing interpretations of governance. The body of knowledge on governance in Thailand is in a state of chaos. For Thais, there is no clear answer as to what exactly is "governance." Governance means different things to different people. It can also mean different things to the same people in different circumstances. Contradiction appears everywhere.

The chapter is divided into two major parts. First, the author argues that so far, there are six major interpretations of governance in Thailand: the new democracy or democratic governance, good governance, the efficiency perspective, the Ten Guiding Principles for the King, the Thaksin system, and the governance as an ethical issue perspective. The origins, assumptions, and problems of each interpretation are explained. These six interpretations present us with hybrids of governance in Thailand. The second part discusses four reform consequences arisen from the import of governance: the difficulty of determining which prototype of governance is the correct one, the problem from cloning deformed hybrids, the confrontation among competing hybrids, and the appropriate level of analysis for governance.

## COMPETING HYBRIDS FROM DIFFERENT INTERPRETATIONS OF GOVERNANCE

The existence of many interpretations of governance in Thailand meant that there is no agreement as to which interpretation is the most suitable. Each interpretation of governance has produced many hybrids that have their own perspectives or frameworks for understanding governance. Since they are different, these hybrids are in a state of competition. The governance puzzle becomes even more complicated if we consider the fact that we cannot agree on the nature of the prototypes that produce the six interpretations of governance. For example, good governance may mean different things for the World Bank and the Overseas Development Agency (ODA).

It is difficult to pinpoint when exactly "governance" entered the Thai polity. As far as the author can recall, the concept of governance arrived in Thailand during the early 1990s. At that time, leading Thai intellectuals were trying to come up with the Thai equivalent of governance. Several alternatives were suggested, for example, *thammarat* (meaning a just state) and *thammapiban* (meaning governing justly). Governance was not alone, as other words such as globalization and the rebirth of liberal democratic values also became the catchwords of the late 1980s and beginning 1990s. When the new 1997 Constitution was promulgated, governance principles and values were incorporated. At the same time, the Chuan II government at the end of 1990s had also requested the Thailand's Development Research Institute (TDRI) to come up with a blueprint for "good governance" in government. As a member of the TDRI team led by former Prime Minister Anand Panyarachun, the author recall that one day, we agreed to experiment with the word *thammapiban* instead of *thammarat*, and since then this word became to signify good governance in Thailand. Later on, the TDRI blueprint of 1999 would develop into an Order of the Office of the Permanent Secretary of the Office of the Prime Minister of 1999, and eventually into a Royal Decree during the Thaksin I government in 2003.

The author will now explain the six postulated interpretations or prototypes of governance in terms of their sources, characteristics, problems, and implications.

## *First Interpretation: Governance as the New Democracy (Democratic Governance)*

The first interpretation of "governance as the new democracy" or "democratic governance" rests on the principle of citizen power. Citizens are the masters of government. The position of the prime minister is temporal, and whoever assumes such a position does so in the name of the citizen who owns the country. Therefore, there should be strong independent mechanisms acting in the interests of the citizens that monitor the government work. This first interpretation of governance reflects the ideas contained in the suggested theories on governance proposed by scholars such as Rhodes (1996), Peters (1996), and Bowornwathana (2006a). It represents the conventional interpretation of governance as understood by contemporary scholars in public administration. As I have suggested before, governance can be seen as the movement away from the old state-centric model of government to a new democracy called "governance" emphasizing citizen power and the dispersal of power from the center (Bowornwathana, 1997, 2001a).

Democratic governance came into Thailand after a major political crisis in 1992. The People's Uprising which resulted in the 1992 May Bloodshed brought the downfall of General Suchinda's military-authoritarian rule. After the regime change, the belief of many Thais was that Thailand needed a major political reform to prevent democracy from military takeovers and other forms of authoritarian rule. A Peoples' Constitution Drafting Committee was set up to draft a new constitution which was promulgated in 1997. In short, the 1997 Constitution was Thailand's answer to governance. Constitutional reform of 1997 represents the author's big bang or tsunami hypothesis on reform (Bowornwathana, 2005a). New ideas about democratic practices were drawn from the experiences of several foreign countries all over the world. Thai reformers were quick and flexible in borrowing the new ideas and mechanisms emerging from foreign countries. For example, the Freedom of Information Act and the Administrative Procedure Act were passed after observing the experiences of developed countries such as the United States and the United Kingdom; an administrative court system was for the first time set up with the help of the French administrative court model; the constitution court was also for the first time established in Thailand by looking at experiences of developed countries; the ombudsman system was also set up for the first time by emulating the Swedish Ombudsman; the Election Commission was influenced by the experiences of India and the Philippines; the National Human Rights Commission was influenced by ideas from the United Nations and countries such as the United States.

The major characteristics of the new democracy adopted by the 1997 Constitution are as follows. First, accountability, transparency, and open government represent the key principles of the new democracy. Accordingly, the central thrust of the new 1997 Constitution is to design new independent accountability institutions which will play the role of check and balance on the exercise of power by the prime minister and the government executive. These independent accountability mechanisms are: the Election Commission, the Ombudsmen, The National Human Rights Commission, the Constitutional Court, the Administrative Courts, the National Counter Corruption Commission, and the State Audit Commission. The choices of commission members and constitutional court members are made by the Senate. Therefore, it is imperative that senators must be neutral and independent from outsiders. The prime minister and government members must not be allowed to influence the decisions of the senators. Therefore, candidates who are likely to be pro-government should not be appointed to these commissions. Another central theme of the 1997 Constitution is freedom of the press and expression. Newspaper or radio or television broadcasting businesses shall enjoy their liberties to present news and express their opinions under the constitutional restrictions without the mandate of any State agency (Section 41). A person shall enjoy the liberty to express his opinion, make speeches, write, print, publicize, and make expression by other means (Section 39). A person shall enjoy an academic freedom (Section 42). In short, the government can be criticized, and the mass media should be allowed to present news from all sides. The prime minister and government should not dictate and introduce censorship on the mass media.

Second, the new democracy also stresses the importance of corruption abatement. Accountability, transparency, and open government cannot be achieved when the polity is plagued with corruption. A strong counter corruption system must be created. International agencies such as the United Nations, the World Bank, the OECD, the ADB, and Transparency International were in harmony in orchestrating the return of the anti-corruption movement. In this regard, the 1997 Constitution laid down a new counter corruption framework: an independent national counter corruption commission is set up (see Section 297–307); and rules for criminal proceedings against persons holding political positions are specified (see Section 308–311 of the 1997 Constitution). New forms of corruption such as conflicts of interest were not to be tolerated. Fairness and justice in government practices were highlighted.

Third, the new democracy or democratic governance supports the idea of a smaller central government that does less. Local governments, the civil society, communities, and NGOs should be strengthened. Many public services undertaken by the central government should be transferred to others. The central government should no longer act as the core or focal actor of all public policies. In Thailand, the 1997 Constitution has emphasized the necessity to decrease the traditional role of central government by providing more autonomy to the local governments (Section 282–290).

## Second Interpretation: Governance as Good Governance

The second interpretation of "governance as good governance" has its origins from the policies of international organizations, in particular the World Bank and the International Monetary Fund (IMF). The argument goes like this. The reason why developing countries are facing economic and social upheavals is due to the lack of good governance. Bad governance meant that "the manner in which power is exercised in the management of a country's economic and social resources for development," (World Bank, 1994, p. xiv) is not carried out properly. The World Bank identified three distinct aspects of governance: (1) the form of political regimes; (2) the process by which authority is exercised in the management of a country's economic and social resources for development; and (3) the capacity of governments to design, formulate, and implement policies and discharge functions (World Bank, 1994, p. xiv). Thus, bad governance can result from having the wrong political regime, the misuse of authority in the management of the country, and low policy capacity of governments. In this regard, the World Bank has made it as a condition that any Third World or developing country that wants to borrow money from the World Bank must reform its government in line with good governance principles of the World Bank. The usage of good governance is usually confined to developing countries. This explains why the word good governance is rarely used when referring to problems in government of developed countries such as the United Kingdom and the United States.

The 1997 economic crisis of Thailand had bankrupted the Thai government. It was necessary for the Thai government to borrow money from the World Bank and the IMF. In this regard, the Thai government in consultation with the World Bank came up with a plan to reform the Thai bureaucracy. According to the plan, several conditions were laid out. For example, in the first three-year loan of $400 million of Thailand's Public Sector Reform Program of 1999, two tracks, public finance (reforms in expenditure management, tax administration, and fiscal decentralization) and public administration (enhancing the quality and efficiency of service delivery by introducing performance-based human resource management systems, and organizational renewal in selected line ministries) were laid out. In practice, several central agencies such as The Civil Service Commission, the Budget Bureau, the National Economic and Social Development Board, the Finance Ministry, the Office of the Juridical Council came up with their own programs for their share of the World Bank loan.

Good governance was regarded as a necessary condition for the recovery of the Thai economy. The Chuan II government requested the TDRI under the leadership of former Prime Minister Anand Punyarachun, to devise a plan for good governance. The TDRI team came up with a "Proposal for Promoting Good Governance of January 1999." The TDRI proposal contained the following suggestions: (1) the promotion of Thai good governance; (2) the promulgation of Good Governance Act as required by the 1997 Constitution; (3) the resulted-oriented public sector reform covering budgeting reform and personnel reform; (4) the solving of government corruption; and (5) building good corporate governance (TDRI, 1999).

TDRI good governance proposal develop into an Order of the Office of the Prime Minister on "building good governance and society of August 10th, 1999." According to the 1999 Order, good governance consisted of managing and promoting Thai society in line with six principles: (1) legal principle (laws must be up-to-date and fair, accepted by society); (2) merit principle (honesty, sincerity, hard-working, tolerance, discipline); (3) transparency principle (mutual trust, transparency of government agencies, freedom and access of government information by the public, devise process allowing the people to check the accountability of government); (4) participation principle (encourage people's participation in major decisions of the country, public inquiry, public hearing, opinion polls); (5) responsibility principle (awareness of one's duties and rights, sense of social responsibility, concern for country's problems, respect of difference of opinion, and the courage to assume responsibilities from one's action); (6) economy principle (use of resources for maximum return, encourage Thais to economize, produce high quality goods and services that are globally competitive, and maintain sustainable development of natural resources).

In 2003, the Office of the Prime Minister Order on building good governance and society of August 10, 1999 was replaced by the Royal Decree on "the principles and methods of good governance" which was enacted in accordance with the revised Public Administration Act of 2534 B. E. (No.5, 2002) which specified that the government must lay out the principles and methods of good governance. According to the new 2003 Royal Decree, good governance refers to the administration of government that meets the following objectives: (1) government practices that are beneficial to the well-being and happiness of the people, peacefulness and safety of society, and provide maximum benefit to the country; (2) government practices must meet the objectives of the state, which meant that government agencies must devise operative plans ahead with stated goals, missions, performance indicators; (3) government practices must be efficient, substantially contributing to the achievements of missions of the State; (4) streamlining of government work so that government services to the public would become faster and more convenient to the public; (5) the revision of government agency's functions in accordance to the public administration plan, cabinet policies, budget capacity, the worth of missions, and changing conditions; and (6) the evaluation of government work by an independent team in terms of objective accomplishment, client satisfaction, and contribution to mission success.

## Third Interpretation: Governance as an Efficiency Problem

Under the Royal Decree on the principles and methods of good governance of 2003, good governance became bureaucratized under the main responsibility of the newly created Office of the Public Sector Development Commission (*ko po ro*) which split-off from the Office of the Civil Service Commission (*ko po*). Good governance was given a narrower meaning with a clear focus on the efficiency dimension of reform, or the nuts and bolts of public policy. Unfortunately, the efficiency value was chosen at the expense of other values such as accountability, honesty, and flexibility. All of the sudden, actions considered to be good governance are making strategic plans, creating one-stop service centers, and conducting performance evaluation. No longer were actions that directly foster accountability, transparency, and clean government important parts of the 2003 Royal Decree on good governance. Again, the changes in the direction of good governance have added to the confusion regarding the interpretation of the governance concept.

Interpreting governance as an efficiency problem fits well with the new public management (NPM) reforms that occurred in several developed countries such as the United Kingdom and New Zealand (Pollitt & Bouckaert, 2004; Bowornwathana, 2001b; Hood, 1991). NPM refers to the introduction of management techniques from the private sector to the public sector. In this regard, strategic planning, balance scorecard, performance measurement, managing by results are all examples of governance. International agencies such as the World Bank encouraged the Thaksin government to emulate the experiences of countries with NPM reforms.

Like all NPM reforms, interpreting governance as an efficiency problem has several problems (Bowornwathana, 2004b, 2000). First, management tools that are suited for businesses may not work well in government. Second, management tools are only fashions, they come and go. They are not really useful in improving governance. Third, management tools from the business school have tendencies to centralize power in the hands of the prime minister and provide opportunities for domain expansion for the focal central agency in charge of the reform. Fourth, management tools can be expensive and a waste of money, such as hiring expensive consultants. Fifth, management tools burden government officials especially at the line agencies by demanding them to follow the new rules of the game, fill in new bureaucratic forms, and obey the instructions of the central agencies. Sixth, management tools can inject the wrong government culture and values, and disregard important basic values such as government ethics.

### Fourth Interpretation: Governance as the Ten Guiding Principles for the King

To interpret governance as the qualities of a good Thai king may sound weird to foreigners. But if you ask a typical Thai who is unaware of the public administration literature on governance or what governance is, he will answer that the idea of governance or *thammapipan* in Thai, is nothing new. To him, governance refers to Buddhist teachings of the Ten Guiding Principles for a King (*tossapitratchatham*). The Ten Guiding Principles for a King are: giving (dana); self conduct (sila); giving up (paricaga); straightness (ajava); gentleness (maddava); perseverance (tapa); non-anger (akkodha); not causing injury (avihimsa); endurance or patience (khanti); and not going wrong (avirodhana).

The problem with interpreting governance as the Ten Guiding Principles for the King is that governance is actually a recent word used to explain a phenomenon under a democratic regime where democratic values such as citizen power and government accountability and transparency are prioritized. Meanwhile, the Ten Guiding Principles for the King have their origins in a thousand-year-long Thai tradition of rule by absolute monarchy. Another problem is that governance is a multi-level concept, while the Ten Guiding Principles for the King is an individual level of analysis. Governance has structural implications as well as individual ones. Nevertheless, thinking of governance in terms of the Ten Guiding Principles for the King finds its way among many Thais because of its nationalistic flavor and simplicity.

### Fifth Interpretation: Governance as the Thaksin System (rabop taksin)

After five years in power, Prime Minister Thaksin Sinawatra developed a government system which came to be called the Thaksin system (*rabop taksin*) by several Thais. When Prime Minister Thaksin and his Thai Rak Thai (TRT) Party came into power, government reform was undertaken with the aim of centralization power in the hands of the prime minister: a phenomenon the author called *prime ministerialization* (Bowornwathana, 2004a). The country is like a company that belongs to the prime minister. The country must be run like a company by using the strong CEO model that allows the super CEO to centralize power. Under the Thaksin system, the aim of government is the complete centralization of power in the hands of the prime minister. Everything must be put under strict control of the prime minister: the bureaucracy; state enterprises; independent organizations in charge of ensuring government accountability such as the constitutional court, the national counter corruption, the election commission; the senate; the police; the judiciary system; and parliament. For example, the Thaksin system supported the idea of a one-party parliament with no opposition. Another rule of the Thaksin system is that all provincial administration and local governments had to be under the super CEO prime minister. The prime minister must be able to control all municipalities, provincial administrative organizations, and sub-district (*tambon*) administrative organizations, and village headmen.

Absolute control by the prime minister was achieved by putting prime minister's men into all these key positions. The mass media, televisions, newspapers, radios must serve the prime minister. Criticism against the prime minister and government was not tolerated. Press censorship was strictly practiced. If possible, the mass media had to be put under the ownership of the prime minister and his men. The role of civil society and NGOs was minimized. To ensure compliance, all means were used: payment, patron–client networks, position promises, verbal and physical threats, taxation inspection, harassment by the mafia and the police. Potential competitors such as other political parties, the opposition, and business enemies must be eliminated.

One may wonder why it is so important for the Thaksin system to have a government with such an authoritarian power in the hands of the Prime Minister (Bowornwathana, 2004c, 2006c). According to the Thaksin system, government must serve business interests of government politicians. The more the control the prime minister has over the government, the better government can serve the business interests of the prime minister. Government, in this regard, is like a big branch of a big company. Another branch consists of companies in the business world owned by the prime minister, cabinet members, and politicians. Government and business conglomerates must complement one another. Government assists the business world so that more profit could be made. Higher profit enables the prime minister to use profit money to strengthen control of government.

If one understands the Thaksin system, one should not be surprised to see that conflicts of interest, policy corruption, and double standards were widely practiced by the Thaksin government (Bowornwathana, 2006b, 2005b, 2005c). Some examples are given below. The government runs THAI International, but Thaksin's family entered airlines business by launching Air Asia to compete with THAI. Government hospitals were forced to subsidize the government 30 baht health care populist policy, while the Thaksin's family took over several middle-size hospitals. Privatization of Thailand's Petroleum Authority (PTT) gave the government politicians the privilege to buy the stocks at low price and reap big gains from the increase in stock prices later. Favorable government polices had enabled the Thaksin family to increase the value of their Shin Corp. stocks and make huge profit from the sale of Shin Corp. to Singapore's government-owned company, Temasek.

One may even wonder more how an authoritarian system such as the Thaksin system can be classified as one interpretation of governance in Thailand? Throughout the years, Prime Minister Thaksin used government propaganda especially television and radio channels to convince Thais that his strong leader model is working in the interests of the people. Populist policies were brought in to please the voters. Claims of political legitimacy were made by using the number of votes (19 million) his TRT Party received during the 2005 elections. From a business point of view, Thaksin became the marketing brand. Everything that is Thaksin was deemed to be good. So the Thaksin system is one form of governance, and governance becomes a political tool of the Thaksin government. However, for opponents of the Thaksin government who prefer the democratic governance version of governance, the Thaksin system is unacceptable because it is completely authoritarian.

### Sixth Interpretation: Governance as an Ethical Issue

Former Prime Minister Thaksin had been criticized by many Thais as a prime minister who does not practice good governance because of widespread nepotism and corruption. The Thaksin system was seen as an instrument of the former prime minister to practice bad governance. Increasingly, the word governance has been used to refer to an ideal government leader who adheres to high ethical standards of behavior. The President of the Privy Council, former Prime Minister General Prem Tinsulanond had given several public lectures conveying the message that governance is an ethical issue. "Corruption" became a major reason why the military staged a coup and overthrew the Thaksin government in September 11, 2006. Because of the political events, the concept of governance was narrowed down to mean the ethics or virtues of the individual leader. A leader with good governance became a person who is honest and corruption-free.

This latest interpretation of governance is still in its formative stage. Confusion arises when one tries to pinpoint what exactly is an honest and corruption-free leader? Many questions need to be clarified. Is a devout Buddhist a good governance person? Is a leader who proclaims himself to follow the King's principles of self-sufficient life-style practicing good governance? Can a military dictator who claims not to practice corruption be called a good governance leader?

## REFORM CONSEQUENCES OF COMPETING HYBRIDS

"Chaos" is a good word to describe the major consequence of the reform diffusion process of governance in Thailand. Everyone is to be blamed for the confusion: Thai governments (such as the Anand, Chuan, Banharn, Chavalit, and Thaksin governments); international organizations (such as the World Bank, UN, ADB, OECD); foreign governments (such as the United Kingdom and the United States governments); Western and Thai scholars; consultant companies; the mass media; the Internet; and social leaders. These persons and organizations have their own interpretations of governance. Even among political scientists who specialize in different subfields such as public administration, international relations, and comparative politics, the word governance can have different interpretations (Kjaer, 2004). As a result, if you ask a Thai government official these days about the meaning of governance, he will come up with at least a hundred indicators.

Such a confusion arisen from the reform process of governance comes from the ignorance of Thais about the complexity of the international body of knowledge on governance. The fact that there are several interpretations of governance by international scholar also added to the complication. Since governance meant several things, it was important that we should be able to rank the priorities of the dimensions of the governance concept. For example, is accountability more important than low corruption, downsizing, or fairness? What is the most important indicator of governance? These questions remain unanswered.

The existence of various interpretations of governance has several implications. First, the six interpretations of governance produce competing and contradictory governance reform hybrids. If the idea of governance has so many meanings, then, is governance still a useful concept? The author believes that the concept of governance can be made meaningful only when we accept the idea that, though governance can mean many things to many people, the way to handle the concept is to pick one singularly important characteristic of governance. To the author, the interpretation of governance as the new democracy, or democratic governance, makes a lot of sense. Governance should above all guarantee the independence of independently accountable organizations that check and monitor the use of government authority by the prime minister.

If accountability is the most important dimension of democratic governance, the implications toward other interpretations of governance are as follows: The good governance interpretation has several characteristics that resemble the democratic governance perspective such as concern for accountability and transparency. The efficiency perspective of governance is rather far from democratic governance. The Ten Guiding Principles for the King are rather out of place. The Thaksin system is a contradiction to the democratic governance because it is authoritarian in nature. The ethical interpretation of governance does not distinguish between an honest authoritarian from an honest elected leader. Democratic governance requires the regime to be democratic in nature.

Now, suppose we choose other interpretations of governance as the guiding perspective – what then happens? If governance is seen as good governance, then the democratic governance, the efficiency approach, the Ten Guiding Principles for the King, the Thaksin system, and the ethical perspectives are rather irrelevant. If governance takes the efficiency perspective, then, the democratic governance, the Ten Guiding Principles for the King, good governance, the Thaksin system, and the ethical perspectives are eliminated. And, if governance is defined as the Thaksin system, then the remaining five perspectives become irrelevant.

Second, the confusion involved in the numerous interpretations of governance has resulted in bad or deformed hybrids of governance. Of course, which one is a good hybrid or a bad hybrid is a subjective matter. Assuming that democracy is preferred over authoritarian rule, the best interpretation of governance is the new democracy or democratic governance. Based on such an assumption, the unacceptable interpretations of governance that produce deformed hybrids are the Thaksin system, the Ten Guiding Principles for the King, and the efficiency perspective. The Thaksin system perspective is the opposite of democratic rule. The Ten Guiding Principles for the King are suitable for an absolute monarchy environment. The efficiency perspective serves the political boss, and therefore can be anti-democracy if the prime minister becomes a tyrant. Only the good governance perspective that emphasizes the accountability and transparency aspects of governance has the capacity to produce good hybrids.

Third, another interesting consequence of the existence of many competing governance hybrids is that it can lead to serious confrontation between persons with different opinions. This is exactly what happened in Thailand between anti-Thaksin and pro-Thaksin groups. The former believes that Prime Minister Thaksin is not following the democratic governance paradigm. To them, Thaksin's style of governance is authoritarian. Meanwhile, the latter believes that Thaksin has his own style of governance. Another example is when those who adhere to the governance as efficiency perspective are in conflict with those who represent the democratic governance perspective. For advocates of the democratic governance, management efficiency is a far less important than accountability and honesty.

Fourth, a possible solution to the problem of competing hybrids may open up once we consider the issue of levels of analysis. There are three levels of analysis: macro, meso, and micro (African Development Bank, 1993). The author believes that the concept of governance is a macro level concept since it deals with regime analysis. Thus, the new democracy or democratic governance is the best interpretation. Good governance, the efficiency perspective, and the Thaksin management style are meso or middle level analysis perspective. They can easily lead us to see trees instead of the forest. The qualities of a Good King are micro level, and can only render our focus even narrower.

## CONCLUSION

The author has argued that the import of governance into the Thai polity has created numerous hybrids of governance. Six interpretations of governance in Thailand are: the new democracy or democratic governance, good governance, the efficiency perspective, the Ten Guiding Principles for the King, the Thaksin system, and the ethical interpretation. Each interpretation of governance has its own origins, assumptions, strengths, and weaknesses. At the end, reform consequences from the competing hybrids are discussed. Future research should focus on whether other countries have shared similar or different experiences when importing governance into their polities.

## REFERENCES

African Development Bank. (1993). *Governance and development in Africa: Issues and the role of the African development bank and other multilateral organizations.* Abidjan: Cote d'Ivoire.

Bowornwathana, B. (1997). The governance of the Bangkok metropolitan administration: The old system, the new city, and future governance. In: J. S. Edralin (Ed.), *Local governance and local economic development: A new role of Asian cities* (pp. 87–114). Nagoya: United Nations Centre for Regional Development.

Bowornwathana, B. (2000). Governance reform in Thailand: Questionable assumptions, uncertain outcomes. *Governance: An International Journal of Policy, Administration and Institutions, 13*(3, July), 1–2.

Bowornwathana, B. (2001a). The politics of governance reform in Thailand. In: A. Farazmand (Ed.), *Handbook of comparative and development public administration* (2nd ed., pp. 421–443). New York: Marcel Dekker.

Bowornwathana, B. (2001b). *Administrative reform abroad: The United States, the United Kingdom, France, New Zealand, Japan, and Sweden.* Bangkok: Office of the Administrative Reform Commission, the Royal Thai Government. (In Thai).

Bowornwathana, B. (2004a). Thaksin's model of government reform: Prime ministerialisation through 'A Country is My Company' approach. *Asian Journal of Political Science, 12*(1), 133–151.

Bowornwathana, B. (2004b). Putting new public management to good use: Autonomous public organizations in Thailand. In: C. Pollitt & C. Talbot (Eds), *Unbundled government: A critical analysis of global trend in agencies, quangos and contractualisation.* London: Routledge, Taylor and Francis Group.

Bowornwathana, B. (2004c). *Government reform under Thaksin: The return of the authoritarian perspective.* A country case report presented at the Regional Forum on Reinventing Government for East and Southeast Asia organized by the Division for Public Administration and Development Management, the United Nations Department of Economic and Social Affairs (UNDESA), Penang, Malaysia, 21–23 August, 2004.

Bowornwathana, B. (2005a). Administrative reform and tidal waves from regime shifts: Tsunamis in Thailand's political and administrative history. *The Asian Pacific Journal of Public Administration, 27*(1), 37–52.

Bowornwathana, B. (2005b). State capture, conflict of interest, business empires and the super patron: Comparison of big businessman Thaksin and Berlusconi in power. Paper presented at the IX IRSPM (International Research Symposium on Public Management), Bocconi University, Milan, Italy, 6–8 April, 2005.

Bowornwathana, B. (2005c). Dynamics and effectiveness of the NCC Commission and the new counter corruption network in Thailand: The story of the struggling tiger. Paper presented at the National University of Singapore's Centennial Conference on Asian Horizons: Cities, States and Societies, The National University of Singapore, Singapore, 1–3 August, 2005.

Bowornwathana, B. (2006a). Transforming bureaucracies for the twenty-first century: The new democratic governance paradigm. In: E. Otengo & N. Lind (Eds), *Comparative public administration: The essential readings.* Oxford: Elsevier.

Bowornwathana, B. (2006b). Big businessmen at the helm: The politics of conflicts of interest in Thailand. In: J. S. T. Quah (Ed.), *Corruption and accountability in Asian Pacific countries.* Singapore: Marshall Cavendish International.

Bowornwathana, B. (2006c). Autonomisation of the Thai state: Some observations. *Public Administration and Development, 26*(1), 27–34.

Hood, C. (1991). A public management for all seasons. *Public Administration, 69*(1), 3–19.

Kjaer, A. M. (2004). *Governance*. MA: The Polity Press.
Peters, B. G. (1996). *The future of governing: Four emerging models*. Kansas: University Press of Kansas.
Pollitt, C., & Bouckaert, G. (2004). *Public management reform: A comparative analysis*. Oxford: Oxford University Press.
Rhodes, R. W. A. (1996). The new governance: Governing without government. *Political Studies, 44*(4), 652–668.
TDRI. (1999). *Proposal for the promotion of Thai thammapiban*. TDRI: January.
World Bank. (1994). *Governance: The World Bank's experience*. Washington, DC: World Bank.

# ADMINISTRATIVE REFORM IN HONG KONG: AN INSTITUTIONAL ANALYSIS OF FOOD SAFETY☆

John P. Burns

## ABSTRACT

*In this chapter I trace the evolution of Hong Kong's political and administrative systems from one dominated by the bureaucracy to one dominated by the political executive. The change has had profound consequences for governance arrangements in Hong Kong and on reform capacity. I illustrate the impact of the change on the institutional arrangements in one policy domain, food safety.*

## INTRODUCTION

As they make policy on administrative reform, political executives operate within discrete political–administrative traditions that influence their calculations of how through reform to maximize political support. The traditions range on a continuum from those where politicians dominate

---

☆ I am grateful for the support of the Hong Kong Research Grants Council in the preparation of this paper.

administrators (e.g., the UK) to those where administrators are relatively autonomous from politicians (e.g., Germany or Japan) (Knill, 1999). These relationships help to determine reform capacities: strong political executives have better capacity to impose administrative reforms. The traditions are also largely path-dependent (Peters, 1999) and they influence the institutional choices of the political executive. Conversely, the institutional choices of the political executive also influence political–administrative tradition: the process is an iterative one. Cases of states changing from one tradition to another in a relatively short period of time are rare. Yet, this is exactly what has happened in Hong Kong. As a result of regime change, the political executive in Hong Kong has improved capacity to impose administrative reform.

I trace the evolution of Hong Kong from a system dominated by the bureaucracy to one dominated by the political executive. This change has had profound consequences for governance arrangements in Hong Kong and on reform capacity. I illustrate the impact of the change on the institutional arrangements in one policy domain, food safety. I draw on official documents, especially Legislative Council papers, other government documents, depositions and petitions submitted by trade representatives, official Hong Kong and mainland websites, and a series of interviews carried out with Hong Kong government officials in August 2006.[1]

## THEORETICAL CONSIDERATIONS

This chapter draws on two theoretical perspectives, historical and rational choice institutionalism. According to historical institutionalism public organizations are path-dependent – historical traditions and informal norms are important for understanding organization reforms. In order to understand contemporary institutions we need to study their political and policy histories. Once governments make their initial institutional choices, the patterns created will persist, unless there is some force sufficient to overcome the inertia created at the inception of the program (Peters, 1999).

Path dependency helps to explain patterns of relationships between politicians and administrators in various political systems. According to Knill (1999) we can explain reform capacities in terms of the relative power relationships between politicians and administrators. In some systems, such as the United Kingdom, strong political executives dominate administrators and are able to impose administrative reforms on government agencies relatively successfully. In other systems, such as Germany or Japan, strong bureaucracies have dominated weak politicians. In these systems bureaucrats are able to veto, significantly modify, or indefinitely delay administrative reforms. An historical institutionalist approach would lead us to expect that types of relationships between politicians and administrators are relatively stable. Yet I also understand that while institutions are enduring, they are also capable of adapting, for example, to the problems that they have created. Critical institutional events, during which a variety of internal or external forces come together, can alter institutional paths. One such event was the regime change that marked the transfer of sovereignty over Hong Kong to China in 1997. A result of this shock, was to move Hong Kong from a system dominated by administrators to one dominated by politicians. In this chapter I illustrate the impact of this change on institutions and administrative behavior by examining the case of food safety.

Historical institutionalism has relatively little to say about institutional design (Peters, 1999). To remedy this problem I draw on the literature of institutional choice from the perspective of transactions costs analysis (Horn, 1995; Williamson, 1999). According to this perspective politicians have a choice of institutions to deliver public services. Generally they choose the institutional arrangements that reduce four kinds of transactions costs including (1) decision-making costs (which implies that they prefer vague solutions if beneficiaries can readily participate in administrative rulemaking ex post); (2) commitment problems, such as the possibility that politicians in the future may undo the policy or institutional choice thus threatening support for politicians; (3) uncertainty costs, the risks associated with complying with government policies or attempting to influence them ex post; and (4) agency problems, that is the problem that the agency will fail to implement the policy as politicians intended due to information asymmetry and/or conflicts of interest between the principal (politicians) and the agent (administrators). This perspective assumes bounded rationality, methodological individualism, and that politicians are concerned to please their constituents.

Combining these two perspectives I explain the changing institutional choice of the political executive in Hong Kong as it moved from a position of weakness to strength vis-à-vis the administration. Combining the two perspectives improves the robustness of the explanation.

## THE CASE OF HONG KONG

The case of Hong Kong demonstrates the utility of combining historical and rational choice institutionalism. Colonial Hong Kong preferred autonomous governance arrangements that could help to address the political executive's legitimacy problems. With the transfer of sovereignty in 1997, the political executive sought to gain political control over the up-to-then bureaucratic state as it addressed new legitimacy problems. Strengthening the political executive was accomplished over time from 1997 to 2002 when the Principal Official Accountability System (POAS) was introduced (see later).

## The Administrative (Colonial) State

The high colonial state (the 1970s and early 1980s) was characterized by bureaucratic rule (Lau, 1982; Scott, 1989, 2005; Miners, 1998). First, all official positions in the colonial government, except the Governor who was appointed by the UK government, were held by civil servants. Civil servants made policy, sold it to the public, and then implemented it. The political executive in this set up was confined to the Governor and his advisors. Second, governors generally were appointed from among British Foreign Office officials and arrived in Hong Kong with relatively little administrative experience, although some may have served briefly as advisors to previous governors. No governor came to the position with expertise in Hong Kong's education, social welfare, housing, transport, or other sectors. Moreover, they brought with them virtually no staff of their own. Accordingly they were heavily dependent on the civil service for policy. This meant that in policy terms, administrators dominated the political executive in all areas, except managing relations with the UK and China. Third, all formal power was centralized in the office of the Governor who was advised by an appointed (until 1991) legislature (the Legislative Council). Although the Legislative Council approved the budget, because of its formally weak (advisory) position, the administration had a high degree of budgetary autonomy. Power over the budget was in practice exercised within the administration by the Financial Secretary, himself usually a career civil servant. This does not mean that bureaus always obtained what they wanted (they did not), but it does mean that the political executive exercised only weak control over the budget. This state of affairs was aided by Hong Kong's huge and relatively consistent budget surpluses. In Knill's (1999) terms, then, the administration dominated the political executive and was able to shape administrative reform to suit its interests. Fourth, the colonial state faced continuous legitimacy problems (Scott, 1989). These were addressed, but not overcome, by cooptation of the local elite into various advisory positions and elected local councils, on the one hand, and by adopting policies that lead to rapid economic growth, which provided some kind of performance-based legitimacy, on the other.

The autonomy enjoyed by Hong Kong's administration was reflected in its approach to public health and food safety. Hong Kong's public health function came into existence in 1843 principally to serve the needs of the government, the British military, the police, and prisoners. Only gradually did it extend its reach to the community. The Medical Department was set up in 1872 and by 1890 included a 'government analyst' whose duties included determining food and water quality (Ho, 2004, p. 169). From at least this period food safety came under the purview of relatively autonomous bureau-type agencies,[2] especially the Department of Health (DH) which took up responsibility for the safety of all imported (that is virtually all) food in Hong Kong.

In 1883 administrators put sanitation (including the cleanliness of wet markets which sold raw, unprocessed food) under the control of a relatively independent Sanitation Board (Ho, 2004). Conflict between influential members of the public and civil servants over whether a more tightly controlled Department of Sanitation, staffed by civil servants, or a more independent Sanitation Board should manage the cleanliness of food markets apparently dates from at least the 1890s (see Lau, 2002). The government preferred the Sanitation Board, but was eventually persuaded to set up a Sanitation Department in 1908. The colonial government's view was that it should be as little involved in food safety and sanitation as possible.

Hong Kong's status as a city also contributed to the decision to put food safety in the public health domain. Being almost completely urbanized, Hong Kong had little local production of agricultural and fishery products (they accounted for only 0.1% of GDP in 2005) and has imported virtually all (95%) of its food since World War II. Accordingly, in Hong Kong the domestic lobby for agriculture and fisheries is small and relatively insignificant. Pressure to frame food safety as an adjunct of agriculture, requiring protection and development for an export market, was almost completely absent in Hong Kong. Indeed a department of agriculture was set up only in 1946 (prior to that time administrators established agencies such as the Government Gardens Department). This sets Hong Kong apart from many places where food safety policy is dominated by agricultural bureaucracies and their producer clients (Ansell & Vogel, 2006; Toke, 2004; Nestle, 2003).

The colonial state's approach to governance (defined here as a preference for autonomous agencies) and its need for legitimacy lead to highly fragmented institutional arrangements including those for food safety. The colonial political executive was not as constrained as post-1997 politicians by the need to please beneficiaries. Still, pleasing beneficiaries (to gain and maintain legitimacy) was not unimportant given the colonial state's legitimacy deficit. The colonial political executive chose autonomous arrangements to manage food safety because of its governance ideology, on the one hand, and to reduce transactions costs, on the other.

According to the transactions cost approach, politicians seek to reduce their decision-making costs by articulating vague policy if they can ensure beneficiaries rights to participate in administrative rule making ex post (Horn, 1995). In a typical regulatory situation such as food safety, beneficiaries (the public) are a large and diffuse group, and accordingly have high participation costs. Those bearing the burden of regulation (for example, in this case importers, wholesalers, retailers, and restaurateurs) are usually a small relatively cohesive group, whose participation costs are low. To ensure that beneficiaries are protected, the political executive will choose more autonomous arrangements, which is exactly what it did in Hong Kong. The political executive's concern that future politicians might undo these arrangements to the detriment of the public also encouraged a more autonomous solution. The political executive sought to reduce agency problems by relying on bureaus, which in principle were characterized by civil service type incentives, including performance-based promotion (Horn, 1995).

At its apogee, the colonial state's political executive chose to manage food safety and environmental hygiene through 11 different departments and agencies (Health and Welfare Bureau, 1998). These included two elected municipal councils, set up to address legitimacy problems, which each had authority to make different by-laws with different standards applicable in their respective (urban and rural) jurisdictions; three policy bureaus, three agencies (departments), and the Hospital Authority. At that time key aspects of food safety were the domain of the DH under the Health and Welfare Bureau. The DH operated mainly through a food surveillance system, testing samples of imported food and spot checks on retailers and restaurants. The Agriculture and Fisheries Department (AFD), where veterinarians were located, managed wholesale markets and supervised the inspection of imported live animals. AFD was managed by the Economic Services Bureau, reflecting its trade facilitation and agriculture and fisheries development functions. The Urban Services and Rural Services departments, both reporting to different elected municipal councils, focused on restaurant licensing and environmental hygiene including the cleanliness of food markets.

These arrangements characterized above all by a high degree of autonomy from the political executive, accorded to colonial governance ideology, on the one hand, and addressed (weakly) the government's legitimacy problems through elected local councils, on the other. They had consequences for policy making and implementation, however.

*Participation Rights*
The beneficiaries of food safety policy (the general public) are a diffuse group with high participation costs. Those burdened by regulation (importers, wholesalers, retailers, and restaurateurs) are relatively well organized and have lower participation costs. To protect the interests of beneficiaries, the colonial political executive chose more autonomous institutional arrangements, which are more difficult for the regulated to influence. In other political systems, more autonomous regulatory commissions are typical choices (Horn, 1995). In Hong Kong, the colonial political executive chose to spread responsibility of food safety among a large number of different agencies which made participation by 'the trade' more difficult. It also addressed the commitment problem by making reform of the arrangements more difficult. Indeed, it was only with the relatively drastic change of regime that reform became possible.

In Hong Kong stakeholders, such as local producers, importers, wholesalers, retailers, and restaurateurs, collectively known as 'the trade,' have formed scores of groups to lobby the government on food safety regulatory issues.

Given their lack of access and the decentralization of the food safety regime, 'the trade' has focused mostly on influencing government policy through its over-representation in the local legislature. Hong Kong's Legislative Council, resembling a bicameral system, is divided equally into two types of constituencies: 30 general constituencies (elected by universal suffrage and representing the public) and 30 functional constituencies (elected by interest groups that represent business and 'the trade'). Among the functional constituencies are Legislative Councilors who speak for food safety in one way or another, such as agriculture and fisheries, catering, wholesale and retail, commerce, and import and export. The trade is represented on the Legislative Council's Panel on Food Safety and Environmental Hygiene, which monitors the government's food safety policy and its implementation. Seven of the 10 members of the panel come from functional constituencies, including agriculture and fisheries, catering, and wholesale and retail, which ensures that the trade has significant representation in any attempts by the government to change food safety law or regulation.

According to Hong Kong's constitution no bill may be passed by the Legislative Council unless a majority of delegates representing both types of constituencies assent to it. This provision gives 'the trade' some influence in the legislature to modify or resist food safety regulation.

*Uncertainty Risks*

Uncertainty over policy preferences and the impact they will have on beneficiaries is a cost to the political executive which it seeks to reduce (Horn, 1995). The colonial state reduced uncertainty costs by operating in a relatively closed environment. Policy was made and implemented by the civil service, with relatively little participation from even attentive publics, such as the trade. The nature of the colonial civil service also served to reduce uncertainty costs. Policy was made by a small group of elite administrative officers, who shared a common background (social class and education), and a common vision of their place in the Hong Kong political system and the role of the state in society. Elite administrative officers met regularly in the Policy Committee, chaired by the Chief Secretary, to make policy. They all knew each other, participated in key decisions, and were bound by common understandings. The administrative officer grade structure itself acted as a coordinating mechanism that reduced uncertainty (Lam, 2005).

*Agency Problems*

Agency problems arise when the agent (the administration in this case) fails to implement the policies of the principal (the political executive [the Chief Executive in this case]). Agency problems result from two general types of structural features of hierarchy, namely, information asymmetry and conflicts of interest (Horn, 1995; Moe, 1984; Williamson, 1999). Both featured prominently in the colonial set up.

The extreme decentralization of Hong Kong's food safety regime meant that no focal point existed to steer and coordinate policy in food safety. No policy bureau had responsibility for the municipal councils and their executive agencies (the Urban Services Department and the Regional Service Department) and the Director of Health's power to make binding decisions on food safety was considerably limited. The fragmented arrangements also undermined the ability of the administration to address large-scale food safety emergencies quickly. In 1997, 2001, and 2002, for example, Hong Kong was the site of a deadly outbreak of avian flu in humans. In these cases authorities established links between public health and the way food was handled. The crises also revealed breakdown in communications that went way beyond the usual information asymmetries that characterize typical government bureaucracies. A lack of communication within agencies in Hong Kong (e.g., the DH, AFD, and the Hospital Authority) and between the Hong Kong and mainland governments was especially damaging.

Conflicts of interest also characterized the decentralized arrangements. As the Permanent Secretary for the Health Welfare and Food pointed out, reflecting on the differences between the current and colonial (in practice, pre-2000) situation: 'If two bureaus [are involved] I have to get another Permanent Secretary to work with me. She may have a different agenda in terms of priority. When it comes to resource allocation we have to spend some time to fight as to who is going to pay for what ... So, from my perspective, now [under the reformed arrangements] I'm the Permanent Secretary for food safety and I can call the shots.' Policy coordination in particular suffered under the pre-2000 arrangements. The different missions of the various policy secretaries, focused on health, economic development, and planning, the environment and lands, undoubtedly undermined effective coordination of food safety policy. Indeed, these arrangements pushed policy coordination up to the Chief Secretary, who was preoccupied with other responsibilities resulting in delay and neglect.

Still, under these fragmented arrangements ties evolved linking food safety agencies at an operational level. Coordination was facilitated through personnel placements (seconding specialized staff from department to department such as, health inspectors from the Urban Services Department to the DH) and by developing standard operating procedures (SOP) that required the involvement of staff of another department, such as the SOP that required doctors in the DH investigating food poisoning cases in restaurants to turn their findings over to the restaurant licensing authorities in the Urban Services Department for action.

Interdepartmental working committees and task forces were used to handle crises, such as the 1997 avian flu outbreak (Poon, 2003). Initially led by the DH because officials viewed avian flu as primarily a health risk, the Urban Services Department was brought in to clean up Hong Kong's wet markets and the AFD to inspect local chicken farms, and then on December 29, 1997 to slaughter all (1.5 million) chickens in Hong Kong, initially planned as a 24 h operation. Only after strong criticism from the legislature, the public, and the trade that the government had acted too slowly did the Chief Executive appoint the Chief Secretary to coordinate follow-up action (Poon, 2003).

Multiple levels of agency problems also characterized the relationship between Hong Kong and central and local mainland bureaucracies, on the one hand, and between the central government bureaucracies and local government agencies on the mainland, on the other. To stop the import of live chickens, for example, the government had to seek the cooperation of the Ministry of Foreign Relations and Trade (later Commerce) in Beijing which controlled livestock quotas. The Ministry, however, did not have information on the incidence of avian flu on mainland farms (this was held by the Ministry of Agriculture). The Ministry of Agriculture in turn was dependent on local agriculture bureaus to report this information.

The colonial political executive chose relatively autonomous arrangements for the management of food safety. If uncertainties were low, so too were participation rights for the private sector (the trade). A result of this institutional choice was relatively high agency costs.

### The Political State

Regime change fundamentally altered the relationship between politicians and administrators in Hong Kong with the balance of power shifting toward politicians. Strengthening the political executive culminated in the introduction of the POAS in 2002 under which fixed-tenure politicians replaced career civil servants as policy secretaries. This move, which dramatically increased the number of politicians, established an entirely new relationship between politicians and administrators. As part of the POAS, the political executive centralized policy making in the hands of the appointed politicians. For the political executive regime change substituted one kind of legitimacy problem with another. Hong Kong's new status as a special administrative region of China addressed the problem of rule imposed through the coercive force of an alien state, but it did not address the problem of the people being disenfranchised. According to the constitution, the central government appoints the Hong Kong government in a process that excludes virtually all citizens in Hong Kong.[3] The shift of power from administrators to politicians was facilitated by the series of crises that engulfed the public health and food safety domains (discussed earlier).

Historical institutionalism is able to explain change in terms of adaptation and learning (Peters, 1999). Incremental adjustment to crises characterized the Hong Kong response as well. By 1998 politicians saw the need for structural changes to strengthen leadership in the coordination of food safety policy and to ensure efficient coordination and prompt response to food safety crises (Constitutional Affairs Bureau, 1998).

To address agency problems the political executive replaced the fragmented and autonomous arrangements with a single more tightly controlled agency. The move sought to address agency problems by centralizing authority over food safety in a single department, (the Food Safety Center within) the Food and Environmental Hygiene Department (FEHD) which was formed from pieces of the DH, the (renamed) Agricultural, Fisheries and Conservation Department (AFCD), and the Urban Services and Rural Services departments. A single policy secretary working with one permanent secretary was put in charge of most of the relevant food safety departments FEHD, AFCD, and Health, and the confused structure of elected municipal councils and urban and rural services departments was abolished. This arrangement provided for a lead department (FEHD) and a single source of policy.

A consequence of these changes, however, was to replace one set of agency problems with new ones.

*Participation Rights*
Under the new more centralized arrangements, the trade has a single entry point to the policy system, namely the FEHD. An FEHD deputy director has regular meetings with various trade groups to consult them on impending changes to laws or regulations. The relationship between FEHD and the trade, however, was less one of bargaining and negotiation and more one of FEHD passing on information. As the former Director of FEHD pointed out: 'Whatever you told them at this stage in a regular meeting they wouldn't say much. But then things changed when you got to Legco. Then all of a sudden at Legco they said you never talked to me and then we pointed out that on such and such a date we told them about it [the policy]. They seemed to have forgotten everything we had told them before.' Given their representation in Legco functional constituencies, the incentive to participate privately may have been low.

Government's relations to the trade are to a large extent hierarchical. Government uses consultation with the trade to inform and to listen to objections. As the former Director of FEHD pointed out: 'We may change the details after talking to them, but yes, we still want to implement [the policy or regulation]. We are fully aware of the political facts. In the last few years all the important things ... we managed to get them all done ... In spite of all the kicking and screaming, they [the policies] were done because they were important.' On lower priority items for the government, such as a scheme for rating restaurants according to their cleanliness and on nutrition labeling, opposition from the trade has resulted in delay. Because the government consults many different groups it may play one off against another to achieve a 'balanced' policy. 'Just because we I can't please both it is unfair to say that we haven't consulted ... we *have* consulted but we haven't listened, that may be true' (Interview, DFEHD, August 21, 2006).

*Uncertainty Risks*

One of the most significant consequences of the introduction of the POAS system was to increase uncertainty risks. Many of the politicians recruited to fill the elite policy positions came from outside the civil service. Accordingly they brought to their positions a wide variety of policy preferences that, because Hong Kong's system eschews political parties, were not molded into a coherent program. Individual preferences assumed an exaggerated importance in such a system. The government also replaced the Policy Committee, which had brought elite civil servants together to make policy, with an Executive Council, on which all political appointees sat. This arrangement fostered a silo effect, which undermined coordination at the top and increased uncertainty. Government policy became less predictable for both the administrators and the public, and increased risks of uncertainty.

*Agency Problems*

The new arrangements addressed some sort of agency problems, but resulted in new problems as well. The new arrangements facilitated the establishment of a new, high level Steering Group on food. The Group brings together senior officials from the bureau and the FEHD (and AFCD and Health as needed) to study longer-term policy issues. The Steering Group is the first such regular policy coordination mechanism for food safety created in the Hong Kong government.

The bureau has also established regular mechanisms to improve coordination including twice monthly meetings that the directors and deputy directors of FEHD, AFCD, and Health had with the policy secretary and the weekly meetings convened by the secretary with his permanent secretary, deputy secretaries, and principal assistant secretaries. Although these are held on a regular basis, their agendas are usually crises driven. The permanent secretary also maintains daily contact with the heads of departments supervised by the bureau. Heads of departments interact with other departments generally to iron out the details of policies set at the bureau (such as which department should pay for a particular exercise).

Policy bureaus turn to more ad hoc coordination mechanisms to handle operational problems that require an explicit policy steer. The interdepartmental working committee chaired by the policy secretary of Health Welfare and Food Bureau (HWFB) to deal with malachite green in eels in 2005 brought together many officials from the policy bureau, FEHD, AFCD, and Health to work intensively over only about a week and according to one source was called an 'interdepartmental working committee' for the sake of a press release 'for ease of comprehension' (Interview, PSHWFB, August 25, 2006). The government gave these informal arrangements more structure to demonstrate to the public that action was being taken (as indeed it was).

In another case, the permanent secretary pulled together an interdepartmental task force to deal with organized crime and food smuggling in a wholesale food market. In this case the permanent secretary of HWFB chaired a task force that included representatives of the Security Bureau, police, customs, FEHD, and AFCD. Initiative for the exercise came from the bureau. The permanent secretary pointed out: 'We have to have a task force because they [the departments] will have to work together ... The bureau gives its blessing. If I need to sort things out I will have to come in. But by and large, I think after one or two interventions all departments worked smoothly together. My intervention is really to fund them to employ additional guards and strengthen the [market] management system.' Fights over resources tended to undermine cooperation among agencies and required this kind of high-level intervention which was facilitated by the new institutional arrangements.

The new arrangements have not reduced problems of conflicts of interest among departments even those housed under one bureau, however. As a result of the reforms the single permanent secretary's position has been split into two, which means turf battles between the two permanent secretaries push disputes between them up to the policy secretary.

Conflicts between policy secretaries as they stake out their programs and compete for resources are more marked after the introduction of the POAS. In the food safety arena, for example, an October 2005 HWFB proposal to create a new Food Safety Inspection and Quarantine Department from parts of FEHD and AFCD prompted the Secretary for Environment, Transport, and Works to demand that AFCD's remaining conservancy functions be transferred to her portfolio. The result would have been to abolish the AFCD, a move vigorously protested by AFCD staff who were supported by the legislature. This opposition scuppered the plan (see Health Welfare and Food Bureau, 2005).

Not surprisingly, the new arrangements have not resolved conflicts of interest among departments, some of which have long standing causes. AFCD's mission to develop agriculture and fisheries in Hong Kong makes it in some sense unsuitable to regulate food safety. As the former Director of FEHD pointed out, 'The two departments [FEHD and AFCD] have very different missions. Because of this, they also have different approaches [to cooperation] ... If you ask the AFCD people, if they are honest with you, they will tell you they are not quite sure what they are doing. They are caught between two bosses now [Health Welfare and Food; Environment, Transport, and Works]. [They say] for my first 20 years in the department my job was to help the industry develop. When it comes to the control side [and FEHD asks] "Hey, can you control the farmers for us?" they will be very reluctant ... But from day one FEHD is the control agent, we don't care whether the pig farm is prospering or not, we want to make sure the food is safe. Therefore we are very control oriented ...'.

Although AFCD has provided support and cooperates at an operational level with FEHD on food safety issues every day, its commitment to food safety was tested to the limit in 2005 when the government blue print for food safety reform essentially called for the AFCD to be abolished. This episode demonstrates the limits to which the department is committed to policy coordination. Survival comes first, and in this case all key players recognized that the department should continue to exist even if food safety policy would be less effectively coordinated. As a deputy secretary pointed out: 'Obviously you cannot dismiss concerns of staff summarily ... We were talking about the breaking up of a very old and traditional department, sparking staff resentment which was something we have to think about ... if you want to force it through to the extent that staff are extremely unhappy, this will not do any good to the new department, nor to the community with its heightened expectations of what we could do and deliver' (Interview DSHWFB, August 21, 2006).

The new arrangements have facilitated improved coordination between the Hong Kong government and mainland authorities. The permanent secretary has regular meetings (three times per year) with officials of Administration of Quality, Supervision, Inspection, and Quarantine (AQSIQ)[4] in Beijing to review food safety policies. Given their policy rather than operational portfolios, informal contact between the permanent secretary and AQSIQ is rare. 'If things come to me [the Permanent Secretary] there is bound to be something serious ...' (Interview, PSHWFB, August 25, 2006). Generally these contacts between the bureau and the AQSIQ are maintained by a deputy secretary in the bureau or the director of

FEHD. Regular meetings were also held between food safety officials in Hong Kong, Guangdong, Shenzhen, and Zhuhai to review operational matters. Contacts between Hong Kong and the mainland have also been strengthened. These include a new notification system contained in protocols signed between the Hong Kong government and AQSIQ and Ministry of Agriculture that requires these agencies to notify the Hong Kong government of any adulteration of food or incidences of animal disease coming from AQSIQ-export registered farms. The two governments have also established a regular annual meeting of the policy secretary for Health, Welfare, and Food (HWF) and the Minister of AQSIQ to review food safety issues and procedures.

In spite of these developments, information asymmetry and conflicts of interest still characterize Hong Kong mainland food safety issues, however. Problems with mainland-sourced food are complex. First, moral hazard problems and information asymmetries characterize the AQSIQ bureaucratic set up. Given the high levels of corruption found in China generally, why should we believe that they are not also found in the licensing and inspection of farms and food processing plants? Indeed, Hong Kong food regulators admit that this may be a problem. As the permanent secretary said: 'Of course there is no fool-proof system, we have to be content with it. We still know that when it comes to matters with a trading interest we still have to grapple with the problem of possible corruption ... their own sort of norm, way of looking at the system...'. Yet, the Hong Kong government believes that because China is a food exporter (all controlled imports [high risk food] to Hong Kong comes through this channel) the incentive for mainland authorities to provide safe food is very high. Given the openness of Hong Kong, any problems here will be quickly picked up by China's trading partners.

Information asymmetries are a particularly difficult problem. Given that Hong Kong cannot send thousands of inspectors to investigate every farm or food-processing factory, the government relies heavily on the AQSIQ bureaucracy. The ministry in Beijing, however, may not know what is going on at local level. During the malachite green scandal, the government pushed the AQSIQ to set up a system of registered fish farms in China from which exports to Hong Kong would come. The authorities issued a list of such farms in short order, but Hong Kong journalists who tried to visit the farms found out that many did not exist.

Hong Kong is thus dependent on the mainland for information and the quality of its regulation. Although AQSIQ in some sense acts as an agent of the Hong Kong government on the mainland, AQSIQ has its own control problems. AQSIQ is also an organization of the central government and thus probably outranks its Hong Kong 'partners' in the bureaucratic pecking order in China. Still, the evidence presented here is that both sides have an increasingly close and institutionalized working relationship driven by China's needs to develop its food export business. This incentive has probably reduced agency problems somewhat.

The post-1997 political executive choose to exercise much tighter control over the food safety bureaucracy, in keeping with new governance ideas and pressure from the public for better service (better protection for beneficiaries). The new centralized arrangements increased uncertainty, however, and provided more focused access to the trade. The introduction of the POAS in 2002 resulted in new agency problems.

## CONCLUSION

Regime change altered the balance of power between politicians and administrators in Hong Kong and improved the capacity of politicians to impose administrative reforms. Dramatic changes to the institutional arrangements for food safety date only from 1997. Politicians replaced the autonomous arrangements preferred by the colonial state with more tightly controlled institutions. Politicians took these steps based on their new understanding of governance and legitimacy, on the one hand, and to reduce transactions costs, on the other. As a result of the reforms, private sector participation became more focused, but uncertainty costs increased. Politicians replaced one set of agency problems with another. In particular the introduction of the POAS system, which was critical to cementing the position of politicians vis-à-vis administrators has led to new problems, which have undermined the coherence of government and policy coordination.

In some sense the reforms of food safety are representative of reforms in other policy domains. They all have occurred within a general framework of shifting politician–administrator relations.

In 2005 the Chief Executive resigned and was replaced by a political appointee with long experience as a career civil servant. He has moved the system partially back to the colonial era, by reinstating the Policy Committee in a move to bring more coherence to the government's program. Given the problems associated with the POAS, however, which continues to be implemented, more coherent policy is unlikely to result.

## NOTES

1. The interviewees were: Permanent Secretary of the Health Welfare and Food Bureau (PS, HWFB); former Deputy Secretary of HWFB (DS, HWFB); former Director of Food and Environment Hygiene Department (DFEHD); and the Comptroller, Center for Food Safety (CCFS).
2. I identify two types of bureaus, the 'autonomous' bureau and the 'tightly politically controlled' bureau, both of which are 'bureaus' as defined by Horn (1995). That is, they are tax funded, their output is opaque, and therefore difficult to measure, they generally lack transparency, their budgets are subject to annual scrutiny by politicians, and they are staffed by civil servants.
3. The Chief Executive (CE) is elected by an 800-member Election Committee, composed mostly of local notables chosen by the Chinese Communist Party. Upon being elected, he is appointed by the Chinese central government. The CE nominates principal officials (ministers) who mostly head various policy bureaus and they together with the CE form the government. The central government also appoints these principal officials. For the constitutional set up in Hong Kong see *The Basic Law of the Hong Kong Special Administrative Region of the People's Republic of China* (1980) which came into force in 1997 when the United Kingdom ceded sovereignty over Hong Kong to China.
4. On the mainland the Hong Kong government's key partner is the General Administration for Quality Supervision, Inspection and Quarantine (AQSIQ), part of the central government in Beijing. The AQSIQ supervises a network of local Entry and Exit Inspection and Quarantine bureaus (the Guangdong province bureau and Shenzhen and Zhuhai bureaus are key regulators for Hong Kong food imports) that implement central government quality controls for all exports, including food. The AQSIQ maintains registers of approved farms and processing plants that may export food to Hong Kong (and the rest of the world).

## REFERENCES

Ansell, C., & Vogel, D. (2006). *What's the beef? The contested governance of European food safety*. Cambridge, MA: MIT Press.
Constitutional Affairs Bureau. (1998). Update on review of district organizations. Paper prepared for the Legislative Council Panel on Constitutional Affairs, 17 September. LC Paper No. CB(2)285/98-99(03).
Health, Welfare and Food Bureau. (2005). Reorganization plan for the food safety regulatory framework. Paper prepared for the Legislative Council Panel on Food Safety and Environmental Hygiene, 17 October. LC Paper No. CB(2) 26/05-06(2).
Health and Welfare Bureau. (1998). Progress on review of structure for discharge of food safety and environmental hygiene. Paper prepared for the Legislative Council Panel on Health Services, 12 October. Accessed on August 20, 2006. Available at http://www.legco.gov.hk/yr98-99/english/panels/hs/papers/hs1210_2.htm
Ho, Pui-yin. (2004). *The administrative history of the Hong Kong government agencies 1841–2002*. Hong Kong: Hong Kong University Press.

Horn, M. J. (1995). *The political economy of public administration.* Cambridge: Cambridge University Press.
Knill, C. (1999). Explaining cross-national variance in administrative reform: Autonomous versus instrumental bureaucracies. *Journal of Public Policy, 19*(2), 113–139.
Lam, Wai-fung. (2005). Coordinating the government Bureaucracy in Hong Kong: An institutional analysis. *Governance, 18*(4), 633–654.
Lau, Siu-kai. (1982). *Society and politics in Hong Kong.* Hong Kong: Chinese University Press.
Lau, Y. W. (2002). *A history of the municipal councils of Hong Kong 1883–1999.* Hong Kong: Leisure and Cultural Services Department.
Miners, N. (1998). *Government and politics of Hong Kong* (5th ed.). Hong Kong: Oxford University Press.
Moe, T. (1984). The new economics of organization. *American Journal of Political Science, 28*(4), 739–777.
Nestle, M. (2003). *Safe food: Bacteria, biotechnology and bioterrorism.* Berkeley: University of California Press.
Peters, B. G. (1999). *Institutional theory in political science: The 'new institutionalism'.* New York: Continuum Press.
Poon Ping Yeung, P. (2003). *A study of the HKSAR government's strategy to manage avian flu outbreaks.* Unpublished MPA dissertation, University of Hong Kong.
Scott, I. (1989). *Political change and the crisis of legitimacy.* London: Hurst.
Scott, I. (2005). *Public administration in Hong Kong: Regime change and its impact on the public sector.* Singapore: Marshall Cavendish.
Toke, D. (2004). *The politics of GM food: A comparative study of the UK, USA, and EU.* London: Routledge.
Williamson, O. (1999). Public and private Bureaucracies: A transaction cost economics perspective. *Journal of Law, Economics and Organization, 15*(1), 306–342.

# CIVIL SERVICE REFORM IN INDONESIA

Prijono Tjiptoherijanto

## ABSTRACT

*An important agency of the government is its civil service or bureaucracy. The civil service has the potential to empower a government to achieve a country's goals, that is, to improve its citizens' standard of living. The ability of a civil service to successfully support the government depends heavily on the characteristics of the civil service. In the case of Indonesia, the civil service is slow; lacks transparency, accountability, initiative; and is sometimes corrupt. Therefore Indonesia's civil service is badly in need of reform, both in relation to its institutional aspects as well as in relation to moral issues.*

> God ... is clearly democratic. He distributes brainpower universally, but He quite justifiably expects us to do something efficient and constructive with that priceless gift. That is what management is all about.
> 
> – McNamara (1968, pp. 109–110)

## INTRODUCTION

The issue of good governance has gained prominence during the past two decades. Good governance has become the new paradigm of public administration, replacing Weber's (1978) old public administration model. The new model involves cooperation among the government, civil society, and the business sector, whereas the old one only took government entities into account.

Reforms in the field of human resource management and civil service administration point to the changing role of public administration. This new role has been shaped by three main models: (a) public administration, (b) public management, and (c) governance. While public administration can be defined as all the processes, organizations, and individuals involved in carrying out laws and other rules adopted or issued by the legislature, the executive branch of government, and the courts, public management redefines the relationship between the government and society.

According to Osborne and Gaebler (1993), the new paradigm of public management calls on governments to focus on achieving results rather than solely conforming to procedures and to adopt competitive, innovative, and entrepreneurial strategies. By contrast, according to the World Bank (1993b), good governance entails sound public sector management (efficiency, effectiveness, and economy), accountability, and exchange and free flow of information (transparency) along with a legal framework for development (justice and respect for human rights and liberties). Hirst (2000, p. 14) offers a more succinct definition of good governance, namely, that it refers to "creating an effective political framework conducive to private economic action: stable regimes, the rule of law and efficient state administration adapted to the roles that government can actually perform and a strong civil society independent of the state."

Table 1 highlights some of the unique characteristics of each of the three main models discussed. Regardless of the model, the civil service has a key role to play in empowering a government to achieve a country's goals and to improve its citizens' standard of living.

## THE INDONESIAN CIVIL SERVICE

To adapt to globalization, the Indonesian government has to improve the structure of its bureaucracy, both in terms of enhancing the quality of government employees and developing a modern and efficient system. The development of human resources would improve the quality of services provided to citizens. This task is currently especially significant in Indonesia as the country is confronting a variety of new developments, such as democratization and decentralization.

*Table 1.* Key Aspects of Three Models of Public Administration.

| Aspect | Public Administration | Public Management | Responsive Governance |
|---|---|---|---|
| Relationship between citizens and the state | Obedience | Entitlement | Empowerment |
| Accountability of senior officials | To politicians | To politicians and citizens/customers | To politicians, citizens, and stakeholders |
| Guiding principles | Compliance with rules and regulations | Efficiency and results | Accountability, transparency, and participation |
| Criteria for success | Output | Outcome | Process |
| Key attribute | Impartiality | Professionalism | Responsiveness |

*Source:* United Nations (2005).

## Civil Servant Numbers

Indonesia has a large number of civil servants: approximately 3.74 million, or 1.7% of the 2005 population. This figure represents a decrease from 1974, during the early years of the so-called New Order Government (1966–1998), when this was about 2.1% of the population. These percentages are similar to those of other countries in the region, such as India (1.2%), Pakistan (1.5%), the Philippines (2.1%), and Vietnam (3.2%) (Schiavo-Campo, 1998). Table 2 shows the number of civil servants at different levels of government.

As shown in Table 2, as of 2002, the number of civil servants assigned to regional levels of government is far higher than the number in the central government. This is in line with the government's objective of providing better quality services to the public, as well as moving government closer to society. Indeed, the main objective of public service reform in most Asian countries is to provide citizens' with enhanced services (see, e.g., Chham, 2006 in relation to reforms in Cambodia).

## Salary System

At the same time, even though the number of civil servants in Indonesia is equivalent to only about 1.7 percent of the total population, the quality of government employees is low. This is partly an outcome of the unattractive salary system. To attract effective, efficient, and uncorrupt government

Table 2. Number of Civil Servants, Selected Years.

| Level of Government | 1974 | | 2002 | | 2003[a] | | 2005 | |
|---|---|---|---|---|---|---|---|---|
| | Number of civil servants | Percentage of all civil servants | Number of civil servants | Percentage of all civil servants | Number of civil servants | Percentage of all civil servants | Number of civil servants | Percentage of all civil servants |
| Central government | 1,312,254 | 78.3 | 915,660 | 24.0 | 840,007 | 23.1 | 896,211 | 24.0 |
| Provincial governments | 362,617 | 21.7 | 2,907,426 | 76.0 | 311,047 | 8.5 | 303,724 | 8.1 |
| Regency or municipality governments | | | | | 2,496,951 | 68.4 | 2,541,560 | 67.9 |
| Total | 1,674,871 | 100.0 | 3,823,086 | 100.0 | 3,648,005 | 100.0 | 3,741,495 | 100.0 |

*Source*: National Civil Service Agency data.
[a] Since 2003, regional civil servants have been divided among provincial governments and regencies or municipalities. This is an outcome of the decentralization of civil servants that started at the end of 2000; however, until 2003, determining the number of civil servants assigned to the two levels was difficult.

employees, they need to be provided with appropriate salaries and benefits. Appropriate compensation will not only have an impact on staff turnover and on employees' productivity and quality of work, but will also reduce tendencies for civil servants to engage in corrupt practices.

Salaries for Indonesian civil servants are determined by the level of responsibility, the type of job, and the cost of living. The salary system for government employees in Indonesia is classified as a combination scale system, because it combines the single scale system and the double scale system. Under a single scale system, employees at the same rank receive the same salary regardless of the type of job and the level of responsibility. Under a double scale system, salaries are determined based on employees' level of responsibility and type of job. Job performance is not generally taken into account. Under the combination scale system, some civil servants might have significantly higher salaries than their colleagues at the same rank.

Civil servants are divided into four ranks, from I (the lowest) to IV (the highest), each with a basic salary scale. Ranks I through III are divided into four grades (a, b, c, and d), and rank IV has five grades (a, b, c, d, and e), making a total of 17 grades from Ia to IVe. Individual civil servants' ranks are based on their educational qualifications and seniority. Ranks III and IV require a university degree. The basic salary for a civil servant at rank Ia (primary and junior high school graduates), regardless of the job held and the level of responsibility, is around US$66 per month, or a little over US$2 per day. The salary for an employee at rank IVe with 32 years of service is only around US$207 per month. This is roughly equivalent to 6 percent of the average salary of a chief executive officer of an Indonesian state-owned enterprise. Table 3 breaks down basic salaries for different ranks and grades of civil servants in recent years.

The ratio between the salaries of the lowest-paid employees and of the highest-paid employees started changing as of 2001. This followed the departure from office of President Soeharto in May 1998, when Indonesia embarked on numerous reforms, one of the main pillars of which was democratization. Thus as of this time, equality was emphasized. As shown in Table 3, in 1993 the ratio between the earnings of the lowest-paid and highest-paid civil servants was 1:7, but by 2001 it was only 1:3.

In recent years, governments have become aware that they need to link civil servants' salaries to those paid in the private sector if they are to attract and retain the talent necessary to improve and sustain public sector performance. When income inequality among staff is deliberately increased, senior management positions become more attractive than was previously

*Table 3.* Basic Salaries for Civil Servants by Rank and Grade, Selected Years (Rp Thousands/Month).

| Rank | Grade a | | | | | Grade b | | | | |
|---|---|---|---|---|---|---|---|---|---|---|
|  | 1993 | 1997 | 2001 | 2003 | 2005 | 1993 | 1997 | 2001 | 2003 | 2005 |
| I | 78.0 | 135.0 | 500.0 | 575.0 | 661.3 | 92.2 | 151.1 | 537.5 | 619.7 | 712.6 |
|  | 150.8 | 254.6 | 689.3 | 767.7 | 882.8 | 173.8 | 271.4 | 723.1 | 809.2 | 930.5 |
| II | 110.1 | 182.9 | 620.0 | 725.6 | 834.4 | 129.0 | 204.8 | 667.3 | 782.0 | 899.2 |
|  | 277.3 | 409.3 | 832.8 | 1,047.1 | 1,204.2 | 294.0 | 425.7 | 868.5 | 1,091.4 | 1,255.2 |
| III | 150.2 | 241.8 | 760.8 | 905.4 | 1,041.2 | 154.0 | 251.5 | 788.3 | 943.7 | 1,088.2 |
|  | 374.2 | 527.9 | 1,129.4 | 1,292.1 | 1,485.9 | 390.8 | 549.0 | 1,170.2 | 1,346.8 | 1,548.8 |
| IV | 168.6 | 282.9 | 878.8 | 1,068.6 | 1,228.9 | 176.4 | 294.2 | 908.4 | 1,113.8 | 1,280.9 |
|  | 450.2 | 617.6 | 1,301.6 | 1,525.1 | 1,753.8 | 474.0 | 612.3 | 1,348.6 | 1,589.6 | 1,828.0 |

| Rank | Grade c | | | | | Grade d | | | | |
|---|---|---|---|---|---|---|---|---|---|---|
|  | 1993 | 1997 | 2001 | 2003 | 2005 | 1993 | 1997 | 2001 | 2003 | 2005 |
| I | 94.7 | 157.1 | 557.1 | 645.9 | 742.8 | 97.2 | 163.4 | 577.2 | 673.2 | 774.2 |
|  | 190.7 | 282.2 | 749.2 | 843.4 | 969.9 | 207.6 | 293.5 | 776.2 | 879.1 | 1,010.9 |
| II | 131.7 | 212.9 | 691.4 | 815.0 | 937.3 | 135.3 | 221.5 | 716.4 | 849.5 | 976.9 |
|  | 314.7 | 442.7 | 1,001.4 | 1,137.6 | 1,308.3 | 336.3 | 460.4 | 1,037.5 | 1,185.8 | 1,363.6 |
| III | 157.8 | 261.6 | 816.7 | 983.6 | 1,310.1 | 161.8 | 272.0 | 816.2 | 1,025.2 | 1,179.0 |
|  | 407.4 | 571.0 | 1,212.5 | 1,403.8 | 1,614.3 | 424.0 | 593.8 | 1,250.2 | 1,463.2 | 1,682.6 |
| IV | 184.2 | 306.0 | 941.2 | 1,160.9 | 1,335.1 | 192.0 | 318.2 | 975.2 | 1,210.1 | 1,391.6 |
|  | 494.6 | 668.0 | 1,367.3 | 1,656.9 | 1,905.4 | 515.2 | 694.7 | 1,447.7 | 1,727.0 | 1,986.0 |

| Rank | Grade e | | | | |
|---|---|---|---|---|---|
|  | 1993 | 1997 | 2001 | 2003 | 2005 |
| I | n.a. | n.a. | n.a. | n.a. | n.a. |
|  | n.a. | n.a. | n.a. | n.a. | n.a. |
| II | n.a. | n.a. | n.a. | n.a. | n.a. |
|  | n.a. | n.a. | n.a. | n.a. | n.a. |
| III | n.a. | n.a. | n.a. | n.a. | n.a. |
|  | n.a. | n.a. | n.a. | n.a. | n.a. |
| IV | 201.6 | 331.0 | 1,010.4 | 1,261.2 | 1,450.4 |
|  | 537.6 | 722.5 | 1,500.0 | 1,800.0 | 2,070.0 |

*Source:* National Civil Service Agency data.
*Note:* n.a. = not applicable. Applicable exchange rates were as follows: in 1993, US$1 = Rp 2,100; in 1997, US$1 = Rp 4,650; in 2001–2005, US$1 = Rp 9,200–10,000.

the case. In theory, an egalitarian pay structure is more attractive to those in the lower ranks of the civil service, whereas a pay structure that more clearly differentiates between staff at different levels is conducive to recruiting and retaining talent that might move to the private sector (United Nations, 2005). However, Indonesia's salary structure is moving toward an egalitarian system, with the result that most of the best graduates from well-known and high-quality universities are not keen to become government employees. Moreover, the low salaries tend to encourage wrongdoing and illegal activities, such as accepting bribes and asking for compensation for services provided.

In Indonesia, as in many developing countries, allowances and in-kind benefits play a substantial role in remunerating public sector employees, which is why determining the right balance between pay and benefits and allowances is so important. In Zambia, for instance, permanent secretaries earn 50 times as much as the lowest-paid civil servants when in-kind benefits (housing, cars, telephones, and so on) are taken into account, but if such benefits are excluded, the difference is only fivefold (Kenleers, 2004). Moreover, where "moonlighting" and corruption prevail, senior civil servants will earn even more than junior ones, as they are likely to have more opportunities to engage in such activities.

## Impact of Regional Autonomy

The situation of extremely low salaries for government employees as described earlier has changed somewhat since the implementation of Indonesia's decentralization policy, which started in early 2001.

Proponents of decentralization see it as a process that enables more efficient allocation of resources, reduces information asymmetries, increases transparency, promotes citizen participation, and enhances accountability, thereby improving governance. Local governments are often more aware of and attuned to the needs of local populations than the central government, which means that local governments may have a clearer sense of which projects and policies people living in their jurisdictions would favor. This will have an impact on the duties of civil servants in different regions.

The other impact of decentralization has been improved conditions for some regional civil servants. For example, in Riau Province in West Sumatra, as of December 2006, a decree by the governor gave civil servants of the lowest rank (Ia) an additional Rp 1.6 million (around US$160) per month, while those at the highest level (IVe) received a pay increase of

Rp 4.5 million (around US$450) per month. Thus the most senior civil servants in Riau are paid more than twice the basic salary that central government civil servants of the same rank receive. With a salary of US$657 (base pay of US$207 plus US$450) per month, civil servants in Riau earn almost as much as middle managers in the business sector in Jakarta, the capital.

In addition to regional civil servants being paid more in line with their rank, their functional professions are also recognized by means of additional functional allowances. For example, in East Kutai Regency in East Kalimantan Province, since 2006, elementary and high school teachers have been paid an additional allowance of Rp 1.2 million (approximately US$120) per month. Therefore these teachers, who are ranked II or III, have monthly incomes of around US$250 to US$290, which is much more than the minimum wage in the province set by government decree of some US$150 a month.

Nevertheless, despite some improvement that followed implementation of the Regional Autonomy Law, Indonesia's public sector still needs to undergo substantial change, especially in relation to establishing good governance that will allow the country to compete in the global arena.

## BASIS FOR CHANGE

The stimulus to embark on changes came from perceptions that the system of public administration was incapable of providing good services to the public. It was viewed as slow and as lacking in transparency and accountability. In Indonesia, as in many other Asian countries, citizens have demanded cheaper, faster, and better public services and more effective and efficient government. To respond to this demand, the country's public management must become more democratic, efficient, and citizen oriented.

Governance is more than just routine government operations. Governance refers to how civil society, the government, the business sector, and all other relevant institutions and bodies interrelate to manage their affairs. Hunter and Shah (1998) developed the following governance quality index based on four sub-indexes:

- a citizen participation index – an aggregate measure based on indexes of political freedom and political stability;
- a government orientation index – an aggregate measure based on indexes of judicial efficiency, bureaucratic efficiency, and lack of corruption;

*Table 4.* Quality of Governance, Selected Asian Countries, 1997.

| Country | Index | Quality of Governance |
|---|---|---|
| Singapore | 65 | Good |
| Japan | 63 | |
| Malaysia | 58 | |
| Korea, Republic of | 57 | |
| Sri Lanka | 45 | Fair |
| Philippines | 44 | |
| India | 43 | |
| Thailand | 43 | |
| China | 39 | Poor |
| Indonesia | 38 | |
| Nepal | 36 | |
| Pakistan | 34 | |

*Source*: Adapted from Hunter and Shah (1998, Table 2.1).

- a social development index – an aggregate measure based on indexes of human development and egalitarian income distribution;
- an economic management index – an aggregate measure based on indexes of outward orientation, central bank independence, and ratio of debt to gross domestic product.

The resulting governance quality index is then used to rate countries as good, fair, or poor. Table 4 summarizes the results for selected Asian countries.

In 2003, the World Bank (Kaufmann, 2003) constructed an index of government effectiveness that compared the quality of public bureaucracy, policy making, and service delivery as one of six elements of a measure of governance.[1] An analysis of data from 175 countries confirmed that government effectiveness contributed to higher national income.

Good governance is an important vehicle for guaranteeing that a state's political and economic activities benefit the whole of society and not just a small group of individuals. In the absence of good governance practices, a lack of transparency in state affairs and opportunities to engage in corruption flourish. This can result in widespread corruption in both the government and state-owned enterprises, in a judicial system that lacks accountability, in poor management of natural resources, and in a lack of responsiveness to civil society. These and other impacts of poor governance undermine development efforts, hinder progress with respect to eradicating poverty, and infringe on human rights (World Bank, 1993b). As shown in

Table 4, Indonesia's governance quality is poor; therefore a reform of its public service is badly needed.

## DIRECTION OF REFORM

A major challenge for countries undergoing rapid change is the establishment of an effective and socially responsible bureaucracy or, in other words, an efficient and innovative civil service. The civil service is an important agency of routine government activities. Accountability, transparency, and public participation are some of the ways in which the behavior of civil servants can be influenced. Many developing states are viewed as weak mainly because of their inability to control their civil servants and obligate them to enforce the will of the state (Fukuyama, 2004). Public services in developing countries are riddled with patronage and corruption, and cleaning them up by implementing "modern" (in terms of recruitment, training, promotion, and discipline) civil service systems has been a central goal of institutional reform (Fukuyama, 2004). Nevertheless, the problem of controlling bureaucrats still exists to varying degrees in most developing Asian countries. One way to achieve the objective of controlling the behavior of civil servants is by means of civil service reform. In this regard, Indonesia is currently focusing on institution building and moral or ethical conduct.

### *Institutional Approach*

The United Nations Development Programme (2003) describes civil service reform as developing the capacity of the civil service to fulfill its mandate by addressing such issues as recruitment, promotion, pay, number of employees, and performance appraisal, and this still constitutes the bulk of national programs concerned with public administration reform. Civil service reform has historically focused on the need to contain the costs of public sector employment through retrenchment and restructuring, but has broadened to focus on the longer-term goal of creating a government workforce of the right size; with the appropriate mix of skills; and with the correct motivation, professional ethos, client focus, and accountability (United Nations Development Programme, 2003).

Furthermore, in a report for the Indonesian government, the World Bank (2001, p. 10) indicates that "the civil service reform strategy should include changes to the incentive system, size of the civil service, recruitment, performance management, remuneration, and probity." Indonesia is planning to launch a number of promising initiatives in these areas. For example, pilot reform initiatives are planned for the ministries of Finance and Education, including a new merit-based pay initiative under Teacher Law No. 14/2005. If successful, these initiatives could be scaled up to the national level. In addition, an independent remuneration commission will advise on pay scales and on modernizing the pay structure for senior officials; a review of the legal framework for the civil service is ongoing; a number of subnational reform initiatives are taking place in Yogyakarta, Jembrana in Bali, Solok in West Sumatra, and elsewhere; and a cabinet-level unit to help implement reforms is planned (World Bank, 2006).

To have an effective and efficient public service, most governments have set up a special institution responsible for human resource management. This body is often referred to as the civil service commission (CSC) or public service commission. In the Republic of Korea, the CSC established in 1999 has been leading the country's major civil service reform initiatives. In 2004, those personnel management functions that still remained under the purview of the Ministry of Government Administration and Home Affairs were transferred to the CSC, thereby resulting in a single, central personnel authority for the Korean government (Kong, 2006). In New Zealand, in 1999 the state service commissioner asked to be given responsibility for developing a solution to the lack of corporate capacity in the public service. Since that time, New Zealand's public service has increasingly moved to address a wide range of service and human resource management issues from a corporate perspective (United Nations, 2005).

Once a CSC has been set up, questions frequently arise pertaining to the commission's relationship with line ministries and agencies, thus once a government decides to establish a CSC, it must clearly delineate the division of responsibilities in relation to resource management among central government departments and agencies. In many countries, responsibilities for human resource management in the civil service are along the lines shown in Table 5.

The structure outlined in Table 5 resembles the model prevalent in the Commonwealth of Nations, especially with respect to the role of the CSC, but countries such as Korea and Thailand have similar arrangements in place.

Indonesia does not yet have a CSC. Even though Law No. 43/1999 of 2000 stated that a CSC should be established, the government does not currently have any plans to establish such a body. Therefore the division of responsibilities in relation to human resources among line ministries and other public sector entities is as shown in Table 6.

*Table 5.* Responsibility for Human Resource Management in Central Government Agencies.

| Agency | Function |
|---|---|
| Office of the Prime Minister | Overall government policy |
| Ministry of Finance | Pay and pensions |
| Ministry of Public Service | Deployment and conditions of service for civil servants |
| CSC | Appointments, promotions, transfers, and discipline |
| National Administrative Staff College | Staff training and development |

*Source:* Adapted from United Nations (2005, Table 6).

*Table 6.* Institutions Responsibility for Human Resource Management in Indonesia.

| Agency | Function |
|---|---|
| Office of the President (State Secretariat and Cabinet Secretariat) | Overall government policies |
| Ministry of Finance | Civil service pay and pensions (state-owned enterprises are responsible for their own pay and pensions under the supervision of the State Ministry for State-Owned Companies) |
| Ministry of Administrative Reforms | Supervision, coordination, monitoring, and evaluation of all civil services matters, including supervision and coordination of the National Agency for the Civil Service and the National Institute of Public Administration |
| National Agency for the Civil Service | Appointments, promotions (except at the highest levels, which are managed by a team chosen by the president), and transfers |
| National Institute of Public Administration | Education, training, and organizational design |

*Source:* Author.

Thus as shown in Table 6, the management of human resources in the civil service is not being carried out by an independent body that reports directly to the president, but by institutions that are part of the government bureaucracy.

*Moral Issues*

In countries such as Indonesia, where civil servants, like politicians, are key government decision makers, government employees are sometimes viewed as community leaders. In this sense, civil servants may be expected to do many things in the communities where they live, following practices established during the Dutch colonial era. Such a role calls for adherence to norms of morality, meaning that civil servants must avoid irregularities and always obey the rules when conducting their activities (Magnis, 1996; Natakusumah, 1990). Therefore civil servants should not engage in any illegal activities, such as bribery and other corrupt acts.

Friederich (1940) noted the growing importance of internal values and moral and professional standards among bureaucrats. In their absence, abuses of power can easily arise in the government sector.

A recent study by Meier and O'Toole (2006) shows that bureaucratic values are far more important in explaining bureaucratic output and outcomes than political factors. This should not be taken to mean that external political control is unimportant, but it does show that paying serious attention to the values of civil servants is important.

Ensuring that civil servants give high priority to honesty, responsibility, and integrity in relation to their day-to-day activities and routine duties can be done through well-planned human resource development. Human resource development for civil servants starts with their recruitment and continues until they leave government service. Recruiters should undertake job and requirement analyses before undertaking recruitment activities. Furthermore, to allow the civil service to select the best candidates, the recruitment process should be fair and open. The next step in human resource development for civil servants is education and training and should be provided regularly for those at every level, as is already done in the armed forces. An objective and selective recruitment process combined with integrated and systematic education and training during the period of service can enhance the quality of government employees. Several Asian countries have adopted such an approach, for example, China, Japan, Korea, and Malaysia. Furthermore, the government should also provide higher education scholarships both in the country and abroad for exceptional government employees. Such a policy is not only good for the individuals concerned, but also for the government and perhaps for the country in the future (World Bank, 1993a).

# CONCLUSION

Since the 1980s, many countries, including Asian countries, have engaged in major efforts to promote administrative reform, focusing on the openness, transparency, and accountability of government administration. All countries, regardless of their economic situation or stage of development, need good governance. For some Asian countries this became particularly important after the 1997 Asian financial and economic crisis.

In Indonesia, following the fall of the New Order Government in 1998, a political movement emerged that pursued reforms in relation to politics, the economy, the judicial system, and public administration. Law no. 22/1999 on Decentralization and Law no. 43/1999 on Civil Service Administration opened up possibilities for public service reform in Indonesia, but the country still has a long way to go in relation to having a high-quality civil service. As with any reforms, strong and determined leadership is crucial. While good governance is a central pillar for dealing with competition in a globalizing world, Indonesia must also undertake civil service reforms to achieve a clean and efficient bureaucracy.

## ACKNOWLEDGMENTS

This chapter was written with assistance from several individuals. I would like to thank Yon Arsal, Ph.D student at the Graduate School of International Cooperation Studies, Kobe University, for helping me to complete the chapter. Chen Kuang-Hui was kind enough to invite me to the school as a visiting professor, while other colleagues helped make my time at Kobe University memorable. I am, however, solely responsible for the content of this chapter and any errors are mine alone.

## NOTE

1. The six indicators are (a) voice and accountability, (b) political stability, (c) government effectiveness, (d) regulatory quality, (e) rule of law, and (f) control of corruption (Kaufmann, Kraay, & Mastruzzi, 2003).

## REFERENCES

Chham, C. (2006). The national program of administrative reform. Paper presented at the Asian Public Reform Forum, Nanning, China.

Friederich, C. J. (1940). Public policy and the nature of administration responsibility. In: C. J. Friederich & E. S. Mason (Eds), *Public policy* (pp. 3–24). Cambridge, MA: Harvard University Press.

Fukuyama, F. (2004). *State-building: Governance and world order in the 21st century*. Ithaca, NY: Cornell University Press.
Hirst, P. (2000). Democracy and governance. In: J. Pierre (Ed.), *Debating governance: Authority, steering, and democracy* (pp. 13–25). Oxford, UK: Oxford University Press.
Hunter, J., & Shah, A. (1998). *Applying a simple measure of good governance to the debate on fiscal decentralization*. (Policy Research Working Paper 1984). Washington, DC: World Bank.
Kaufmann, D. (2003). Governance redux: The empirical challenge. World Bank Policy Research Department Working Paper. Available at http://www.worldbank.org/wbi/governance/pubs/govredux.html
Kaufmann, D., Kraay, A., & Mastruzzi, M. (2003). *Governance matters III: Governance indicators for 1996–2002*. Washington, DC: World Bank. Available at http://www.worldbank.org/wb1/governance/govdata2002/index.html
Kenleers, P. (2004). *Key issues for consideration when assisting civil service personnel management reforms in developing countries*. Unpublished paper, United Nations Development Programme, Subregional Resources Facility for the Pacific, Northeast, and Southeast Asia, Bangkok.
Kong, D. (2006). Reinventing South Korea's bureaucracy toward open and accountable governance. Paper presented at the Asian Public Reform Forum, Nanning, China.
Magnis, S. F. (1996). Morality in bureaucracy (in Indonesian). Paper presented at the meeting on the Efficiency and Effectiveness of Bureaucratic Work Patterns and the Quality of Nine Years of Elementary Education in Relation to the Era of Globalization, Especially in 2003 and Beyond, Jakarta.
McNamara, R. (1968). *The essence of security*. New York: Harper & Row.
Meier, K. J., & O'Toole, L. J., Jr. (2006). Political control versus bureaucratic values: Reframing the debate. *Public Administration Review, 66*(2), 177–192.
Natakusumah, P. (1990). *Quality improvement of Government employees* (in Indonesian). Jakarta: Lembaga Administrasi Negara, R.I. (National Institute for Administration).
Osborne, D., & Gaebler, T. (1993). *Reinventing government*. Reading, MA: Addison Wesley.
Schiavo-Campo, S. (1998). Government employment and pay: The global and regional evidence. *Public Administration & Development, 18*, 457–478.
United Nations. (2005). *World public sector report 2005: Unlocking the human potential for public sector performance*. New York: Department of Economic and Social Affairs.
United Nations Development Programme. (2003). *Public administration practice note*. New York: Bureau for Development Policy.
Weber, M. (1978). *Economy and society: An outline of interpretive sociology*. Berkeley, CA: University of California Press.
World Bank. (1993a). *The East Asian miracle: Economic growth and public policy*. Oxford, UK: Oxford University Press.
World Bank. (1993b). *Governance*. Washington, DC: World Bank.
World Bank. (2001). *Indonesia: The imperative for reform*. Report 23093-IND. World Bank, Jakarta.
World Bank. (2006). *Country assistance strategy progress report for Republic of Indonesia*. Washington, DC: World Bank.

# COMBATING CORRUPTION AS A POLITICAL STRATEGY TO REBUILD TRUST AND LEGITIMACY: CAN CHINA LEARN FROM HONG KONG?

Anthony B. L. Cheung

### ABSTRACT

*Despite an intensified anti-corruption campaign, China's economic growth and social transition continue to breed loopholes and opportunities for big corruption, leading to a money-oriented mentality and the collapse of ethical standards, and exposing the communist regime to greater risk of losing moral credibility and political trust. In Hong Kong, the setting up of the Independent Commission Against Corruption (ICAC) in 1974 marked the advent of a new comprehensive strategy to eradicate corruption and to rebuild trust in government. The ICAC was not just an anti-corruption enforcement agency per se, but an institution spearheading and representing integrity and governance transformation. This chapter considers how mainland China can learn from Hong Kong's experience and use the fight against corruption as a major political strategy to win the hearts and minds of the population and reform governance in the absence of more fundamental constitutional reforms, in a situation similar to Hong Kong's colonial administration of the 1970s–1980s deploying administrative means to minimize a political crisis.*

## INTRODUCTION

The year 2006 sounded a great alarm to corrupt officials in China. Former Communist Party Politiburo member and party chief of Shanghai, Chen Liangyu, was removed from office and investigated in connection with a RMB3 billion (approximately US$395 million) social security fund corruption scam. Other top officials charged with corruption included Qiu Xiaohua, former chief of the National Bureau of Statistics, and Zheng Xiaoyu, former Vice Director of the State Administration of Food and Drug; the latter was even given a death sentence. By now there is no doubt that China's fourth-generation leadership under President Hu Jiantao and Premier Wen Jiabao has embarked on a new high-profile campaign against corruption in pursuit of the construction of a harmonious society.

This is not the first time that China has engaged in a conspicuous exercise to fight corruption. Indeed, as academic research (e.g. Wedeman, 2005) puts it, China has depended largely on a strategy of 'enforcement swamping' or campaign-style enforcement, using periodic intensive anti-corruption campaigns and intensive crackdowns, so as to create a deterrence effect. Such strategy might result in some concurrent decrease in petty corruption but ironically there has been observable increase in more serious corruption cases involving huge sums of money and more senior and top officials. It is argued that this strategy aims at controlling corruption rather than eradicating it as the costs of eradication are too high and there lacks the political will and enforcement capacity for vigorous eradication (Wedeman, 2005). As the anti-corruption campaign intensifies and as China's economic growth and social transition breed loopholes and opportunities for big corruption (e.g. bank loans, financial deals and land clearance and development), leading to a money-oriented mentality and the collapse of ethical standards, the present communist regime is in the risk of losing its moral credibility and political trust.

Colonial Hong Kong by the early 1970s also faced the same moral and legitimacy crisis caused by extensive corruption. However, three decades later, Hong Kong now stands far ahead of the rest of China in the eyes of the international community (see Table 1).

**Table 1.** Hong Kong and China According to Corruption Perception Index (CPI), 2001–2006.

|  | 2001 | 2002 | 2003 | 2004 | 2005 | 2006 |
|---|---|---|---|---|---|---|
| CPI score of Hong Kong (out of 10) | 7.9 | 8.2 | 8.0 | 8.0 | 8.3 | 8.3 |
| Country ranking | 14 (out of 91) | 14 (out of 102) | 14 (out of 133) | 16 (out of 146) | 15 (out of 159) | 15 (out of 163) |
| CPI score of mainland China (out of 10) | 3.5 | 3.5 | 3.4 | 3.4 | 3.2 | 3.3 |
| Country ranking | 57 (out of 91) | 59 (out of 102) | 66 (out of 133) | 71 (out of 146) | 78 (out of 159) | 70 (out of 163) |

*Source:* Transparency International (2007).

Most analysts would attribute Hong Kong's achievement to the setting up of the Independent Commission Against Corruption (ICAC) in 1974, which marked the advent of a new comprehensive strategy to eradicate corruption and at the same time rebuild trust in a government that suffered from an inherent legitimacy deficit because of its colonial and undemocratic nature. The ICAC was not just an anti-corruption enforcement agency per se, but an institution spearheading and representing integrity and governance transformation. This chapter considers how mainland China can learn from Hong Kong's ICAC experience and use the fight against corruption as a major political strategy to win the hearts and minds of the population and reform governance in the absence of more fundamental constitutional reforms, in a situation similar to Hong Kong's colonial administration of the 1970s–1980s deploying administrative means to minimize a political crisis.

## HONG KONG'S ANTI-CORRUPTION EXPERIENCE

The establishment of the high-powered ICAC in Hong Kong in 1974 by the colonial Governor Murray MacLehose had proved to be greatly successful in breaking up corruption syndicates within government departments and in detecting corrupt practices in both the public and private sectors. In the words of MacLehose himself, the ICAC 'has changed much in Hong Kong that many regarded as unchangeable' (quoted in King, 1980, p. 115). Indeed, this very indigenous setup had in no insignificant degree created a new phase of political development in Hong Kong and was credited as a kind of 'charismatic institution', with immense symbolic and organizational capabilities and being able to command a high degree of public commitment which in turn provided it with some of its own institutional resources (King, 1980, p. 115).

The ICAC was an outcome of both evolution and revolution. It was not a sudden product. As Kuan (1981) pointed out, the formation of the ICAC came after over 20 years of government efforts to develop stricter and more severe legal measures against corruption. The first proper anti-corruption legislation passed in Hong Kong was the 1948 Prevention of Corruption Ordinance which was based on an equivalent law in Britain. An Anti-Corruption Branch was set up in the Police Force. From 1956 a Standing Committee on Corruption was established to advise the government on anti-corruption measures. This Committee was reorganized in 1961 to include an unofficial member each from the Legislative and Executive Councils in response to public pressure for an independent commission of enquiry. The first local legislation on corruption, the Prevention of Bribery Ordinance, was enacted in 1971. In 1973, because of the unexplained escape from Hong Kong of a corruption suspect, Chief Police Superintendent Peter Godber, there were mass demonstrations and calls for quick and tough action by the government whose legitimacy had now suffered further erosion. As King remarked, the government was defenceless in the face of the public outcry over the Godber escape and 'to say that there was an authority crisis is no exaggeration' (King, 1980, p. 117). The then newly arrived reform-minded governor was thus able to seize upon the opportunity to appoint a Commission of Inquiry under Justice Alastair Blair-Kerr in 1973, who eventually recommended the setting up of an ICAC answerable directly to the governor. MacLehose was determined 'to represent the cause of the people' and through the ICAC to launch a 'silent revolution' to provide Hong Kong with 'a clean society and a clean government' (Kuan, 1981, p. 41).

However, as Lee observed, the change in social awareness suggested that corruption as a social problem had 'both an objective and a subjective aspect' (Lee, 1981, p. 6). Corrupt activities were widespread (objective aspect) in Hong Kong for more than a century, but corruption only came to be recognized (subjective aspect) as a serious problem within the 1970s, particularly following the establishment of the ICAC.[1] That the colonial government was prepared to target corruption for major reform in the 1970s but not previously, needs to be explained by the post-1967 change in the government's political agenda,[2] particularly after MacLehose's arrival, manipulating the 'political opportunity' created by the Godber crisis to re-establish the legitimacy of the government. The ICAC was in effect an administrative response to a more fundamental political problem facing British colonial governance in Hong Kong at the time:

> Many thought that government was run only in the interests of those who held office. More believed that officials and the police, in particular, were corrupt and that it was necessary to pay bribes to obtain services. ... For a government anxious to establish its legitimacy on a basis of positive support, it was clearly important that it should be seen to be strongly opposed to graft. When the opportunity arose to demonstrate government's commitment to the prevention of corruption, MacLehose was quick to seize it. (Scott, 1989, p. 146)

In this respect, as Scott analyzed, colonial governments faced constant, if often latent, challenges to their legitimacy – 'a regime established and ultimately reliant on force cannot easily win the consent of the governed' (Scott, 1989, p. 322). Legitimacy is not just about strength and the capacity to govern. It is also about the moral basis of the government's authority. In the case of colonial Hong Kong, the government's justification of its right to rule rested mainly on five contingent factors:

- Its record of past performance-proven capacity in delivering public goods, i.e. its administrative efficiency;
- The right to rule as legitimized by epistemocratic authority, i.e. its claims to specialized knowledge and wisdom (bureaucratic paternalism);
- Its ability to maintain its position by interpreting what it said was the consensus, through a rationalization process of 'consultation and consent' (the advisory system);
- The 'sheer habituation' or apathy of the population, i.e. the people's acquiescence of the status quo; and
- Economic prosperity as an important support for legitimacy.

Against this backdrop, the problems created by widespread corruption to the government's legitimacy were twofold. Corruption had become dysfunctional to both economic development and the modernization of government administrative capacity, which were crucial to improving its performance on the legitimacy front. By grasping an anti-corruption agenda, the reformist colonial administration under MacLehose was able to demonstrate its epistemocratic authority and consensus-interpretation capacity (Scott, 1989, pp. 323–324) by way of a major strategic response to a crisis considered no longer tolerable by all quarters of society. Doing something about what everybody wanted to be eradicated, and doing it right the first time, was a sure way of winning support and legitimacy. As the ICAC scheme subsequently showed, the innovative way of combating corruption through a high-powered agency was able to underscore both the *moral* determination as well as the *organizational* effectiveness of the new administration to finally do something about corruption. The worth of government was thus proven.

Since its inception in 1974, ICAC has adopted a comprehensive and all-embracing strategy (the three-pronged approach emphasizing enforcement, prevention and community education). Unlike anti-corruption reforms elsewhere, the building blocks of such a strategy were based on the realization that corruption involved complex interactions between state and society; that cultural values played a major role in defining the operational and practical meanings of corruption; and that legal reforms, if they were to be effective, had to be closely linked to those values (Lo, 2001, p. 25). ICAC was indeed given wide-ranging powers to investigate government and business dealings, some of which would be politically impossible in other countries and even deemed draconian by current-day Hong Kong standards. In addition to the ICAC, the colonial administration had also embarked on extensive measures of civil service modernization and public sector reform in the final decades of colonial rule (Cheung, 1999, 2006).

By now the ICAC is one of the largest anti-corruption agencies in the world and a role model emulated by other countries (notably Australia and South Korea). According to its 2006 commissioned survey (ICAC, 2007), 65.4% considered corruption uncommon, and 82.2% expected less corruption or a steady corruption situation in the coming year. On a 0–10 point scale (0 representing total rejection and 10 total tolerance), the mean scores for public tolerance of corruption in the civil service and the business sector were extremely low, at 1.1 and 1.8, respectively. The ICAC has also become one of post-1997 icons of Hong Kong, to mark the city's difference from mainland China under the 'one country two systems' framework; hence official publicity has emphasized that '*Hong Kong has the ICAC!*' Looking back, it is clear that Hong Kong's anti-corruption efforts have worked not only because of ICAC's three-pronged strategy, but also due to the presence of a strong political will on the part of government, as sustained by an equally strong public consensus, to make Hong Kong a clean society.

## CORRUPTION IN CHINA: FEATURES AND CAUSES

In China, corruption is usually described as the using of public authority (and public resources) for private interests (and purposes) ('*yiquan musi*'). According to Articles 382–396 of the Criminal Law of the People's Republic of China (PRC), corruption crimes occur when any state functionary, by taking advantage of his office, appropriates, steals, swindles public money or property or by other means illegally takes it into his own possession; extorts money or property from another person, or illegally accepts another person's money or property in return for securing benefits for the person; for the purpose of securing illegitimate benefits, gives money or property to a state functionary, or introduces a bribe to a state functionary; misappropriates public funds for his own use or for conducting illegal activities or for profit-making activities; divides up state-owned assets in secret, and so on.

Both Heidenheimer (1989) and White (1996) suggested a three-class categorization of corruption in China. In a gist, *public office-centered corruption* includes graft, bribe, fraud, embezzlement, extortion, smuggling, tax evasion, etc., which may be regarded as economic crimes. *Market-centered corruption* includes 'unhealthy practices' such as extravagance and waste, and spending public money to support luxurious work conditions and/or life style of senior officials; as well as 'institutional corruption' whereby officials of public institutions use their institutional power to increase the revenue of their institutions and improve the welfare of their staff through various legal, semi-legal and illegal means, including engaging in business activities and imposing fines or collecting all sorts of administrative fees and so-called service charges (which Chinese critics called '*guan tao*' during the late 1980s to early 1990s). *Public-interest-centered* corruption refers to those practices constituting a kind of 'common practice' of social life, including all forms of nepotism and favoritism, often alluded to as the relationship networks (or '*quanzi*').

Despite rapid economic development and growing affluence, mainland China has scored poorly in Transparency International's corruption perception index (Table 1). Corruption problems are perceived to be particularly acute in the real estate and banking sectors (Political & Economic Risk Consultancy Ltd., 2007, p. 7). What makes matters worse is that 'the local judicial system has a poor record of prosecuting corruption and judges and police are frequently seen as being more apart of the problem than the solution' (*ibid.*). According to the Supreme People's Procuratorate (Ye, 2006),[3] corruption crimes nowadays display the following characteristics:

- Corruption crime cases have become more numerous, of which the proportion of the major and important cases is high. In 2005 alone, some 41,500 state functionaries were investigated for involvement in bribery, embezzlement and malfeasance crime cases, of which some 8,500 involved accepting bribes of RMB100,000 and above, or misappropriations of pubic funds of RMB1 million and above. Among the culprits, about 2,800

were at county/division head level and above, of whom 196 were at departmental head level in provincial and central governments and 8 were at provincial leadership or ministerial level.
- Corruption crimes spread along with the development and transformation of the economy. In the early 1980s, officials took advantage of the loopholes resulting from prices differentials existing in the 'double track system' as the planned economy transited towards a market economy system. In the mid- to late-1980s, corruption crimes and embezzlement cases arose in the communication and transportation fields which were the 'bottlenecks' of economic reform. From the 1990s onwards, corruption crimes spread to the financial system, particularly in the approval of bank loans. As more construction projects of highways were launched, bribery and embezzlement crimes involving transport bureaus became common.
- Corruption crimes frequently involve collusion among several or even tens or hundreds of suspected officials in a cluster of related cases. In certain local governments, it was estimated that collusion cases took up over 30% of the total caseload.
- There seems a trend of 'corruption succession' among different holders of the same position, so that even after the predecessor was punished for corruption crime, the successor fell into the same path of corruption, in what is described in Chinese as the phenomenon of 'goes the former, follows the latter' (*qianpu houji*).
- Corruption crimes often involve the whole family, where two or more members of a family collectively engage in bribery and corruption, such as collusion between husband and wife, parents and children, and in-laws.
- Trading in official positions is becoming rampant. Owing to the lack of transparency in the cadre personnel system, some officials either take advantage of their authority over the transfer, appointment and removal of cadres to amass a fortune, or become the target of bribery by those pursuing official positions illegally in order to seek access to power and privileges.

China's fight against corruption has taken several twists and turns over the past half-century. Each period represents a different interpretation of the problems of corruption, resulting in the state's particular strategic response to them.

*Maoist Period: Combating Corruption as Bureaucratic Failure*

In the early years of the PRC following the rise to power of the Chinese Communist Party (CCP), corruption was seen as a result of either the moral/ideological breakdown of cadres or their behaviors of bureaucratism. In spite of the relatively puritan features of early PRC rule, where cadres as revolutionary vanguards and champions of the mass line ('from the masses, to the masses'), were expected to live a simple life and not to become parasites of the masses, abuse of power and economic crimes were recognized quite early on as the new social ills of the young revolutionary regime; hence the *san-fan* ('three anti') and *wu-fan* ('five anti') campaigns in the early- to mid-1950s against economic crimes and waste as the country went through the initial stage of economic reconstruction and socialist transformation. Until the end of the Cultural Revolution in the mid-1970s, such social ills were regarded as the problems of bureaucratic failure, not the nature of the socialist economy and society which was deemed superior to capitalism, nor the nature of the communist political order of one-party dictatorship which was portrayed as even more democratic and accountable to the masses than Western-style liberal democracy.

Bureaucratic failure and bureaucratism were blamed on the lack of revolutionary fervor and a proper state of thought (the correct ideological and political lines) on the part of the cadres. Problems were perceived within the context of ethical norms and ideological correctness rather than in terms of legal and structural inadequacies. Maoist prescriptions to bureaucratic problems took the forms of re-education, rectification and purges, aiming at reinstituting a correct socialist moral and ideological frame (like the mass line, and the campaign to learn from Lei Feng[4]) that could contain and minimize the abuse of cadre power and deviant behaviors. In a totalist, one-party state which centralized all powers and functions – political, economic, social and cultural, it was understandable that any defects in its cadre bureaucracy were bound to cause great ramifications across various spheres. In the same vein, all political, economic and social problems were easily reduced to being problems of bureaucratic failure. Harding (1981) identified three broad approaches used by the CCP to deal with the problem of bureaucracy including corruption:

- *Rationalization* – seeking to perfect the bureaucracy (on the assumption that problems arise if the system departs from the bureaucratic ideal);
- *External remedialism* – subjecting the bureaucracy to effective outside (external) supervision and control, including the masses; and
- *Internal remedialism* – introducing non-bureaucratic elements into the bureaucracy to alleviate problems arising from bureaucratic organization.

In the 1950s, a system of formal networks of cadre control was instituted similar to that in the Soviet Union – with a state Procuratorate; a Ministry of Supervision and its network of local supervisory offices to investigate cases of administrative malfeasance; and the party's Central Control Commission and local control commissions to control party members. Redefined procedures, standards and rules were promulgated for the management of cadres. There was initially reduced reliance on mass campaigns as a method for implementing policy as higher priority was given to *regularized* bureaucratic practice rather than mass mobilization. However, when more institutional means of perfecting and disciplining the bureaucracy failed to achieve results, more radical and non-institutional means were resorted to, such as open-door rectification in the late 1950s and early 1960s, and the radical revolutionary style of mass campaigns and purges witnessed during the Cultural Revolution (1966–1976) (the period of *Radicalism* in Harding's words).

### *Reform Period: Corruption as Bureaucratic-Cum-Economic Rent-Seeking*

The Cultural Revolution had much weakened the CCP both ideologically and politically, resulting in what were characterized by intellectuals as the 'three confidence crises' (*sanxin weiji*) – lack of trust in the party, lack of confidence in the future and lack of faith in the Communist ideology. There was widespread distrust of open door rectifications and campaigns and the radical approach was discarded when the old guards led by Deng Xiaoping and Chen Yun returned to power in the late 1970s. External remedial measures were restored to enforce a better regulated cadre system, notably through the introduction of new laws and regulations, re-establishment of the Ministry of Supervision in the government system, a re-styled and strengthened Central Commission on Disciplinary Inspection (CCDI) in the party system and various personnel management reform measures.

During the socialist era of state planning and control, the state bureaucracy centralized all economic resources and surpluses of society and the decisions on their distribution and use under what was sometimes described as 'an economy based on positions' (*zhiquan jingji*), giving rise to bureaucratic rent-seeking behaviors rooted in interdependency relationships among cadres. The advent of economic reform and opening-up after the Cultural Revolution, culminating in the introduction of a full-fledged market economy in the 1990s, should have in theory ended the previous 'positions economy'. However, the new but underinstitutionalized market nurtured by a state which still exercised immense administrative power had led to the rise and rapid spread of various bureaucratic-cum-economic rent-seeking activities. Instead of terminating the old vicious cycle, new opportunities were opened up to corruption which was brought to record highs. By 1995, some Chinese observers maintained that there were 'no officials who were not corrupt' (White, 1996, pp. 151). Corruption had so permeated various sectors of society that the phenomenon was described as 'whole people corruption', satirically paraphrasing the official term of 'whole people' ownership [meaning state ownership] of the economy in the Maoist past (*ibid.*). According to He (2000), there were some common explanations of such rise of corruption in Reform China:

1. The co-existence of dual economic systems (i.e. a state-planned sector and a market-commodity sector) during the whole transition period provided plenty of incentives and opportunities for corrupt practices.
2. The breakdown of the prior distribution of national income among different social strata (i.e. the relative reduction of officials' income) drove government officials and public institutions to seek extra income to supplement their own or their staff's relative low and fixed official salaries.
3. The loopholes in, and weakness of, regulatory policies and institutions, certain policy failures, and a lack of experience and technology in the anti-corruption agencies tackling the new forms of corruption, all contributed to the growth of corruption.
4. The incompleteness of political reform and the weakness of the current political system undermined anti-corruption efforts which, in turn, promoted the further proliferation of corruption.
5. The decline in the moral costs of corruption had stimulated its further spread.
6. Certain traditional factors (such as the feudal and absolutist traditions) and international factors (such as the impact of globalization) also contributed to the growth of corruption.

# THE FIGHT AGAINST CORRUPTION IN CHINA

Over the past three decades of reforms, combating corruption was without exception put at the forefront of the CCP's political agenda each time a new leadership came to power. According to Hu and Hu (2005, p. 537), two major anti-corruption campaigns were launched in late 1978 (when Deng Xiaoping replaced Mao's designated successor Hua Guofeng as the new strongman of the party) and 1989 (following the Tiananmen crackdown on the pro-democracy movement), respectively. On both occasions, the CCP was deemed at the verge of organizational breakdown and embroiled in a serious legitimacy crisis.

### Rehabilitation of Party and State Control Mechanisms after Cultural Revolution

At the Third Plenum of the 11th CCP Central Committee held in December 1978, the CCDI was established to enforce strict discipline in a party which had been torn apart by a decade of rebellion, purges, unruliness and anarchism during the Cultural Revolution. The people's procuratorate and people's courts systems were also revived. The National People's Congress (NPC) returned to normal functioning after a new state constitution was promulgated in December 1982. This represented a strategy of returning to the rational-bureaucratic approach of the 1950s. In 1982, as economic reform unfolded, Deng warned his fellow comrades at the Central Committee Politburo meeting:

> Since our implementation of the twin policies of opening up externally and reinvigorating our economy internally, it has taken no more than one to two years' time to see quite many of our cadres becoming corrupted. Those involved in economic criminal activities are by no means small in number; they constitute a large number. ... This wave is coming hard on us. If our party does not take it seriously, to stop it resolutely, our party and country would truly encounter the question of whether they would 'change face'. This is not an exaggerating warning. (Deng, 1994, pp. 402–403)

Between 1979 and 1989, 23 pieces of rules and decisions on combating corruption were made (Hu & Hu, 2005, p. 537).

In the aftermath of the 1989 Tiananmen crisis, despite political setback, Deng insisted on continuing economic reform but urged the new leadership headed by Jiang Zemin to take strong actions to control and penalize corrupt activities, particularly at the senior levels, in order to restore people's confidence in the party. After all, corruption by public institutions and officials (*quan tao*) was a key cause of student resentment that led to the protests and hunger strike at Tiananmen Square in the spring of 1989. Soon after becoming party General Secretary, Jiang told a national conference of chiefs of organization department in August 1989,

> The spread of corruption has seriously damaged the relations between the party and the masses, and become the excuse for our enemies inside and outside the country to subvert us. The struggle against corruption is crucial to the life and death of the party. (Selected Important Documents since the Thirteenth Party Congress, 1991, p. 580)

From 1989 to 2001, another 32 pieces of anti-corruption rules and decisions were made (Hu & Hu, 2005, p. 537). Despite these exhortations, corruption as a political disease and social illness continued to escalate in scale and degree, causing rising public concern. For example, a 1996 survey found that Chinese workers ranked corruption as the social problem that concerned them the most, above problems like wage reform, inflation and law and order.[5] Surveys by the Chinese Academy of Social Sciences in 2001 found that the urban and rural respondents named corruption as the top and second top factors affecting social stability, respectively (cited in Hu & Hu, 2005, p. 542, Table 2).[6] Middle to senior party and state cadres (district/department level and above) polled also pointed to corruption as the most serious problem (Hu & Hu, 2005, p. 544, Table 4).

## Under the Current Hu-Wen Leadership

Three decades of economic reform have enabled China to experience a boom not seen before in the contemporary period. There is much talk of the new rise of China in the 21st century. However, as the new leadership of President and party General Secretary Hu Jiantao and Premier Wen Jiaao took over power at the 16th Party Congress in 2002, it had obviously felt the mounting pressure to upscale efforts to control corruption. The growing discontent by the general public (especially from a better educated and informed younger generation) towards worsening corruption and abuse of power by officials, amidst widening gaps in income and welfare in society, would make people lose faith not only in the party, but also in the present economic marketization and reform policies which are perceived to have allowed corruption to proliferate. It is also threatening social stability and cohesion, contrary to the kind of 'harmonious society' that the Hu-Wen leadership seeks to build to mark the new approach of people-based governance.[7]

Enforcement actions have been intensified. At the 3rd session of the 10th NPC in March 2006, the Procurator-General of the Supreme People's Procuratorate, Jia Chunwang reported that 2,960 officials at or above country level were investigated for corruption charges – among whom 11 officials were at provincial or ministerial level (*People's Daily Online*, 9 March, 2005). Prominent senior officials convicted included former Minister for Land and Resources Tian Fengshan, former Guizhou provincial party secretary Liu Fangren, and former Hubei provincial party deputy secretary and governor Zhang Guoguang, who were given sentences ranging from 11 to 12 years to life imprisonment (*ibid.*). According to the Chief Justice Xiao

*Table 2.* Corruption in China – Conservative versus Liberal Claims.

|  | Conservative | Liberal |
| --- | --- | --- |
| Causes of corruption | • Structural causes as indirect or external, motivational factors as direct and fundamental<br>• Corruption as caused by market reforms. While market economy can raise efficiency, it also leads to money fetishism by sanctioning monetary value and self-interest as highest goals. Corruption results when individuals commercialize all human transactions | • Structural causes as fundamental<br>• Corruption only a byproduct of market reforms; it is an incomplete and obstructed market, rather than the market per se, that is the real culprit<br>• Roots of corruption lie in the intervention and destruction of economic activities by administrative power – rent-seeking by bureaucrats |
| Harms of corruption | • Corruption shakes public confidence in the government and party, damages their legitimacy and provides pretext for 'bourgeois liberals' to incite anti-government sentiments | • Corruption casts doubts on the future of reform and prevents market from functioning properly<br>• Economic development is top priority and some irregular activities are to be tolerated as necessary trade-off |
| Remedies of corruption | • Eradicating corruption requires reconsidering and halting market reforms<br>• State and ideological control needs to be strengthened, not weakened | • Retreat of government from the economy<br>• More genuine market reforms necessary |

*Source:* Sun (2001).

Yang, president of the Supreme People's Court, in a separate report to NPC, the court system penalized 772 corruption officials and dealt with 24,148 cases involving graft, bribe-taking and other corrupt activities in 2004 (*ibid.*). In 2004, the party's CCDI handled a caseload of 166,705 crimes and punished 170,850 party members found to have misbehaved, including 16 provincial/ministerial officials and 432 at or above prefecture level, according to a meeting on clean government held in February 2005 (*ibid.*). What was disturbing was that a total of 345 procurators, 411 judges and 681 revenue collectors were also punished for graft charges in 2004 (*ibid.*). Corruption figures had not subsided in 2005. Jia Chunwang told the 4th session of the 10th NPC held in March 2006, that of a total of 41,447 government officials were probed for corruption and dereliction of duty, 30,205 were brought to court (The Central Government of the People's Republic of China website, 11 March, 2006). At total of 2,799 officials above the county level – including 196 at prefecture and 8 at provincial and ministerial levels – were investigated. In addition, 9,117 executives of state-owned companies were probed for misappropriating or embezzling company assets (*ibid.*).

Under the new leadership, various policy statements, rules and legislations were introduced aimed at curbing corruption and malpractices. At the Fourth Plenum of the 16th CCP Central Committee held in September 2004, a core document titled *Implementation Outline for Building and Improving the System to Punish and Prevent Corruption* (hereinafter '*Implementation Outline*') was considered, and subsequently promulgated in January 2005 (Xinhua Net, 16 January, 2005), which advocated a three-pronged approach with equal emphasis on education (as fundamental), institution-building (as guarantee) and supervision and monitoring (as the key) to combat and prevent corruption. A holistic approach to deal with the roots and sources of corruption in addition to the symptoms and crimes was promised. The document also highlighted the needs of strict enforcement against any breaches of the law, especially in the major cases. Primary targets were the abuse of power and misappropriations in central organs and among senior cadres. It was aimed that the basic framework of an anti-corruption system covering both punishment and prevention be put in place by 2010. The goal is to ultimately establish an effective long-term ideological and ethical mechanism, an institutionalized anti-corruption system and a monitoring system of the exercise of power.

Since 2005, some 26 new rules, administrative measures and decisions directly or indirectly related to corruption control were made, notably: the *Party Regulations on Intra-Party Monitoring and Supervision* (25 August, 2005); *Provisions on the Responsibility System of Building a Fine Party Style of Work and a Clean and Honest Government* (16 January, 2005); *Provisional Guiding Principles for Honest and Clean Government by Party Members as Leading Cadres* (16 January, 2005) and *Provisional Rules Requiring Party Members as Leading Cadres to Report on Work and Anti-Corruption Performance* (26 February, 2006). Various rules, notices and opinions have also been issued to curb the involvement of government and party officials in commercial activities. In October 2005, the Standing Committee of the NPC approved China's access to the United Nations Convention Against Corruption. In September 2006, the Chinese government promulgated the *Declaration of Honest Government in China's Public Security*, requiring all police officers to take an oath of conduct, undertaking, inter alia, to lead an honest life while serving the public.

Besides anti-corruption measures and enforcement, Hu Jintao also launched a spiritual rejuvenation campaign known as the 'Eight Honours and Eight Disgraces' (*barong bachi*) Campaign in March 2006.[8] A 'Clean Government Channel' specializing in anti-corruption news and information is set up at Xinhua News Net. In March 2007, the establishment of a new National Corruption Prevention Bureau (NCPB) was approved, with ministerial status directly under the State Council and given a wider range of anti-corruption responsibilities including cadre education, institution building and international cooperation (*Wen Wei Po*, 21 March, 2007). The new Bureau, to be headed concurrently by the Minister of Supervision, will deal with corruption problems at their roots and work hand in hand with CCDI, the Ministry of Supervision and the Supreme People's Procuratorate.

## ANALYZING CHINA'S CORRUPTION CONTROL STRATEGY: CONSTRAINTS AND CHANGES

Despite the enhanced importance attached to fighting corruption by the top leadership, and after several decades of anti-corruption drives from the Maoist era of ideological campaigns to the current period of using law enforcement and disciplinary inspection, corruption continues to flourish. China's corruption control efforts are often frustrated by its enforcement constraints and caught in a dilemma in conceptualizing the politics of corruption. Nevertheless, there are signs of changes in the most recent years.

## ENFORCEMENT PROBLEMS: FROM CAMPAIGN ENFORCEMENT TO INSTITUTIONALIZATION

As Wedeman described vividly,

> the repeated ebb and flow of China's war against corruption have ... left many with the strong impression that anticorruption campaigns are a form of Beijing Opera in which the actors rush about the stage amid great sound and fury in a drama that ultimately

signifies nothing because, after the din dies down and the actors leave the stage, corruption abides. (Wedeman, 2005, p. 94)

China's strategy of 'enforcement swamping', relying on intensive periodic campaigns targeted at cracking down some big fish was credited by some as being successful in the sense that it helped to push corruption rates back below the 'tipping point' beyond which further increases would have overwhelmed the regime's enforcement resources and led to a 'crisis of corruption' (Manion, 1999). It was suggested that such a strategy was necessitated by the lack of enforcement resources and capacity (including policy capacity) to wipe out corruption. Campaign enforcement involves the consequential steps of increasing the intensity of internal monitoring, then increasing prosecutorial efficiency, then changing the incentive structure by offering 'clemency' to those who surrender, and finally mobilizing extra-judicial monitoring mechanisms, including the masses. Whether used in a randomized or reactionary manner, the primary function of campaign-style enforcement is more to *control* corruption than to *eradicate* it, irrespective of the rhetoric accompanying such campaigns (Wedeman, 2005, p. 98). It worked through a process of changing the calculus of cadres and their incentive structures by temporarily increasing their risk of being caught and the severity of punishment, and by creating uncertainly about the future risk of detection (*ibid.*).

The short-term goal is to reduce the rate of corruption by capturing corrupt officials, so that in the long term, there is deterrence effect because lowering the rate of corruption will enhance the efficacy of routine policing by improving the balance between enforcement capabilities and the rate of corruption. However, given this kind of 'kitten-and-mice' strategy, it would also mean that corruption is not meant to be eradicated entirely because there does not exist a policy of 'zero tolerance'. Campaign enforcement may also lay the seeds for more high-level corruption – so long as routine detection rates remain relatively low and only soar up during periods of hyper-enforcement (i.e. during campaign periods), campaigns are likely to deter low-level corruption but not high-stakes high-level corruption. Cadres engaged in high-stakes corruption will have stronger incentives to sit tight than those engaged in petty corruption. By deterring low-level and petty corruption without deterring high-stakes high-level corruption – and perhaps even contributing to high-states corruption by encouraging corrupt cadres to demand bigger bribes – campaign enforcement might have by default actually caused the subsequent intensification of corruption (Wedeman, 2005, pp. 114–115). Tentative comparative data analysis also suggests that there has been a significant decrease in the odds that corrupt officials will get caught over the past decade, thus widening the gap between actual rate of corruption and reported rate of corruption (Wedeman, 2007).

Although its rhetoric still resembles that of mass movements, Sapio (2005) contends that the anti-corruption strategy nowadays consists of a far more complex set of measures marking a clear departure from the past style of enforcement, as exemplified by the multiple legal and administrative measures introduced in recent years. Instead of ad hoc campaigns, there is now growing institutionalization of a three-pronged policy where preventive measures are taken alongside repressive and propagandistic ones, underpinned by improved legal foundations and better-trained legal personnel (Sapio, 2005, p. 4). However, selective implementation is still discernible in three aspects: *selective sanction*, i.e. letting the party deal with corruption crimes using 'organizational measures' (*zuzhi chuli*) rather than disciplinary or criminal sanctions; *selective prosecution*, i.e. graft and passive bribery being more likely prosecuted than active bribery and misappropriations of public funds; and *selective sentencing*, i.e. the inconsistency of sentencing by the courts (*ibid.*, pp. 40–41). Such selectivity could be explained by local protectionism and the broad and unchecked regulatory powers enjoyed by local anti-corruption organs, resulting in eschewing the implementation of anti-corruption laws enacted by the center, and tolerating illegal practices seen as promoting short-term local economic interests:

> Acts of misappropriation are aimed at different purposes. Notwithstanding the absolutely negative impact sorted by corruption on long term economic growth, misappropriation can often result in a boost of local growth, albeit one standing on shaking foundations.
> 
> Active bribery can sort the same effect. Starting from the nineties bribery has been employed to get access to resources needed to fulfill the plans for local economic growth. (Sapio, 2005, pp. 37–38)

In other words, the developmental priorities of local party bosses and their concern for local economic and revenue growth, in light of the new emphasis on local achievements as judged by hard data, are at least partly responsible for the institutionalization of economic rent-seeking in the form of corrupt practices. Another problem is the existence of corruption even within anti-corruption agencies, including the procuratorate and courts. For example, a total of 144 provincial-level anti-corruption officials were dismissed and expelled from the party in 2004 (Guang, 2005). In June 2004, Han Jianlin, Director of the Anti-Corruption Bureau of the Jiangsu Provincial Procuratorate, was dismissed because of corruption charges (Sina net, 19 June, 2004). As Manion (2004, p. 201) observed, 'in a setting of widespread corruption, corrupt enforcers and a shortage of enforcement resources, relative to the scope of the problem, pose significant obstacles'.

## CONCEPTUALIZING CORRUPTION: FROM A CRISIS OF THE SYSTEM TO THE PRODUCTION OF LEGITIMACY

The rampant situation of corruption within the context of rapid economic reform and social transformation has triggered two opposing calls for rectification: the traditionalist or *socialist-conservative* tendency blames the market as the source of all evils and urges more government control and regulation; whereas the *liberal–reformist* tendency blames the government (and hence the power of officials) as the source of evil and advocates full-fledged marketization and the withdrawal of state interference. To the latter, alluding to Huntington's theory of modernization (Huntington, 1968, 1970), corruption is sometimes functionally unavoidable given the existing structural constraints of a government controlled and interfered market. The claims and counterclaims are illustrated in Table 2.

As Sun (2001) remarked, the two forces appear more or less equally matched, at both the political and intellectual levels. Such contestation in the corruption discourse is expected to persist as the economic, social and political transition of China deepens. Whether one takes the conservative or liberal view, corruption would still seem to stay as a permanent feature because on the one hand, as there is no prospect of the existing one-party state system coming to an end soon, state power would continue to be politically unchecked, thus restraining market autonomy and encouraging bureaucratic rent-seeking (the structural cause of corruption in the eyes of the liberals); while on the other hand, with the party-state being unlikely to put a brake on market reforms, the opportunities for corruption caused by the re-interfacing of bureaucracy and market would remain abundant. The deepening of reform may ironically contribute to further intensification of corruption by progressively reducing the structural opportunities for low-level corruption while creating new opportunities for the high-level high-stakes corruption (Gong, 1997; He, 2000).

While it may be true that corruption will persist as a major social and political problem to China in the foreseeable future, the party leadership's latest response to it has seen a strategic shift, in turning it around to become a political narrative that helps shore up the legitimacy of the state. As Hsu

(2001) explained, in the 1980s, political critics, dissidents and disgruntled intellectuals all drew upon the traditionalist collective narrative of corruption to blame the leadership and the political system for various social problems, and in so doing threatened the political authority of the party-state (as happened in the Tiananmen protests of 1989). Since the 1990s, however, party leaders and the official media had revised the story of corruption so that it was no longer a sign of government failure, but that of the party-state fighting corruption on behalf of its people in order to bring them economic opportunities, better living standards and social stability. Corruption, as public enemy number one, is now blamed by the state for harming economic development by 'debilitating the party-state's ability to implement its policies of economic construction, economic reform, and "opening up" to the outside world' (Hsu, 2001, p. 44).

In re-articulating the narrative of corruption, the state turns around the traditional narrative as promoted by dissidents that interpreted corruption as a sign of an incompetent and immoral regime; instead, the economic management narrative translated anti-corruption into the symbol of the state's efforts to improve economic development. As Hsu saw it, the new narrative succeeded not only in co-opting the issue of corruption, but also in becoming a commonly borrowed collective narrative that was used even by the critics (Hsu, 2001, p. 46). It may also be added that within the factional power politics of the CCP, corruption sometimes provides a convenient premise for removing political rivals or insubordinate senior cadres by exposing their corruption crimes even though the motive for action against them is essentially a political one. The removal of former Beijing municipal party chief Chen Xitong by ex-party General Secretary Jiang Zemin in 1995 (Wedeman, 1996), and the latest removal of former Shanghai municipal party chief Chen Liangyu by current party General Secretary Hu Jintao, both on corruption charges, are widely seen as political moves to foil a major challenge by a powerful local party boss to the consolidation of the new party leadership's authority at the center.

## CAN CHINA LEARN FROM HONG KONG?

In terms of both enforcement and the political strategy to achieve legitimacy, the Chinese leadership can learn from Hong Kong's past anti-corruption initiative. Mainland China today is similar to colonial Hong Kong in the 1970s: corruption becoming rampant and somewhat institutionalized; the government suffering from a serious legitimacy crisis;

and there being no opportunity to have more fundamental constitutional reform in order to re-legitimize government politically, but every possibility for the leadership to seize upon the window of opportunity induced by the crisis of corruption to launch a 'silent revolution' to regain some degree of political trust and legitimacy. Using Kingdon (1984)'s model, both the 'problem' and the 'politics' are present, even the 'policy' may be around if the Hong Kong anti-corruption approach could be adopted to bring about effectiveness (which seems plausible given that the new NCPB is clearly modeled on Hong Kong's ICAC).

Quah identifies three distinct patterns of corruption control (Quah, 2003, pp. 16–17): *Pattern 1* occurs when there are anti-corruption laws but no specific agency to implement these laws. *Pattern 2* involves the combination of anti-corruption laws and several anti-corruption agencies. *Pattern 3* involves the impartial implementation of comprehensive anti-corruption laws by a specific anti-corruption agency (ACA). Singapore and Hong Kong, both world-acclaimed to be highly successful in keeping a clean government and clean society through vigorous corruption control efforts, belong to Pattern 3. Mainland China is an example of Pattern 2. The question is: *Can China learn from Hong Kong and move from Pattern 2 to Pattern 3?* Based on his comparative study of four Asian countries (Singapore, Hong Kong, Thailand and South Korea), Quah (in this issue) further sets out six pre-conditions for the effectiveness of an ACA:

1. the ACA must be incorruptible;
2. the ACA must be independent from the police and from political control;
3. there must be comprehensive anti-corruption legislation;
4. the ACA must have adequate staff and funding;
5. the ACA must enforce the anti-corruption laws impartially; and
6. political will is crucial for minimizing corruption.

The related question is: *Can China's ACAs satisfy these pre-conditions, or are these pre-conditions critical to anti-corruption effectiveness in China?*

## ENFORCEMENT MODEL – MULTI-AGENCY STRUCTURE TO REMAIN

There is no doubt that during recent years, there have been increasing voices among policy advisers and researchers urging the Chinese government to move in a single-agency direction. For example, Hu Angang, director of

Tsinghua University's China Studies Research Centre, has been advocating the enactment of an Anti-Corruption Law[9] and the establishment of a Central Anti-Corruption Authority (by amalgamating the Major Cases Unit of the CCDI and the Anti-Corruption Bureau of the Supreme People's Procuratorate), as part of the new third-generation anti-corruption strategy of the Hu-Wen leadership (as contrasted with the Deng and Jiang strategies). Recent anti-corruption emphasis has also certainly pointed to the move towards a three-pronged approach similar to the Hong Kong ICAC model in fighting corruption on the three fronts of enforcement, prevention and education. The latest *Implementation Outline* adopted in January 2005 underscores such an approach. Addressing an international corruption studies course organized by the University of Hong Kong in November 2006, a Vice-Director of the Ministry of Supervision, Guo Hongliang, made it quite clear that Hong Kong was a role model for the mainland in its anti-corruption offensive: 'Hong Kong is such a good example in its fight against bribery' (*South China Morning Post*, 7 November, 2006). Modeling on ICAC's three-pronged strategy, however, is not necessarily the same as adopting its single-ACA approach. On the contrary, as the latest launch of the NCPB indicates, China is to stay put with a three-agency approach – meaning CCDI (as the party anti-corruption organ), Ministry of Supervision (that acts concurrently through the NCPB) and the Supreme People's Procuratorate (and its Anti-Corruption Bureau). All of these agencies have investigative powers and sometimes operate jointly as special 'work teams' on big cases.

Hong Kong (and also Singapore) is the pioneer of the single-agency approach to fight corruption. Compared with the multiple-agency approach used in other countries, this is more ambitious in that while creating a super-powerful 'lead' organization, it may also pose a higher power risk by possibly upsetting the balance and separation of governmental powers. The organizational politics of the Chinese system have to be taken into consideration in any process of transplanting the Hong Kong experience. In both Hong Kong and Singapore, the single-agency option was chosen because there was a crisis of legitimacy that threatened investor confidence and political stability (Meagher, 2005). Normally anti-corruption agencies need to be strategic in defining their focus because an unlimited mandate might well jeopardize its effectiveness. Hong Kong's ICAC is arguably the exception in that it is given a very broad anti-corruption jurisdiction over both the public and private sectors, in effect covering the whole of society, coupled with a 'zero-tolerance' mission. This kind of comprehensive model that seeks to eradicate rather than merely controlling corruption would be a far cry from the current situation in mainland China where selective enforcement and a multi-agency (involving party and state organs, with decentralizing of investigation and prosecution powers to local agencies) approach would still prevail, not to mention the fact that local economic protectionism often condones or even encourages bribery, misappropriations and others corrupt practices.

A related question is whether in the current political system of China, it is possible to establish a single ACA that stands even above party organs, and is accountable, independent, mandated with high power (both legislatively and administratively), and given reassurance of staff and budget resources. In practice, ACAs work not just on their own, but have to rely on the availability of adequate laws and procedures, and a proper system of the rule of law – accompanied by functional courts, free and active media, an energetic community of NGOs and public interest groups, and other capable agencies of restraint such as supreme audit and central bank (Meagher, 2005, p. 98). As China stands presently, it is desperately in need of such institutional mechanisms to create and sustain a habitat conducive to strong actions against corruption. In other words, anti-corruption is a key to more extensive reforms to the system of governance, but administrative and governance reforms in other aspects also need to be launched at the same time in order to give well-designed anti-corruption measures a conducive environment to bear fruit and become effective. As previous discussion shows, corruption within ACAs is a serious problem in China. In addition, ACAs in China cannot be free of political control within the party-state configuration. Since 1993, the Ministry of Supervision has in effect been operating with the CCDI under the so-called 'one working team, two organizational labels' model, a phenomenon also common in other function areas. A more optimistic view might be that given the overriding power of CCDI, which in effect leads other ACAs, a *quasi-single-agency model* is already in place by default.

However, the effectiveness of the party's own anti-corruption apparatus can be circumscribed. The 'dual leadership' system which local Disciplinary Inspection Committees work under – they are led vertically by CCDI *and* horizontally by the corresponding local party committee – can often frustrate anti-corruption investigations. Political interference, especially at the local levels, remains a major obstacle to anti-corruption work. As Gong (2006) points out, the local party boss who has great control over resources and personnel as a result of power decentralization from the center to various local levels, can easily become free from effective institutional oversight and disciplinary surveillance (dubbed the 'number one person phenomenon', *diyibashou xianxiang*). Party and state regulations relating to corruption remain quite scattered and a comprehensive anti-corruption law has yet to be enacted. Hence the overall ACA structure does not meet all of the preconditions found to be essential by Quah for effectiveness. Having said that, the fact that China remains a country tightly run by a party-state means that if the party leadership decides to take strong action against corrupt activities, its organizational capability is still a force to be reckoned with.

## The Politics of Corruption

It is generally believed that Hong Kong and Singapore were highly successful in eliminating widespread entrenched corruption at a time of accelerating economic takeoff three decades ago because the top officials in government undertook a dramatic – and credible – program of suppressing corruption (Meagher, 2005, p. 99). Anti-corruption efforts are unavoidably political. The causes and consequences of corruption, as well as the solutions for it, tend to be intertwined (Jain, 2001, p. 72). Should the political elites be corrupted, they would likely attempt to reduce the effectiveness of the legal and judicial systems through the manipulation of resource allocation and appointments, which in turn would weaken the effectiveness of the system to combat corruption. On the other hand, the politics of corruption also shows that the leadership's self-preservation could be a strong motivating force behind anti-corruption cleanups (Gillespie & Okrunhlik, 1991). Meagher's (2005, p. 88) review of the emergence of ACAs suggested that the 'constitutional moment' of their establishment was critically important, i.e. by capturing the momentum created by scandal and crisis, gaining consensus on a reasonably clear and realistic strategy and mobilizing the resources to implement it. During the post-1967 crisis of legitimacy in Hong Kong, by building up strong public expectations for combating corruption, and seizing the opportunity of an administration that was weakened by the crisis and thus internally less resistant to drastic reforms, MacLehose was able to accomplish what previously was thought almost impossible, either because of a lack in political will or the difficulty to secure intra-governmental consensus.

In today's China, corruption is clearly seen as a major crisis that hurts the political leadership in addition to the well-being of the ordinary citizens. The economic management narrative of corruption, though partly an attempt to snatch the corruption agenda from the critics and political dissidents by the party-state, also underscores the perceived long-term threat of corruption to the new leadership's mission to restore a harmonious society and regain political trust and legitimacy. The incumbent leadership clearly has the self-preservation motive. Regardless of the innovation in terminology and language employed in the current anti-corruption and governance reform campaigns – such as enhancing the democratic rule of the party, higher transparency, respect for the law, enhancing the governance capability of the party, institutional building of a corruption-free government, and so on – its ultimate goal is to curb corruption in the party and government in order to improve the quality of governance by the party-state, and thereby to reinvent the legitimacy of CCP rule in China against mounting internal discontent and international pressures and threats to the 'socialist' regime.[10]

The present anti-corruption offensive should not be read as just another round of spontaneous or ad hoc responses, but may be placed at the core of a reinvention agenda to be unveiled at the 17th Party Congress scheduled for late 2007. Indeed, the massive efforts in researching and planning anti-corruption work during recent years had come along with the 16th CCP Party Congress in 2002. They are part of a 'regime saving' project, mingled by political struggles and power consolidation means in 2005–2006, after the Hu-Wen strategy had faced challenges from different fronts, ranging from the so-called 'Shanghai circle', the emerging upper-middle class, to the giant domestic interests and the 'New Left' faction (i.e. the 'reform or not to reform' controversy).[11] The complexity of the present situation somewhat resembles that of the former British colonial government desperate to improve itself to maintain its rule in a developing and more educated Hong Kong in the 1970s, and a number of parallels in terms of problem, policy and politics (a la Kingdon, 1984) can be drawn (Table 3). This may well present a window of political opportunity for China to move into a steady and enhanced anti-corruption path in the years to come.

## CONCLUDING REMARKS

To conclude, so long as there is the perceived threat to the leadership's political security (i.e. a corruption-induced crisis), there should be a correspondingly strong political will to take mitigating or remedial action. The Hu-Wen leadership may have its own political motives and agenda (such as strengthening CCP rule), just as MacLehose had his own in colonial Hong Kong, but if such politically motivated strategy could be aligned with the general population's strong resentment towards widespread corruption and its rising expectations for some clear-cut actions against corruption,

*Table 3.* Comparing Present-Day China with Colonial Hong Kong in 1970s in Anti-Corruption Efforts Using Kingdon's Model.

|  | China (now) | Hong Kong (1970s) |
| --- | --- | --- |
| Problem | • Corruption becoming rampant and institutionalized hurting credibility of both party-state and economic reforms<br>• Corruption as officially defined 'problem' helping to underscore regime's determination to improve economy and people's livelihood – the economic management narrative | • Syndicated corruption becoming dysfunctional to both economic development and modernization of government to cope with new challenges<br>• Corruption as officially defined 'problem' helped to demonstrate colonial government's epistemocratic authority and consensus-interpretation capacity |
| Policy | • *Implementation Outline* (2005) marked new three-pronged approach (education, institution-building and supervision & monitoring) emphasizing both punitive and prevention actions<br>• Debate over need to move to single-agency approach | • Setting up super-strong ICAC and adopting three-pronged approach (enforcement, prevention and education) |
| Politics | • Hu-Wen leadership seeking to promote party and government reforms without questioning CCP rule in China<br>• Anti-corruption can be means to improve quality of public sector and regain people's trust and political legitimacy for the party | • MacLehose seized on political opportunity in early 1970s to use anti-corruption as means to underscore government reforms and to gain political trust and legitimacy, in the absence of constitutional reform |

*Source:* Author.

then there is the possibility that a new consensus can be achieved that is conducive to a more comprehensive and sustainable anti-corruption strategy. China may not follow exactly the path of Hong Kong and Singapore, in terms of shifting towards a single-ACA approach, and its anti-corruption drive will remain shaped by political factors and institutional constraints as discussed in this chapter, but this should not mean that the country is not able to make some good progress in fighting corruption and plugging some institutional loopholes. It is clear, though, that combating corruption involves not just the ACA front, but more wide-ranging efforts in institutional and governance reforms.

## NOTES

1. This is somewhat similar to the conceptual distinction made between 'condition' and 'problem' in agenda setting by Kingdon (1984). Condition is an objective situation while 'problem' is how the policy-makers define the condition for subsequent action.
2. The Chinese communist-inspired riots against the British colonial administration exposed serious gaps between the ruling elites and the masses, and a crisis of legitimacy of colonial rule. In the aftermath of the riots, the government began to embark on major administrative reforms in order to modernize the civil service and to build links between government and people through the City District Officer scheme (see King, 1981; Cheung, 1999).
3. Ye Fe is the Director General of the International Judicial Cooperation Department, Supreme People's Procuratorate, PRC.
4. Lei Feng, a young soldier, was claimed to have died heroically in order to save the lives of his comrades.
5. Survey conducted by the Institute of Opinion Research of the People's University of China, June 1996 (cited in Hsu, 2001).
6. In the rural survey, financial burden on peasants was named the top one factor affecting social stability. This referred to all kinds of fees and charges levied by local officials on the peasants, again a symptom of bureaucratic corruption and abuse of power.
7. The goal of 'building a socialist harmonious society' was first put forward at the Fourth Plenum of the 16th Central Committee in September 2004. Accordingly, a harmonious society 'should feature democracy, the rule of law, equity, justice, sincerity, amity and vitality. Such a society will give full scope to people's talent and creativity, enable all the people to share the social wealth brought by reform and development, and forge an ever closer relationship between the people and government' (*Xinhua News Agency*, 27 June, 2005).
8. The eight 'honours' and eight 'disgraces' are presented as follows: 'Love the mother country is honourable, harming the mother country is disgraceful; serving the people is honourable, neglecting the people is disgraceful; upholding science is honourable, blindness and ignorance are disgraceful; hard work is honourable, idleness is disgraceful; unity and cooperation are honourable, using others for profit is disgraceful; honesty and keeping one's word are honourable, seeing personal gain and forgetting justice is disgraceful; respecting laws and regulations is honourable, disobeying laws and regulations is disgraceful; suffering for the struggle is honourable, conceit and lasciviousness are disgraceful' (as translated by The University of Hong Kong China Media Project, 2007).
9. In the mid-1990s, there was a great debate about enacting an anti-corruption law. Disagreements in the NPC on a draft anti-corruption bill forced it to be withdrawn from voting at the session. One key area of contention was the scope of the bill. Eventually the Law on Administrative Supervision was passed in May 1997 instead (Sun, 2001, p. 251).
10. In response to internal demands and external pressures for democratic reforms, the State Council published a White Paper on democracy in China in October 2005, which reflected current party leadership thinking (The State Council, People's Republic of China, 2005).

11. The author thanks Siu Hoi-yin, who visited the Chinese Academy of Social Sciences in 2005–2006, for providing this perspective based on her own research on corruption in China and her interviews with some senior academics and officials in Beijing.

## ACKNOWLEDGMENT

The author gratefully acknowledges the support from the Governance in Asia Research Centre of the City University of Hong Kong.

## REFERENCES

Cheung, A. B. L. (1999). Administrative development in Hong Kong: Political questions, administrative answers. In: H. K. Wong & H. S. Chan (Eds), *Handbook of comparative public administration in the Asian-Pacific Basin* (pp. 219–252). New York: Marcel Dekker.
Cheung, A. B. L. (2006). Reinventing Hong Kong's public service: Same NPM reform, different contexts and politics. *International Journal of Organizational Theory & Behaviour*, 9(2), 212–234.
Deng, X. (1994). *Selected writings of Deng Xiaoping* (Vol. 2). Beijing: People's Press.
Gillespie, K., & Okrunhlik, G. (1991). The political dimensions of corruption cleanups: A framework for analysis. *Comparative Politics*, 24(1), 77–95.
Gong, T. (1997). Forms and characteristics of China's corruption in the 1990s: Change with continuity. *Communist and Post-Communist Studies*, 30(3), 277–288.
Gong, T. (2006). Corruption and local governance: The double identity of Chinese local governments in market reform. *The Pacific Review*, 19(1), 85–102.
Guang, J. (2005). Wu Guanzheng, Secretary of the Central Commission for Discipline Inspection, tenders his resignation. *Cheng Ming Monthly* (September), 19–20 (in Chinese).
Harding, H. (1981). *Organizing China: The problem of bureaucracy 1949–76*. Stanford: Stanford University Press.
He, Z. (2000). Corruption and anti-corruption in reform China. *Communist and Post-Communist Studies*, 33(2), 243–270.
Heidenheimer, A. J. (1989). Perspectives on the perception of corruption. In: A. J. Heidenheimer, M. Johnston & V. LeVine (Eds), *Political corruption: A handbook* (pp. 8–11). New Brunswick, NJ: Transaction Publishers.
Hsu, C. L. (2001). Political narratives and the production of legitimacy: The case of corruption in Post-Mao China. *Qualitative Sociology*, 24(1), 25–54.
Hu, A., & Hu, L. (2005). *Transition and stability: How China can achieve long-term governance (Zhuanxing Yu Wending: Zhongguo Ruhe Chang Zhi Jiu An)*. Beijing: People's Press (in Chinese).
Huntington, S. (1968). *Political order in changing societies*. New Haven: Yale University Press.
Huntington, S. (1970). Modernization and corruption. In: A. J. Heidenheimer (Ed.), *Political corruption: Readings in comparative analysis*. New York: Holt, Reinhart and Winston.

Independent Commission Against Corruption. (2007). Press release, May 11, Hong Kong.
Jain, A. (2001). Corruption: A review. *Journal of Economic Surveys*, 15(1), 71–121.
King, A. Y. C. (1980). An institutional response to corruption: The ICAC of Hong Kong. In: C. K. Leung, J. W. Cushman & G. Wang (Eds), *Hong Kong: Dilemmas of growth* (pp. 115–142). Canberra and Hong Kong: Research School of Pacific Studies, Australian National University and Centre of Asia Studies, The University of Hong Kong.
King, A. Y. C. (1981). Administrative absorption of politics in Hong Kong: Emphasis on the grass roots level. In: A. Y. C. King & R. P. L. Lee (Eds), *Social life and development in Hong Kong* (pp. 127–146). Hong Kong: The Chinese University Press.
Kingdon, J. (1984). *Agendas, alternatives and public policies*. Boston: Little Brown.
Kuan, H.-chi. (1981). Anti-corruption legislation in Hong Kong – A history. In: R. P. L. Lee (Ed.), *Corruption and its control in Hong Kong: Situation up to the late seventies* (pp. 15–44). Hong Kong: The Chinese University Press.
Lee, R. P. L. (1981). Introduction: Definitions and patterns. In: R. P. L. Lee (Ed.), *Corruption and its control in Hong Kong: Situation up to the late seventies* (pp. 1–14). Hong Kong: The Chinese University Press.
Lo, J. M. K. (2001). Controlling corruption in Hong Kong: From colony to special administrative region. *Journal of Contingencies and Crisis Management*, 9(1), 21–28.
Manion, M. (1999). Corruption by design: Corruption control through enforcement swamping. Paper presented at the American Political Science Association annual meeting, September, Atlanta, USA.
Manion, M. (2004). *Corruption by design: Building clean government in mainland China and Hong Kong*. Cambridge, MA: Harvard University Press.
Meagher, P. (2005). Anti-corruption agencies: Rhetoric versus reality. *The Journal of Policy Reform*, 8(1), 69–103.
*People's Daily Online*. (2005, March 9). China pledges more efforts in uphill fight against corruption. Available at http://english.peopledaily.com.cn/200503/09/eng20050309_176181.html. Retrieved on 1 February 2007.
Political & Economic Risk Consultancy Ltd. (2007). *Asian Intelligence*, March 14, Hong Kong.
Quah, J. S. T. (2003). *Curbing corruption in Asia: A comparative study of six countries*. Singapore: Eastern University Press by Marshall Cavendish.
Sapio, F. (2005). Implementing anticorruption in the PRC: Patterns of selectivity. Working Paper No. 10. Centre for East and South-East Asian Studies, Lund University, Sweden.
Scott, I. (1989). *Political change and the crisis of legitimacy in Hong Kong*. Hong Kong: Oxford University Press.
Selected Important Documents since the Thirteenth Party Congress (middle volume). (1991). Beijing: People's Press (in Chinese).
Sina net. (2004, June 19). First provincial rank anti-corruption bureau chief Han Jianlin of Jiangsu was implicated, and Zhang Junyuan was under double restrictions. Available at http://finance.sina.com.cn/careerlife/20040619/0907823577.shtml. Retrieved on 5 July 2007.
*South China Morning Post*. (2006, November 7). HK a role model for mainland, corruption official says, Hong Kong.
Sun, Y. (2001). The politics of conceptualizing corruption in reform China. *Crime, Law & Social Change*, 35, 245–270.
The Central Government of the People's Republic of China website. (2006, March 11). *Facts and figures: China's procuratorial work in 2005*. Available at http://english.gov.cn/2006-03/11/content_225012.htm. Retrieved on 1 February 2007.

The State Council, People's Republic of China. (2005). White Paper on building of political democracy in China. Available at http://www.idcpc.org.cn/english/events/051019.htm. Retrieved on 4 January 2007.

The University of Hong Kong China Media Project. (2007). Available at http://cmp.hku.hk/look/article.tpl?IdLanguage = 1&IdPublication = 1&NrIssue = 1&NrSection = 50&NrArticle = 593. Retrieved on 6 July 2007.

Transparency International. (2007). Corruption Perception Index (various years). Available at http://www.transparency.org/policy_research/surveys_indices/global/cpi. Retrieved on 6 July 2007.

Wedeman, A. (1996). Corruption and politics. In: Kuan H.-chi. (Ed.), *China Review 1996* (pp. 61–94). Hong Kong: Chinese University Press.

Wedeman, A. (2005). Anticorruption campaigns and the intensification of corruption in China. *Journal of Contemporary China, 14*(42), 93–116.

Wedeman, A. (2007). Win, Lose, or draw? China's quarter century war on corruption. Paper presented at the Workshop on 'Building Clean Government in China: Institutional Design and Policy Capacity', organized by Department of Public and Social Administration, 17–18 May, City University of Hong Kong.

*Wen Wei Po.* (2007, March 21). National Corruption Prevention Bureau's personnel composition modeled on Hong Kong's ICAC, Hong Kong, p. A9 (in Chinese).

White, G. (1996). Corruption and the transition from socialism in China. *Journal of Law and Society, 23*(1), 149–169.

Xinhua Net. (2005, January 16). Implementation outline for building and improving the system to punish and prevent corruption. Available at http://news.xinhuanet.com/newscenter/2005-01/16/content_2467898.htm. Retrieved on 6 July 2007.

*Xinhua News Agency.* (2005, June 27). Hu: Building harmonious society crucial for progress. Available at http://www.china.org.cn/english/government/133254.htm. Retrieved on 17 May 2006.

Ye, F. (2006). The characteristics of the corruption crimes and anti-corruption in China. Presented at The Third ICAC Symposium, 9–11 May, Hong Kong.

# ANTI-CORRUPTION AGENCIES IN FOUR ASIAN COUNTRIES: A COMPARATIVE ANALYSIS☆

Jon S. T. Quah

## INTRODUCTION

Corruption is a serious problem in many Asian countries, judging from their ranking and scores on Transparency International's Corruption Perceptions Index (CPI). To combat corruption these countries have relied on three patterns of corruption control. The first pattern relies on the enactment of anti-corruption laws without a specific agency to enforce these laws. For example in Mongolia, the Law on Anti-Corruption that was introduced in April 1996 is jointly implemented by the police, the General Prosecutor's Office, and the courts (Quah, 2003a, p. 44)[1]. The second pattern involves the implementation of anti-corruption laws by several anti-corruption agencies. In India, the Prevention of Corruption Act (POCA) is implemented by the Central Bureau of Investigation (CBI), the Central Vigilance Commission (CVC), and the anti-corruption bureaus and vigilance commissions at the state level (Quah, 2003a, p. 66). Similarly, the Philippines has relied on 18

---

☆Revised version of paper presented at the Sixth Asian Forum on Public Management on "Comparative Governance Reform in Asia: Democracy, Corruption, and Government Trust" organized by the Department of Public Administration, Chulalongkorn University in Bangkok, Thailand, January 12–13, 2007.

anti-corruption agencies to enforce the many anti-corruption laws since the Integrity Board was formed by President Quirino in May 1950 (Batalla, 2001, p. 47; Oyamada, 2005, pp. 99–101).

The third pattern of corruption control was initiated by Singapore when it established the Corrupt Practices Investigation Bureau (CPIB) in October 1952 to implement the Prevention of Corruption Ordinance (POCO). Malaysia followed Singapore's example by forming the Anti-Corruption Agency (ACA) in October 1967 (Quah, 2003a, p. 17). Hong Kong was the third country to adopt the third pattern in February 1974, when the Independent Commission Against Corruption (ICAC) was created (Quah, 2003a, p. 140). The success of the CPIB and ICAC in curbing corruption in Singapore and Hong Kong respectively has popularized the third pattern among other Asian countries. The Counter Corruption Commission (CCC) was set up in Thailand in February 1975, but was ineffective and replaced by the National Counter Corruption Commission (NCCC) in November 1999. The Korea Independent Commission Against Commission (KICAC) was formed in South Korea in January 2002 (Quah, 2003a, pp. 17–18). Finally, Indonesia adopted the third pattern when the Corruption Eradication Commission (CEC) was established in December 2003 (Quah, 2006, p. 178).

However, even though the third pattern of corruption control is popular not all the Asian countries which have adopted this pattern have been effective in curbing corruption. Indeed, Jeremy Pope (2000) has lamented that "unfortunately, Anti-Corruption Agencies have been more often failures than successes" (p. 104). What are the preconditions for the effectiveness of ACAs? This chapter compares the performance of the CPIB, ICAC, KICAC, and NCCC by assessing the extent to which these four ACAs have met these six preconditions.[2] Before proceeding to discuss these preconditions, it is necessary to describe the mission and functions of the four ACAs.

## MISSION AND FUNCTIONS OF ACAS

ACAs are specialized agencies established by governments for the specific aim of minimizing corruption in their countries. John R. Heilbrunn (2006) has identified four types of ACAs:

1. The *universal model*, with its investigative, preventive, and communicative functions, is typified by Hong Kong's ICAC.
2. The *investigative model* is characterized by a small and centralized investigative commission as it operates in Singapore's CPIB.

3. The *parliamentary model* includes commissions that report to parliamentary committees and are independent from the executive and judicial branches of the state (for example, the New South Wales Independent Commission Against Corruption).
4. The *multi-agency model* includes a number of agencies that are autonomous, but which together weave a web of agencies to fight corruption. The United States Office of Government Ethics, with its preventive approach, complements the Justice Department's investigative and prosecutorial powers, and together these organizations make a concerted effort to reduce corruption (p. 136).

## Singapore's CPIB

Corruption was a serious problem in Singapore during the British colonial period. In 1871, corruption was made an illegal offence with the enactment of the Penal Code of the Straits Settlements of Malacca, Penang and Singapore. In 1879, a Commission of Inquiry into the causes of inefficiency of the Straits Settlements police force found that corruption was prevalent among the European inspectors and the Malay and Indian junior officers. Similarly, another Commission of Inquiry into the extent of public gambling in the Straits Settlements in 1886 confirmed the existence of systematic corruption in the police forces in Singapore and Penang (Quah, 1979, pp. 24–26). An analysis of the 172 reported cases of police corruption in Singapore during 1845–1921 found that bribery was the most common form (63.4%), followed by direct criminal activities (24.4%), opportunistic theft (5.8%), corruption of authority (5.2%), and protection of illegal activities (1.2%) (Quah, 1979, p. 24, Table 6).

However, the enactment of the POCO as the first anti-corruption law in Singapore, Malacca, and Penang on December 10, 1937, did not improve the situation. On the contrary, the problem of corruption deteriorated during the Japanese occupation (February 1942–August 1945) because the rampant inflation made it difficult for civil servants to live on their low wages. Trading in the black market was "a way of life" as "everyone was surviving on some sort of black marketing." Furthermore, "nepotism and corruption was perfectly acceptable and everyone resorted to connections, friends and relatives" to get jobs (Lee, 2005, p. 142).

The Japanese occupation bred corruption as "bribery, blackmail and extortion grew out of the violence and fear, the mechanisms with which the

Japanese ruled their occupied territories" (Lee, 2005, p. 205). Indeed, according to Lee Gek Boi (2005):

> Bribery worked wonders. From generals to the ordinary soldier, gifts and money smoothed the way. Nothing was transparent and everything was about connections and payoffs. Nothing was impossible with the right connections ... Shortages created the black market and a culture of thievery to fuel the market. Everyone – the Japanese included – did black marketing. The Japanese Occupation culture brought out the basic survival instincts in people and produced a society where all manner of evils could be justified because it was all about survival ... It would take years to undo the corruption and address the social evils that Japanese military occupation bred in Singapore. (p. 205)

Conditions worsened after the war and corruption spread among civil servants as a result of their meager salaries and inflation and their inadequate supervision by their superiors, which provided them with many opportunities for corruption with a low probability of being caught (Quah, 1982, pp. 161–162). In other words, corruption was a way of life for many Singaporeans during the post-war period.

In 1950, the Commissioner of Police, J.P. Pennefather-Evans, reported that corruption was rife in government departments. A few days later, the Chief of the Anti-Corruption Branch (ACB) of the Criminal Investigation Department (CID), which was responsible for tackling corruption, indicated that the problem of corruption had become worse. These reports on the prevalence of corruption led to criticisms of the ACB's ineffectiveness and the colonial government's "weak and feeble attempt" to fight corruption by Elizabeth Choy, a member of the Second Legislative Council on February 20, 1952. She urged the colonial government to take stronger measures to eradicate corruption by removing the ACB from the police force and expanding its size, and by strengthening the POCO (Quah, 1978, p. 14).

The ACB was ineffective in curbing corruption for three reasons. First, it was a small police unit consisting of 17 men who were given a difficult task to perform i.e., the eradication of corruption in the police and other government departments. Second, as the CID's top priority was to deal with serious crimes like homicide, the task of fighting corruption received lower priority and the ACB had to compete with the other branches for limited manpower and resources (Quah, 2003a, p. 113).

The third and most important reason for the ACB's ineffectiveness was the prevalence of police corruption in colonial Singapore. In October 1951, a consignment of 1,800 pounds of opium worth S$400,000 (US$133,333) was stolen by a gang of robbers, which included three police detectives. A special team appointed by the British colonial government to investigate the robbery found that there was widespread police corruption especially among those policemen involved in protection rackets. This opium hijacking scandal made the British colonial government realize the importance of creating an independent ACA that would be separate from the police. Accordingly, it replaced the ACB with the CPIB in October 1952 (Quah, 2003a, pp. 113–114).

The CPIB's mission statement is: "To combat corruption through Swift and Sure, Firm but Fair Action" (CPIB, 2004, p. ii). To fulfill its mission, the CPIB performs these three functions:

1. To receive and investigate complaints alleging corrupt practices;
2. To investigate malpractices and misconduct by public officers with an undertone of corruption; and
3. To prevent corruption by examining the practices and procedures in the public service to minimize opportunities for corrupt practices (CPIB, 2004, p. 3).

The Corrupt Practices Investigation Programme is described in the national budget as the administration of the CPIB and "the investigation of corruption and malpractices, the review of administrative weaknesses in the public sector that provides avenues for corruption and the screening of officers for appointment in the public sector" (Republic of Singapore, 1994, p. 638). Thus, in addition to the three functions mentioned above, the CPIB also ensures that candidates selected for positions in the Singapore Civil Service (SCS) and statutory boards in Singapore are screened to ensure that only those candidates without any taint of corruption or misconduct are actually recruited.

The CPIB comes under the jurisdiction of the Prime Minister's Office (PMO) and is divided into the Operations Division and the Administration and Specialist Support Division. As the CPIB's major function is the investigation of offences under the POCA, the Operations Division has four investigation units including the Special Investigation Team, which handles the more difficult and major cases. These four units are assisted by the Intelligence Department, which collects intelligence and undertakes field research. The Administration Unit is responsible for administrative and personnel matters, provides screening services to government departments and statutory boards, and conducts strategic planning for the CPIB. The other three units in the Administration and Specialist Support Division deal with prevention and review, computer information system, and plans and projects (CPIB, 2004, pp. 3–4).

## Hong Kong's ICAC

Similarly, corruption was also a serious problem in Hong Kong during the British colonial period. Leslie Palmier (1985) contended that corruption was already a way of life in Hong Kong when the British acquired it in 1841 because

> The Chinese who formed its population had long been accustomed to a system where most of an official's income depended on what he was able to extort from the public. Not surprisingly, during the first decades of the colony's history corruption prospered at all levels of government. (p. 123)

Bertrand de Speville (1997), a former ICAC Commissioner, has attributed the rampant corruption in Hong Kong before the advent of the ICAC in 1974 to four reasons. First, the rapid population growth after 1945 severely strained the social services, government resources, and manpower in Hong Kong and contributed to corruption as "everything was in short supply." Second, the Chinese immigrants to Hong Kong paid bribes to the police and other civil servants to avoid being harassed by them. Third, the government's monopoly and regulations of various activities and the discretion of civil servants responsible for these activities provided many opportunities for corruption. The final factor was the widespread police corruption, which prevented the police from resolving the problem of corruption (pp. 13–14).

To cope with the increase in corruption after the World War II, the British colonial government enacted the POCO in 1948. It adopted the same method of corruption control employed in Singapore in Hong Kong by forming the ACB as a special unit of the CID of the Royal Hong Kong Police Force (RHKPF) to deal with the investigation and prosecution of corruption cases (Kuan, 1981, p. 24). The ACB was separated from the CID in 1952 but it still remained within the RHKPF. However, the ACB was not effective as its prosecution of corruption offences resulted in between two to 20 court convictions per year (Wong, 1981, p. 45).

The ACB initiated a review of the POCO in 1968 and sent a study team to Singapore and Sri Lanka during the same year to examine how their anti-corruption laws worked in practice. The study team was impressed with the independence of their ACAs and attributed Singapore's success in curbing corruption to the CPIB's independence from the police (Wong, 1981, p. 47). However, the RHKPF rejected the recommendation to separate the ACB by upgrading it into an Anti-Corruption Office (ACO) in May 1971 (Wong, 1981, pp. 47–48; Quah, 2003a, p. 138).

prepared an anti-corruption draft bill to supplement the inadequate Penal Code. The draft bill was approved by the Cabinet in December 1974 and the Counter Corruption Act (CCA) was passed by the National Assembly in February 1975 (Quah, 2003b, p. 253).

The ACC was transformed by the CCA into the CCC. However, the CCC was ineffective for three reasons: it lacked the power to punish corrupt officials; the public perception among Thais that corruption is acceptable and not against the national interest; and the constant conflict between the Cabinet and senior civil servants (Quah, 2003b, p. 253). The CCC was a "paper tiger" as it lacked the "direct authority to punish public officials" and it could not take action against corrupt politicians as it only had "the power to investigate a bureaucrat following a complaint" (Amara, 1992, p. 240).

The CCC's ineffectiveness in curbing corruption during its 24-year existence led to its dissolution and replacement by the NCCC in November 1999. To avoid the weaknesses encountered by its predecessor, the NCCC's jurisdiction was changed from the Office of the Prime Minister to the Senate. Unlike its predecessor, the NCCC is not a toothless paper tiger as it has been empowered to investigate corruption complaints against both civil servants and politicians.

Section 19 of the Organic Act on Counter Corruption B.E. 2542 (1999) has described in detail the various powers and duties of the NCCC (ONCCC, 2006a, pp. 10–11). The NCCC performs three major functions. First, it is responsible for inspecting and verifying the declaration of the assets and liabilities submitted by politicians and civil servants. Those officials who do not declare their assets or make false declarations are reported to the Constitutional Court by the NCCC. Those found guilty are removed from their positions and barred from holding political office for five years.

The NCCC's second function is to prevent corruption in three ways: (1) to make recommendations on preventing corruption to the Cabinet and other government agencies; (2) to enhance the integrity of the officials and public by organizing contests, meetings, and seminars on fighting corruption among the people and civil servants; and (3) to foster cooperation among the public by conducting seminars on countering corruption in Bangkok and the other provinces.

Thirdly, the NCCC is also empowered to suppress corruption by taking disciplinary action against corrupt politicians and civil servants. More specifically, it investigates complaints of corruption against politicians and civil servants and has the power to impeach them for having "unusual wealth," or for committing corruption, malfeasance, or abuse of power.

The ACO was given more manpower but its credibility was under[mined] on June 8, 1973, when a corruption suspect, Chief Superintendent [P.] F. Godber, escaped to the United Kingdom. Godber's escape angere[d the] public and the government reacted by appointing a Commission of In[quiry] to investigate the circumstances contributing to his escape. Conseque[ntly,] the Governor, Sir Murray MacLehose, was forced by public criticis[m to] accept the Blair Commission's recommendation to establish an indepen[dent] agency, separate from the RHKPF, to fight corruption.

Accordingly, the ICAC was formed on February 15, 1974, "to root [out] corruption and to restore public confidence in the Government" (Wo[ng,] 1981, p.45). More specifically, the ICAC's *raison d'etre* is to perfo[rm] "a trinity of purpose comprising investigation, prevention and educatio[n." ] Indeed, the ICAC's "three-pronged approach" is critical for developi[ng] "a new public consciousness" and is reflected in its organizational structu[re] of the three Departments of Operations, Corruption Prevention, a[nd] Community Relations (ICAC, 1989, pp. 28–29).

## Thailand's NCCC

Corruption remains a serious problem in Thailand and its origins can be traced to the Ayudhya period in the second half of the 14th century. Corruption became a national problem after the World War II and the first anti-corruption law ("An Act Specifying Proceedings Against Public Servants and Municipal Officials Who Conduct Malfeasance or Lack Ability") was enacted in 1945 (Preecha, 2001, p. 105).

The first ACA in Thailand was formed in September 1972 with the establishment of the Board of Inspection and Follow-up of Government Operations (BIFGO). Consisting of five members, the BIFGO's role was to investigate allegations of corruption against government agencies and officials. Unfortunately, the BIFGO was ineffective as its members were found guilty of corruption themselves. Consequently, the BIFGO was dissolved after the October 1973 Revolution (Quah, 1982, pp. 171–172).

In May 1974, Prime Minister Sanya appointed an Anti-Corruption Committee (ACC) to investigate charges of corruption against public officials and to report its findings to the prime minister or minister in charge of the ministry concerned. As an investigatory agency, the ACC did not have any quasi-judicial powers and has to rely on the Civil Service Commission (CSC) and the Court of Justice to take legal action against corrupt officials. Apart from investigating corruption cases, the ACC

## South Korea's KICAC

The origins of corruption in South Korea can be traced to the Yi dynasty (1392–1910). However, corruption only became a serious problem after the 16th century because of the ineffective anti-corruption measures and the participation of the King's relatives in politics and public affairs led to nepotism and bureaucratic corruption (Quah, 2003a, p. 155). In their analysis of South Korean public administration, Jong S. Jun and Myung S. Park (2001) contended that "deeply rooted corruption" was a major reason for the incapability of Korean public administration and the 1997 financial crisis. They wrote:

> Corruption is the cancer of Korean society, and it is found at every level of Korean society, from top officials down to minor civil servants ... Corruption at high-level is widespread, but scandals involving bureaucrats, particularly those who collect taxes and enforce customs regulations, are often reported in newspapers as well. (pp. 8–9)

President Park Chung Hee assumed office in May 1961 and he initiated the fight against corruption in South Korea in 1963 when he merged the Board of Audit and the Commission of Inspection to form the Board of Audit and Inspection (BAI) to act as a direct check on the economic bureaucracy. In other words, the BAI was the first *de facto* ACA in South Korea (Quah, 2003a, p. 161). More specifically, the BAI performs these three functions:

> to confirm the closing accounts of the state's revenues and expenditures; to audit the accounts of the central government agencies, provincial governments and other local autonomous bodies, and government-invested organizations to ensure proper and fair accounting; and to inspect the work done by government agencies and the duties of public officials to improve the operation and quality of government services. (Quah, 2003a, p. 164)

After winning the December 1997 presidential election, President Kim Dae Jung assumed office in February 1998 and showed his commitment to curb corruption by implementing a comprehensive anti-corruption strategy consisting of six components. The first and most important component was the formation of an Anti-Corruption Committee to coordinate the anti-corruption programmes and activities, and the formulation of the anti-corruption law to provide protection for whistle-blowers, to strengthen citizen watch and participation in anti-corruption movements, and to reinforce detection and punishment for corrupt practices (Quah, 2003a, p. 165).

Another important reform introduced by President Kim was the establishment of the Regulatory Reform Committee (RRC) in 1998 to make South Korea more business friendly by eliminating unnecessary or irrational economic and social regulations that hindered business activities or interfered with people's lives. For example, to obtain a permit to build a factory, a company had to prepare an average of 44 documents and wait for several months for approval. These excessive regulations encourage corruption as businessmen are prepared to bribe the relevant officials to bypass the cumbersome and tedious procedures for obtaining a factory permit (Kim, 1997, pp. 261–262). After its first year of operations, the RRC abolished 5,226 or 48% of 11,125 administrative regulations (Quah, 2003a, p. 168).

In April 1999, the Seoul Metropolitan Government launched an "Online Procedure Enhancement for Civil Applications (OPEN)" system to improve civil applications covering 54 common procedures, which could be filed through the Internet.[3] By May 2000, the OPEN system had processed 28,000 cases of civil applications and more than 648,000 persons had visited its website. Thus, the OPEN system has improved "customer-oriented delivery of public services" and "transparency of city administration" as those officials responsible for permit or approval procedures (usually perceived to be corruption-prone) are "required to upload their work reports and documents to the Internet" to enable citizens to monitor the progress of their applications (Moon, 2001, p. 41).

As President Kim's strategy met with stiff resistance, it took more than two years before the Anti-Corruption Act was passed on July 24, 2001. Six months later, the KICAC was formed on January 25, 2002, as the *de jure* ACA in South Korea (Quah, 2003a, p. 169). Chapter 2, Articles 10–24 of the Anti-Corruption Act (2001) specify the creation, functions, and composition of the KICAC (pp. 7–16). The original eight functions of the KICAC were specified in Article 11 (Anti-Corruption Act, 2001, pp. 7–8). However, in its *Annual Report 2005*, the KICAC (2006) has identified its major functions as:

1. *Policy-maker*. To formulate and coordinate anti-corruption policies by organizing on a regular basis the Inter-Agency Meeting on Corruption.
2. *Evaluator*. To evaluate the levels of integrity and anti-corruption practices of public-sector organizations.
3. *Observer*. To monitor corruption and protect whistle-blowers by handling reports on alleged corrupt conduct and protecting and offering rewards for whistle-blowers.

4. *Partner.* To promote cooperation for the fight against corruption by encouraging civil society involvement and public-private partnership against corruption, and engaging in the global fight against corruption.
5. *Legal-reformer.* To improve the legal and institutional frameworks to remove laws and practices which encourage corruption.
6. *Ethics-leader.* To inculcate ethical values in society by promoting public awareness on the risks of corruption, and by enforcing the code of conduct for public-sector employees (pp. 4 and 7).

Unlike the CPIB, ICAC, and NCCC, the KICAC cannot investigate corruption cases itself as it has to rely on the BAI and other agencies to do so. Indeed, the KICAC's inability to investigate corruption cases is its Achilles heel. The second limitation of the KICAC is that it focuses only on public-sector corruption and does not deal with private sector corruption, such as the bribery of a banker or an auditor.

# PRECONDITIONS FOR THE EFFECTIVENESS OF AN ACA

## The ACA Must be Incorruptible

The ACA must be incorruptible for two reasons. First, if the ACA's personnel are corrupt, its legitimacy and public image will be undermined as its officers have broken the law by being corrupt themselves when they are required to enforce the law. Second, corruption among the ACA's staff not only discredits the agency but also prevents them from performing their duties impartially and effectively (Quah, 2000, p. 111). As indicated earlier, BIFGO, Thailand's first ACA, was dissolved after one year because it five members were found guilty of corruption. More recently, the NCCC's efforts in combating corruption in Thailand suffered a setback when its nine commissioners resigned in May 2005. They were found guilty by the Supreme Court of Thailand of abusing their powers in August 2004, when they issued an executive decree to increase their monthly salaries by 45,000 baht (US$1,125). However, this episode also shows that the NCCC members are not above the law and are accountable for the abuse of their powers (Quah, 2007, p. 14).

To ensure its integrity, the ACA must be staffed by honest and competent personnel. Overstaffing should be avoided and any staff member found guilty of corruption must be punished and dismissed. Details of the punishment of corrupt staff must be widely publicized in the mass media to serve as a deterrent to others, and to demonstrate the ACA's integrity and credibility to the public (Quah, 2000, pp. 113–114). For example, after a senior CPIB officer was caught cheating a businessman in Singapore in 1997, the CPIB director, Chua Cher Yak, ordered polygraph tests for all his staff, including himself, to demonstrate their integrity. Indeed, the CPIB's reputation remained untainted as Chua and his staff passed the polygraph tests (Fong, 2005, p. H7).

### The ACA Must be Independent from the Police and from Political Control

As discussed above, the experiences of Singapore and Hong Kong in fighting corruption clearly show the importance of not allowing the police to be responsible for corruption control especially when the police was corrupt. In other words, the police was the biggest obstacle to curbing corruption in Singapore and Hong Kong before the establishment of the CPIB in October 1952 and the ICAC in February 1974 because of the prevalence of police corruption in both city-states.

Accordingly, the success of the CPIB and ICAC in combating corruption has confirmed that the first best practice in curbing corruption is: do not let the police handle the task of controlling corruption as this would be like giving candy to a child and expecting him or her not to eat it (Quah, 2004, p. 1). Singapore has taken 15 years (1937–1952) while Hong Kong has taken 26 years (1948–1974) to learn this important lesson. Unfortunately, many Asian countries (India, Japan, and Mongolia) have still not learnt this lesson yet as they continue to rely on the police to curb corruption.

Apart from independence from the police, the ACA must also be independent from control by the political leaders in two respects. First, the political leaders must not interfere in the daily operations of the ACA. Second and more importantly, the ACA must be able to investigate all political leaders and senior civil servants without fear or favor.

In Singapore, when the CPIB was formed in October 1952, it came under the jurisdiction of the attorney general. From 1959 to 1962, the CPIB was under the purview of the Ministry of Home Affairs. The CPIB was under the jurisdiction of the PMO from 1963 to 1965 and under the purview of the attorney general again from 1965 to 1968. However, since 1969, the CPIB has been under the PMO's purview (CPIB, 2003, p. 16.109).

As the CPIB's Director reports to the prime minister in Singapore, policy makers who are interested in adopting the CPIB model are concerned with the CPIB's independence and the possibility that the prime minister or president can use the CPIB-style agency against the opposition political parties.[4] Indeed, the "alacrity in pursuing corruption allegations against [Deputy Prime Minister] Anwar Ibrahim" by Malaysia's ACA in 1998 indicates that the ACA, which comes under the jurisdiction of the Prime Minister's department, is not independent (RIAP, 2001, p. 131).

How independent is the CPIB? There are two committees which review the CPIB's activities. In 1973, the Anti-Corruption Advisory Committee (ACAC) was formed on the prime minister's advice to enhance its efforts to curb corruption in the SCS. The ACAC was chaired by the Head of the SCS and included all the permanent secretaries as its members. The ACAC was dissolved in 1975 but it was revived in 1996 on the recommendation of the Anti-Corruption Review Committee (ACRC) to review the CPIB's investigative and preventive measures. The ACRC was established in 1996 to review Singapore's anti-corruption measures. Like the ACAC, it consists of senior civil servants and is chaired by the Head of the SCS (Tan, 1999, p. 61; CPIB, 2003, p. 8.71).

As the CPIB has been under the PMO's purview since 1969, it has investigated all allegations of political corruption in Singapore as the incumbent government is committed to minimizing corruption. Indeed, the CPIB has not hesitated to investigate allegations of corruption against political leaders and senior civil servants in Singapore. In his speech to Parliament on March 30, 1993, then Prime Minister Goh Chok Tong declared:

> I have every intention to make sure that Singapore remains corruption free ... And everybody should know that corruption in any form will not be tolerated. I expect all Ministers, all MPs and all public officers to set good examples for others to follow ... *If there is any allegation against any MP* [Member of Parliament] *or Minister of assets wrongfully gained or corruptly gained, the CPIB will investigate.* If the MP concerned is unable to explain how he had acquired these assets, or why he had not declared them, he will be charged for corruption. (Quoted in CPIB, 2003, p. 2.17, emphasis added)

The introduction of the elected president in 1991 has enhanced the CPIB's independence as Article 22G of the Constitution of Singapore empowers the CPIB's director to continue his investigations of ministers and senior civil servants even if he does not have the prime minister's consent to do so if he obtains the consent of the elected president (Thio, 1997, p. 114).

Lee Hsien Loong, who was then deputy prime minister, referred to this check on the prime minister in his speech to Parliament on March 13, 2003:

> the Prime Minister is responsible for the integrity of the whole civil service, the public sector, as well as the Judges and the Ministers. It is his responsibility to keep the system clean. If he does not, and we have a corrupt Prime Minister, then we are in serious trouble. We have safeguarded that situation, because under the Constitution if the Prime Minister would not give leave to the CPIB to pursue a case, the CPIB can go to the President, and the President can give leave to proceed. So, *even the Prime Minister can be investigated.* (Quoted in CPIB, 2003, p. 2.16, emphasis added)

In short, while the CPIB's director can obtain the consent of the elected president to investigate allegations of corruption against ministers, MPs, and senior civil servants if the prime minister withholds his consent, the fact remains that the CPIB is not immune from the prime minister's influence and control as it comes under his jurisdiction. While the PAP government has remained committed to minimizing corruption and has not used the CPIB as a weapon against opposition political leaders during the past 48 years, the CPIB's lack of complete independence from the PMO makes it an unattractive model for those Asian countries which are concerned about the possibility of their political leaders using a CPIB-style agency against their political foes. In other words, the concern is whether the political leaders in other Asian countries will resist the temptation of employing the CPIB-style agency against their political rivals.

Unlike the ACAC and ACRC in Singapore, the ICAC in Hong Kong relies on these four committees made up of citizens appointed by the Chief Executive after July 1997 to scrutinize its activities:

1. The Advisory Committee on Corruption reviews the ICAC's overall policy and reviews the work of the three departments and the Administration Branch.
2. The Operations Review Committee reviews the work of the Operations Department.
3. The Corruption Prevention Advisory Committee reviews the work of the Corruption Prevention Department.
4. The Citizens Advisory Committee on Community Relations reviews the work of the Community Relations Department.

However, as the ICAC Commissioner reports directly to the Chief Executive, the ICAC is not completely free from political control. While the Chief Executive does not interfere in the ICAC's daily operations, it would be difficult for the Commissioner to initiate investigation into allegations of corruption against the Chief Executive.

In Thailand, the CCC was not independent as it came under the jurisdiction of the Office of the Prime Minister (OPM). Accordingly, to enhance the NCCC's independence from the OPM, several measures were introduced by the 1997 People's Constitution, which was designed to minimize the problem of corruption and to enhance political participation. The nine members of the NCCC are appointed by the King on the recommendation of a 15-member selection panel (consisting of three judges, seven academics, and five political party representatives) for a single non-renewable term of nine years. The NCCC reports to the Senate instead of the Prime Minister and can "freely conduct investigations in cases of unusual wealth or corruption, including verification of public figures' asset and liability declarations" (Borwornsak, 2001, pp. 188–189).

According to Section 58 of the Organic Act on Counter Corruption (1999), the Senate has the power to initiate the removal of persons in high-ranking positions if they are found guilty of corruption, malfeasance in office, malfeasance in judicial office, or intentionally exercising power contrary to the Constitution or the law (ONCCC, 2006a, p. 23). However, the control of the Senate by the *Thai Rak Thai* party during Prime Minister Thaksin Shinawatra's term of office meant in practice that the NCCC was not free from political control.

In spite of its resource constraints, the NCCC has done a creditable job as it has investigated corruption cases involving politicians and senior bureaucrats. In December 2000, the NCCC charged Prime Minister Thaksin Shinawatra with concealing assets worth 4.5 billion baht, accusing him of registering these assets in the names of his employees. Thaksin was later acquitted by the Constitutional Court in an 8 to 7 split decision (Quah, 2007, p. 13).

In addition to strengthening the NCCC, the 1997 People's Constitution was also concerned with reducing potential conflicts of interest for public officials. It prohibited cabinet members from holding partnerships, owning shares of more than 5% in business companies, and participating in commercial transactions with state agencies. However, critics of Thaksin accused him of "policy corruption" by formulating policies and implementing projects that favored himself and his cabinet colleagues (Quah, 2007, pp. 13–14).

Prime Minister Thaksin's government was overthrown in a bloodless military coup on September 19, 2006. The 1997 Constitution was suspended and martial law was introduced by the Council for Democratic Reform (CDR) led by army chief, General Sonthi Boonyaratkalin. If the coup had not occurred, it was likely that Thaksin and his *Thai Rak Thai* party would have won the October 2006 general election. This would have resulted in a continuation of Thaksin's rule and the policy corruption that grew during his term of office. If the CDR keeps its promise of holding elections after formulating a new constitution within a year after the coup, there is hope that the situation in Thailand might improve (Quah, 2007, p. 14).

## *There Must be Comprehensive Anti-Corruption Legislation*

Comprehensive anti-corruption legislation is an important prerequisite for combating corruption effectively. More specifically, the anti-corruption laws in a country must (1) define explicitly the meaning of corruption and its different forms and (2) specify clearly the powers of the director and/or members of the ACA. For example, the POCA of 1960, defines "gratification" and identifies the CPIB's director in Section 2. Furthermore, sections 15–20 provide details of the powers of the CPIB's director and his officers (Quah, 1978, pp. 11–12).

Similarly, Section 12 of the ICAC Ordinance 1974 describes the Commissioner's duties as the investigation and prevention of corruption including the "education of the public against the evils of corruption and the enlisting and fostering of public support in combating it" (Quoted in Lethbridge, 1985, p. 104). The ICAC Ordinance also enables the director of the Operations Department to authorize his officers to restrict the movement of a suspect, to examine bank accounts and safe deposit boxes, to restrict disposal of a suspect's property, and to require a suspect to provide full details of his financial situation (Quah, 2003a, p. 143).

The Organic Act on Counter Corruption (1999) defines "corruption" and other terms in Section 4. Section 7 describes how the nine commissioners of the NCCC are selected and sections 19–31 specify their powers and duties (ONCCC, 2006a, pp. 3–5 and 10–14). In the same way, the Anti-Corruption Act of 2001 defines the "act of corruption" and other terms in Article 2. Chapter 2 is devoted to the formation, functions, and composition of the KICAC. Finally, an innovative feature of the Anti-Corruption Act of 2001 is its focus on whistle-blowing, which is described in articles 25–39 in Chapter 3 (pp. 2–3, 7–30).

Apart from being comprehensive, the anti-corruption laws must be reviewed periodically to remove loopholes or deal with unanticipated problems by introducing amendments or, if necessary, new legislation. For example, Singapore's POCA was amended in 1966 to ensure that Singapore citizens working for their government in embassies and other government agencies abroad would be prosecuted for corrupt offences committed outside Singapore and would be dealt with as if such offences had occurred in Singapore (Section 35) (Quah, 1978, p. 13).

### The ACA Must have Adequate Staff and Funding

As fighting corruption is expensive in terms of skilled manpower, equipment, and financial resources, the incumbent government must demonstrate its political will and support by providing the required personnel and budget needs of the ACA.

Table 1 shows that in terms of personnel, the ICAC is the largest ACA with 1,194 members, followed by the NCCC (701 members), the KICAC (205 members), and the CPIB (82 members). Similarly, the ICAC ranks first with its huge budget of US$85 million and per capita expenditure of US$12.32. The CPIB is fourth with its budget of US$7.7 million and second in terms of its per capita expenditure of US$1.71. The KICAC has the second largest budget of US$17.8 million but it ranks third with its per capita expenditure of US$0.37. Finally, the NCCC has the third lowest budget of US$8.6 million and the lowest per capita expenditure of US$0.13.

In his analysis of the NCCC's staffing situation in 1999, when it took over from the CCC, Borwornsak (2001) lamented that the NCCC did not have enough staff to handle its heavy workload of investigating "5,741 asset and liability declarations of politicians and high-ranking officials; 530 accusations launched against holders of public office; 1,967 cases of corruption transferred from the now defunct CCMC [or CCC]; 19 criminal cases transferred from investigation and prosecution police in the Supreme

*Table 1.* Comparative Analysis of Personnel and Budget of Four ACAs, 2004–2005.

| Item | CPIB | ICAC | NCCC | KICAC |
|---|---|---|---|---|
| Personnel | 82 | 1,194 | 701 | 205 |
| Budget | US$7.7m | US$85m | US$8.6m | US$17.8m |
| Population | 4.5m | 6.9m | 63.5m | 48.0m |
| Per capita expenditure | US$1.71 | US$12.32 | US$0.13 | US$0.37 |

*Sources:* The 2005 data for CPIB, ICAC, and KICAC are compiled from Republic of Singapore (2007, pp. 371–372), ICAC (2006, p. 28), KICAC (2006, p. 6). The 2004 data for the NCCC are compiled from the ONCCC (2006b, pp. 85, 87).

Court's Criminal Division for Persons Holding Political Positions; 73 cases of unusual wealth; and 48 urgent cases" (p. 199). Referring to the NCCC's plight in 2001, Borwornsak warned that:

> Staff and funding are critical factors in agency performance because control agencies cannot operate effectively without qualified personnel and adequate resources .... Without adequate funding for new staff and an appropriate pay scale, it is difficult to imagine how the NCCC is to operate effectively. If the situation is not improved the NCCC risks being labeled a "paper tiger" – an appellation often assigned to the CCMC [or CCC]. In such a case the blame rests squarely on the shoulders of the government. (pp. 198–199)

In sum, Table 1 above demonstrates clearly that Hong Kong's ICAC and Singapore's CPIB are well funded and have adequate staff for performing their functions effectively. On the other hand, South Korea's KICAC and Thailand's NCCC are inadequately staffed and funded as manifested in their extremely low per capita expenditure of US$0.37 and US$0.13, respectively.

*The ACA Must Enforce the Anti-Corruption Laws Impartially*

The anti-corruption laws must be impartially enforced by the ACA. The ACA's credibility will be undermined if it devotes it efforts to petty corruption by convicting "small fish," and ignores grand corruption by the rich and powerful in the country. If the "big fish" are protected and not prosecuted, the ACA is ineffective and will probably be used by the political leaders against their political rivals.

Singapore's CPIB has "enhanced its credibility by pursuing allegations of corruption at the highest levels of government" (Tan, 1999, p. 64). In 1975, a Minister of State, Wee Toon Boon, was found guilty of accepting bribes from a property developer and was sentenced to four and a half years of imprisonment. In 1979, a MP and prominent trade unionist, Phey Yew Kok, was convicted of criminal breach of trust and other offences, but he jumped bail and fled to another country. In 1986, Teh Cheang Wan, the Minister for National Development, was investigated for accepting bribes from two property developers. However, he committed suicide before he could be charged in court. In 1991, the Director of the Commercial Affairs Department, Glenn Knight, was jailed and fined after being charged in court for corruption and cheating. In 1993, Yeo Seng Teck, the Chief Executive Officer of the Trade Development Board, was sentenced to four year's jail for corruption, cheating, and forgery. Finally, in 1995, the Deputy Chief Executive of the Public Utilities Board (PUB), Choy Hon Tim, was charged for accepting bribes from PUB contractors and sentenced to 14 years' imprisonment (Tan, 1999, pp. 64–65).

Similarly, Hong Kong's ICAC has earned the public's confidence by ensuring that all reports of corruption, no matter how small, are investigated (Quah, 2003a, p. 144). As corruption is viewed as a "high risk, low reward" activity in Hong Kong, it is not surprising that Robert P. Beschel Jr. (1999) found that a person committing a corrupt offence in Hong Kong was 35 times more likely to be detected and punished than his counterpart in the Philippines (p. 8).

In May 1997, the Joint Standing Committee on Foreign Affairs, Defence and Trade (1997) of the Australian Parliament voiced its concern about corruption in Hong Kong after the handover to China in July 1997 when it stated that "the corruption, rampant in China, if extended to Hong Kong, could prove disastrous for the territory" (p. 98). This concern was not original as it had been expressed earlier by Emily Lau in 1988, and Michael Yahuda in 1996 when he referred to the "pervasive fear" of the "seepage of corruption" from mainland China to Hong Kong after July 2007 (Lau, 1988, p. 29; Yahuda, 1996, pp. 128–129).

In 2001, the then Commissioner of the ICAC, Alan N. Lai, referred to the "considerable trepidation in the community concerning Hong Kong's ability to preserve its essentially corruption-free culture" and posed these two questions:

> Would the SAR Government have the will and determination to fight graft? Now that the territory had reintegrated with mainland China, would the irregular practices so common across the border spill over to Hong Kong? (p. 51)

His answers to these two questions were "Yes" and "No" respectively:

> Four years have passed since the 1997 sovereignty change and today, Hong Kong can say with pride that her credentials as a champion in fighting graft have remained as strong as ever. The ICAC continues to tackle the corrupt without fear or favour, and our track record of catching not only small flies, but also big tigers remains unblemished. Since July 1997, ICAC activities have regularly hit the headlines ... Once known to the ICAC, no one can escape our scrutiny. (Lai, 2001, pp. 51–52)

In sum, there must be impartial and not selective enforcement of the anti-corruption laws by the ACA.

## Political Will is Crucial for Minimizing Corruption

Political will is perhaps the most important precondition for the effectiveness of an ACA. The political leaders in a country must be sincerely committed to the eradication of corruption by showing exemplary conduct and adopting a modest lifestyle themselves. This means that those found guilty of corruption must be punished, regardless of their status or position in society. Political will is absent when the "big fish" or rich and famous are protected from prosecution for grand corruption, and only the "small fish" or ordinary people are caught and punished for petty corruption.

Political will refers to the commitment of political leaders to eradicate corruption and exists when these three conditions are met: (1) comprehensive anti-corruption legislation exists; (2) the independent ACA is provided with sufficient personnel and resources; and (3) the anti-corruption laws are fairly enforced by the independent ACA (Quah, 2004, p. 4). Indeed, political will is "the most important prerequisite as a comprehensive anti-corruption strategy will fail if it is not supported by the political leadership in a country" (Quah, 2003a, p. 181). Thus, the commitment of the political leaders in fighting corruption ensures the allocation of adequate personnel and resources to the anti-corruption effort, and the impartial enforcement of the anti-corruption laws by the ACA.

In 1985, the then prime minister of Singapore, Lee Kuan Yew, argued that political leaders should be paid the top salaries that they deserved to ensure honest government. If ministers and senior civil servants were underpaid, they would succumb to temptation and indulge in corruption (Quah, 1989, p. 848). However, the plausibility of this argument is debatable as Singapore had initiated its anti-corruption strategy in 1960 with the reduction of opportunities for corruption by strengthening the POCA and the CPIB, since the government could not afford to reduce the incentive for corruption through raising salaries until after 1972 (Quah, 2003c, p. 157).

In the final analysis, an ACA in a country is only as effective as its incumbent government wants it to be. In other words, an ACA can only be effective if it is supported by a government that is committed to eradicating corruption in the country. The former CPIB Director, Chua Cher Yak, alluded to this in November 2002:

> It is far easier to have a good, clean government administering a good, clean system than it is for a good anti-corruption agency to clean up a corrupt government and a crooked system. In the latter case, the result is almost predictable: the anti-corruption agency is likely to come off second best. Clearly most governments will possess enough fire power to overwhelm even the most intense, well-meaning anti-corruption agency. (Chua, 2002, p. 3)

## CONCLUSION

In its comparative study on the institutional arrangements employed by 14 countries to combat corruption, the UNDP Regional Centre (2005) in Bangkok concluded that there were more advantages than disadvantages in relying on ACAs to curb corruption. While the third pattern of relying on an independent ACA is popular in many Asian countries, its adoption does not automatically result in success without political will or a favorable policy context.

If political will exists and the country has a favorable policy context, the best method for curbing corruption is to establish an ACA and equip it with adequate powers, personnel, and funding. The examples of Hong Kong and Singapore show that, "apart from political will, they have succeeded in curbing corruption because of their favorable policy contexts: they have small populations; stable governments; high standards of living; efficient civil service systems; and well developed infrastructure" (Quah, 2004, p. 4). On the other hand, apart from being less committed to fighting corruption, the governments of Thailand and South Korea have also a less favorable policy context as they are larger countries with more population, less efficient civil services, and lower standards of living. The fact that the KICAC cannot investigate corruption reports is a reflection of a lack of political will in curbing corruption in South Korea. Hence, it is not surprising that Table 2 below shows that both Singapore and Hong Kong have higher scores on the 2006 CPI and World Bank indicator on the control of corruption than South Korea and Thailand.

*Table 2.* CPI Ranking and Score and Control of Corruption Percentile Rank for Four Asian Countries in 2006.

| Country | CPI Ranking and Score | Control of Corruption Percentile Rank |
|---|---|---|
| Singapore | 5th (9.4) | 98.1 |
| Hong Kong | 15th (8.3) | 92.7 |
| South Korea | 42nd (5.1) | 64.6 |
| Thailand | 63rd (3.6) | 50.5 |
| Number of countries | 163 | 212 |

*Sources:* http://www.transparency.org for the 2006 CPI ranking and score; and http://info.worldbank.org/governance/wgi2007/sc_chart.asp for the 2006 data on the World Bank's sixth indicator on the control of corruption.

However, if there is no political will to curb corruption, the danger exists that the political leaders in a country can use the ACA as a weapon against their political enemies. There must be checks to prevent this from happening if a country decides to establish an independent ACA to curb corruption.

Thus, in spite of their popularity, care should be taken by political leaders before adopting independent ACAs to curb corruption. Richard Rose (2005) has advised that a policy lesson can only be applied if three prerequisites are met:

> Even if a lesson appears desirable and the pressure of events creates a demand for political action, this does not guarantee that you can apply it at home. For this to happen, there must be space to introduce a new programme into an already crowded set of government commitments; there must be the resources to implement it; and there must not be crosscultural misunderstandings that lead to a mismatch between what a lesson requires and the beliefs and practices of the government adopting it. Only if all three conditions are met can you hope to apply a lesson in practice. (p. 116)

Finally, in view of the contextual differences between Singapore and Hong Kong and the other Asian countries, and the absence of political will, it is unlikely that these countries can successfully transplant the CPIB or ICAC model. Indeed, as Michael Johnston (1999) has rightly cautioned: "ICACs [Independent Commissions Against Corruption] are unlikely to be right for every country" (p. 225). In other words, the CPIB and ICAC and their favorable policy contexts have enabled Singapore and Hong Kong to curb corruption effectively. Political leaders in Asian countries who wish to curb corruption must demonstrate their political will by allocating the required resources and legislation for the CPIB or ICAC-style agency to perform its task of impartially enforcing the comprehensive anti-corruption laws.

## NOTES

1. Mongolia finally established an Independent Authority Against Corruption (IAAC) in December 2006, eight years after the present author had recommended its formation as part of the National Anti-Corruption Plan he presented to the Government of Mongolia as the Lead Consultant for the United Nations Development Programme Mission to Ulaanbataar in September and October 1998 (see Quah, 1998, 1999).

2. The ACA in Malaysia and CEC in Indonesia are excluded from this analysis because of the lack of comparative data on these two ACAs.

3. For more details on the OPEN system, see http://open.metro.seoul.kr

4. These questions were posed to me by some Mongolian policy-makers during my visit to Ulaanbataar in October 1998 as the lead consultant for the UNDP mission to Mongolia.

# REFERENCES

Amara, R. (1992). Bureaucracy vs. Bureaucracy: Anti-corrupt practice measures in Thailand. In: R. K. Arora (Ed.), *Politics and administration in changing societies: Essays in honour of Professor Fred W. Riggs* (pp. 220–244). New Delhi: Associated Publishing House.

Anti-Corruption Act. (2001). Seoul: Office for Government Policy Coordination.

Batalla, E. C. (2001). De-institutionalizing corruption in the Philippines: Identifying strategic requirements for reinventiing institutions. In: A. C. Pedro, Jr. (Ed.), *Combating corruption in East Asia* (pp. 41–78). Manila: Yuchengco Center for East Asia, De La Salle University.

Beschel, R. P., Jr. (1999). *Corruption, transparency and accountability in the Philippines.* Manila: Asian Development Bank.

Borwornsak, U. (2001). Depoliticising key institutions for combating corruption: The new Thai constitution. In: P. Larmour & N. Wolanin (Eds), *Corruption and anti-corruption* (pp. 177–203). Canberra: Asia Pacific Press.

Chua, C. Y. (2002). Corruption control: What works? Paper presented at the Seminar on Promoting Integrity and Fighting Corruption in Guiyang, China, November 19–21. Available at http://www.oecd.org/dataoecd/43/4/2408212.pdf

Corrupt Practices Investigation Bureau (CPIB). (2004). *Corrupt Practices Investigation Bureau.* Singapore.

CPIB. (2003). *Swift and sure action: Four decades of anti-corruption work.* Singapore: CPIB.

De Speville, B. (1997). *Hong Kong: Policy initiatives against corruption.* Paris: Development Centre, Organisation for Economic Cooperation and Development.

Fong, T. (2005). The day anti-graft chief took lie test. *Straits Times*, June 30, p. H7.

Heilbrunn, J. R. (2006). Anti-corruption commissions. In: R. Stapenhurst, N. Johnston & R. Pelizzo (Eds), *The role of parliament in Curbing corruption* (pp. 135–148). Washington, DC: The World Bank.

ICAC. (1989). *Fighting corruption: The mission continues.* Hong Kong: ICAC.

Independent Commission Against Corruption (ICAC). (2006). *2005 Annual report by the commissioner of the independent commission against corruption of Hong Kong special administrative region.* Hong Kong: ICAC.

Johnston, M. (1999). A brief history of anti-corruption agencies. In: A. Schedler, L. Diamond & M. F. Plattner (Eds), *The self-restraining state: Power and accountability in new Democracies* (pp. 217–226). Boulder: Lynne Rienner Publishers.

Joint Standing Committee on Foreign Affairs, Defence and Trade. (1997). *Hong Kong: The transfer of sovereignty.* Canberra: Parliament of the Commonwealth of Australia.

Jun, J. S., & Park, M. S. (2001). Crisis and organisational paralysis: The lingering problem of Korean public administration. *Journal of Contingencies and Crisis Management*, 9(1), 3–13.

Kim, M. S. (1997). Regulation and corruption. In: Y. H. Cho & H. G. Frederickson (Eds), *The white house and the blue house: Government reform in the United States and Korea* (pp. 253–269). Lanham: University Press of America.

Korea Independent Commission Against Corruption (KICAC). (2006). *Annual Report 2005.* Seoul: KICAC. Available at http://www.kicac.go.kr/english/E_PubPublicationR.jsp

Kuan, H. C. (1981). Anti-corruption legislation in Hong Kong – A history. In: R. P. L. Lee (Ed.), *Corruption and its control in Hong Kong: Situations up to the late seventies* (pp. 15–43). Hong Kong: The Chinese University Press.

Lai, A. N. (2001). Keeping Hong Kong clean: Experiences of fighting corruption post 1997. *Harvard Asia Pacific Review*, 5(2), 51–54.
Lau, E. (1988). Graft-busters and 1997: Concern arises over anti-corruption commission's future. *Far Eastern Economic Review*, 8, 29.
Lee, G. B. (2005). *The synonan years: Singapore under Japanese rule 1942–1945*. Singapore: National Archives of Singapore and Epigram.
Lethbridge, H. J. (1985). *Hard graft in Hong Kong: Scandal, corruption and the ICAC*. Hong Kong: Oxford University Press.
Moon, S. Y. (2001). The utilization of the internet technology in the public services of Korea. *Asian Review of Public Administration*, 13(1), 30–45.
Office of the National Counter Corruption Commission (ONCCC). (2006a). *Anti-corruption laws and regulations*. Bangkok: ONCCC.
ONCCC. (2006b). *The National Counter Corruption Commission (NCCC) Thailand*. Bangkok: ONCCC.
Oyamada, E. (2005). President Gloria Macapagal-Arroyo's anti-corruption strategy in the Philippines: An evaluation. *Asian Journal of Political Science*, 13(1), 81–107.
Palmier, L. (1985). *The control of bureaucratic corruption: Case studies in Asia*. New Delhi: Allied Publishers.
Pope, J. (2000). *Confronting corruption: The elements of a national integrity system*. Berlin: Transparency International.
Preecha, L. (2001). Institutionalizing strategies to combat corruption in Thailand. In: A. C. Pedro, Jr. (Ed.), *Combating Corruption in East Asia* (pp. 105–119). Manila: Yuchengco Center for East Asia, De La Salle University.
Quah, J. S. T. (1978). *Administrative and legal measures for combating bureaucratic corruption in Singapore*. Singapore: Department of Political Science, University of Singapore, Occasional Paper No. 34.
Quah, J. S. T. (1979). Police corruption in Singapore: An analysis of its forms, extent and causes. *Singapore Police Journal*, 10(1), 7–43.
Quah, J. S. T. (1982). Bureaucratic corruption in the ASEAN countries: A comparative analysis of their anti-corruption strategies. *Journal of Southeast Asian Studies*, 13(1), 153–177.
Quah, J. S. T. (1989). Singapore's experience in curbing corruption. In: A. J. Heiden-heimer, M. Johnston & V. T. LeVine (Eds), *Political corruption: A handbook* (pp. 841–853). New Brunswick: Transaction Publishers.
Quah, J. S. T. (1998). National anti-corruption plan for Mongolia. Confidential report prepared for UNDP and the Mongolian Government, November, 41pp.
Quah, J. S. T. (1999). *Combating corruption in Mongolia: Problems and prospects*. Working Paper no. 22. Department of Political Science, National University of Singapore, Singapore.
Quah, J. S. T. (2000). Accountability and anti-corruption agencies in the Asia-Pacific region. In: *Combating corruption in Asian and Pacific economies* (pp. 101–124). Manila: Asian Development Bank.
Quah, J. S. T. (2003a). *Curbing corruption in Asia: A comparative study of six countries*. Singapore: Eastern Universities Press.
Quah, J. S. T. (2003b). Causes and consequences of corruption in Southeast Asia: A comparative analysis of Indonesia, Philippines and Thailand. *Asian Journal of Public Administration*, 25(2), 235–266.

Quah, J. S. T. (2003c). Paying for the 'best and brightest': Rewards for high public office in Singapore. In: C. Hood, B. G. Peters & G. O. M. Lee (Eds), *Reward for high public office: Asian and Pacific rim states* (pp. 145–162). London: Routledge.
Quah, J. S. T. (2004). Best practices for curbing corruption in Asia. *The Governance Brief* (11), 1–4. Available at www.adb.org/Documents/Periodicals/GB/Government Brief11.pdf
Quah, J. S. T. (2006). Curbing Asian corruption: An impossible dream? *Current History*, *105*(690), 176–179.
Quah, J. S. T. (2007). *National integrity systems in East and Southeast Asia 2006 regional overview report*. Berlin: Transparency International.
Republic of Singapore. (1994). *The budget for the financial year 1994/1995*. Command 2 of 1994. Singapore: Budget Division, Ministry of Finance.
Republic of Singapore. (2007). *The budget for the financial year 2007/2008*. Singapore: Ministry of Finance.
Research Institute for Asia and the Pacific (RIAP). (2001). *Public sector challenges and government reforms in South East Asia report 2001*. Sydney: RIAP, University of Sydney.
Rose, R. (2005). *Learning from comparative public policy: A practical guide*. London: Routledge.
Tan, A. L. (1999). The experience of Singapore in combating corruption. In: R. Stapenhurst & S. J. Kpundeh (Eds), *Curbing corruption: Toward a model for building national integrity* (pp. 59–66). Washington, DC: The World Bank.
Thio, L. (1997). The elected president and the legal control of government: *Quis custodiet ipsos custodies*. In: K. Y. L. Tan & P. E. Lam (Eds), *Managing political change in Singapore: The elected presidency* (pp. 100–143). London: Routledge.
United Nations Development Programme Regional Centre. (2005). *Institutional arrangements to combat corruption: A comparative study*. Bangkok: UNDP Regional Centre.
Wong, J. H. K. (1981). The ICAC and its anti-corruption measures. In: R. P. L. Lee (Ed.), *Corruption and its control in Hong Kong: Situations up to the late seventies* (pp. 45–72). Hong Kong: The Chinese University Press.
Yahuda, M. (1996). *Hong Kong: China's challenge*. London: Routledge.

# REGULATORY REFORM AND BUREAUCRACY IN SOUTHEAST ASIA: VARIATIONS AND CONSEQUENCES

David S. Jones

## ABSTRACT

*Reform of government regulation of private business has been considered a cornerstone of good governance and a necessary condition for economic growth.* Part of regulatory reform is reducing and streamlining administrative or procedural regulations imposed on business by government bureaucracies. Such regulations impose burdens on firms in terms of the time and effort required to file forms, delays in processing documents and applications and in granting approvals, transactional costs if charges are levied, and obstacles resulting from arbitrary decisions by government officials during the process. The chapter will consider the burdens on business caused by regulatory procedures imposed by bureaucracy in the countries of Southeast Asia, and how the reform of such procedures has varied across region, with a particular focus on certain key business functions, viz. starting a business, importing and exporting, paying taxes, and constructing a commercial building. The chapter will posit explanations of why such variation exists and will discuss links between reform of regulatory procedures and the level of *social and economic development of a country. In conclusion, the scope for reform of regulatory procedures in those countries where they remain especially burdensome, will be examined, with consideration given to what reforms are necessary and feasible.*

## INTRODUCTION

The regulation of private business by the state involves imposing restrictions and compulsions on businesses to protect the public from the perceived social and economic harm of the free market such as negative externalities, informational imbalances, and anti-competitive behavior (market failure). Examples, to name but a few, are price controls, trade permits, zoning restrictions, restrictions on lending, regulations to reduce pollution, and work safety stipulations (Baldwin & Cave, 1999, pp. 9–17). Alongside such regulations (which may be referred to as substantive regulations), businesses are often obliged to follow a chain of bureaucratic procedural requirements in relation to key functions they undertake (administrative or procedural regulations), in some cases to determine compliance with a substantive regulation. Such procedural regulations may themselves create obstacles and inconvenience for businesses, and so contribute to their overall regulatory burden.

In recent years, it has been recognized that regulatory reform is crucial to economic and social development and a hallmark of good governance, not least in Southeast Asia. Regulatory reform involves: (a) reducing the number of substantive regulations which impede business activity with no substantial benefit to the public or the economy (deregulation) and (b) creating new regulations which are beneficial to the public and the economy (re-regulation). Equally important, regulatory reform necessitates streamlining the procedures and reducing the red tape which exist alongside and sometimes in conjunction with a substantive regulation as mentioned above (procedural or administrative deregulation). This leads to a more efficient and less burdensome application of the procedural regulations, reducing the amount of time and effort business managers have to spend in ensuring compliance, avoiding undue delays in carrying out key business functions, and lowering the costs in the form of compulsory payments to be made in following the required procedures (Baldwin & Cave, 1999, pp. 81, 82, 85; Hafeez, 2003, pp. 5–8; OECD, 1997; Hopkins, 1992; Khan, 2000, p. 7). Linked to administrative deregulation are also reforms to make bureaucratic procedures clearer and more transparent, so reducing the discretionary and arbitrary power of officials.

In the last 10–15 years, as part of the policy to reform regulatory systems in Southeast Asia, reform of administrative procedures has also been undertaken. However, the extent of reform has varied across the region. Some countries have significantly streamlined procedures, reducing red tape, and cutting compliance costs, whilst ensuring that the procedures which remain are clear and transparent. Other countries by contrast have only taken initial steps to reform regulatory procedures, leaving scope for more far-reaching reforms. The chapter will examine the extent of the regulatory burden arising from bureaucratic processes affecting key business functions in the countries of Southeast Asia. It will distinguish those countries where major reform of procedural regulations has occurred from those where it has not. The chapter will consider why such variation exists and how it corresponds with differences in social and economic development of Southeast Asian states. In conclusion, the scope for reform of regulatory procedures in those countries where they remain numerous and unwieldy, will be examined, with consideration given to what reforms are necessary and feasible. Part of the evidence on regulatory procedures will be taken from the World Bank's database on regulations and its yearly surveys, *Doing Business: How to Reform*.

## THE EXTENT AND BURDEN OF ADMINISTRATIVE REGULATION

As part of regulatory framework imposed by the state, businesses are obliged to adhere to a set of bureaucratic procedural requirements in respect to their key functions – submitting forms and certificates to regulatory, licensing and other public authorities, undergoing inspections and valuations, and obtaining approvals from the authorities mentioned earlier (comprising licenses, permits, certificates, registrations, and signatures). Some of the procedures are little more than formalities involving no major decisions though they can be time consuming and costly. Other procedures exist in order to determine if certain conditions have been fulfilled and may result in an application being rejected, an approval withheld, or an inspection test being failed. Such procedures are more than formalities and entail decisions by officials that affect the business. This is particularly so, as pointed out later, if procedures are unclear and opaque (Hafeez, 2003, p. 7).

The extent to which private firms are subject to procedural regulation can be measured in various ways depending upon the business activities being regulated. Common to most of them is the total list of steps involved: the number of procedures to be followed, documents and forms to be completed and submitted, approvals to be obtained, and inspections and valuations to be undertaken. A second common measure is the time taken for these activities to be completed whilst a third are the costs which arise as a result of the fees and charges levied for any of these requirements. Using these measures, the extent and burden of procedural regulation in the various countries of Southeast Asia can be gauged.

The chain of bureaucratic procedures that must be followed to enable a business function to be undertaken or to ensure that conditions mandated by a substantive regulation have been met can readily add to the burdens of a business, if unduly cumbersome and inefficiently administered. The procedures can encroach upon the time of business managers (such as the hours and days spent in obtaining advice, completing forms, submitting documents, and visiting government departments), which increases if the services of notaries and lawyers are required. In addition, costs have to be borne if charges are levied for processing applications and paperwork, verifying documents, and undergoing inspections and valuations, with extra expenses if notaries and lawyers are engaged. Serious delays may occur in consequence of the time taken by regulatory, licensing, and other public authorities in undertaking the required procedures. If complex and numerous, becoming a drain upon the time of managers, imposing extra costs, and creating undue delays, they may serve to prevent or discourage engagement in business activities. The upshot is to make businesses less efficient, competitive, and profitable, with, what's more, significant disincentives to undertake further investment and expand the scale of operations.

A further concern is that administrative regulations, which otherwise should be straightforward, are not so due to their ambiguity. This allows officials of the relevant agency discretion to determine the conditions and actions required in following a procedure as well the charges to be levied. Given the ambiguity, such discretion may be exercised arbitrarily to restrict or prohibit a business activity. To make matters worse, firms may not always be aware of how an unclear procedural regulation is interpreted, thereby increasing the chances of not meeting the conditions and completing the paperwork in accordance with the stipulations of the agency.

By way of example, the nature and consequences of unclear and opaque procedures in Vietnam have been repeatedly expressed by the Vietnam

Chamber of Commerce and Industry in recent years through its regular bulletin. In one issue in 2006, it stated that "the decision to grant a license is heavily subject to the judgment of officials which increases the prospect for discretion" as result of the fact that "the criteria to grant a license are unclear." If an application is rejected, "the reasons given for refusal are unsubstantiated" (Vietnam Chamber of Commerce and Industry [VCCI], 2006a, p. 1). In the same vein, one Vietnamese bank official has pointed out the impact on businesses which, in trying to comply with administrative requirements, "are hassled or may be required by the licensing authorities to meet many other arbitrary conditions," and in consequence "may have to give up business opportunities" (VCCI, 2006a, p. 2). These observations are fairly typical of the business regulatory system of several countries in the region.

Thus, a key challenge facing governments in Southeast Asia, alongside lessening unnecessary substantive regulations, is to pursue administrative deregulation as well, so as to reduce and simplify the lengthy and complex bureaucratic processes which businesses must follow. Equally important is to make regulatory procedures clearer and their application more transparent so as to reduce the arbitrary control of regulatory and licensing authorities. However, in Southeast Asia, considerable differences remain in the extent to which states have undertaken reform of bureaucratic processes affecting businesses. This can be exemplified in four areas of business activity, as discussed later: starting a business, importing and exporting goods, paying taxes, and constructing a commercial building.

## ADMINISTRATIVE REGULATIONS IN KEY ASPECTS OF BUSINESS IN SOUTHEAST ASIAN STATES

### Starting a Business

A key stage in business activity which is subject to administrative regulation is the setting up of an enterprise, the central requirement of which is its registration with its name and description entered into an official business registry. This is necessary, amongst other things, to accord the business legal status, to enable it to export and import goods, to obtain credit and acquire property, to facilitate the payment of taxes, to ensure proper enforcement of contracts, and to protect employees' rights (World Bank [WB], 2006a, pp. 9–14). As shown in Table 1, in several countries of Southeast Asia, the

*Table 1.* Starting a Business.

| | Number of Procedures | Time Taken (Days) | Costs (% of Income per Head) |
|---|---|---|---|
| Cambodia | 12 | 37 | 173 |
| Indonesia | 12 | 151 | 102 |
| Laos | 9 | 198 | 15 |
| Malaysia | 9 | 30 | 30.5 |
| Philippines | 11 | 48 | 20 |
| Singapore | 6 | 6 | 1 |
| Thailand | 8 | 33 | 6 |
| Vietnam | 11 | 50 | 51 |

*Source:* WB (2007). The World Bank survey does not include Myanmar and Brunei.

procedural requirements in setting up a business are unwieldy, protracted, and costly whilst in others the process has been reformed with the streamlining of procedures, which have become as a result more expeditious and less costly (Djankov, La Porta, de Silanes, & Shleifer, 2002, pp. 1–37; Fonesca, Lopez-Garcia, & Pisarides, 2001, pp. 692–705).

The bureaucratic process for setting up a business in Indonesia is one of the most cumbersome and protracted in the region. Twelve procedures must be followed before a company can become legally operational. The first of these is to ensure that another company is not using the same name. The standard form of the company deed must be obtained from the Ministry of Justice and Human Rights. After completion, it must then be verified by and submitted through a notary, in order to secure clearance for the company's name by the Ministry. Once this is done, the company can then reserve the name for itself. The next step is for the company founder to sign the deed of establishment before a notary, after which the company is obliged to apply for and obtain a taxpayer's registration number, a VAT collector number, and an entrepreneur tax identification number if it is a large company. Following this, the firm is required to obtain a domicile certificate from the local or municipal authority, and to open a bank account in the company's name with a deposit of the paid up capital reserve stipulated for a new business together with the submission to the bank of the company's articles of association and copies of ID cards of the proposed authorized signatories. Only after a bank account has been opened, with the requisite paid up capital, and a tax code number created, can the company apply for the approval of the deeds of establishment from the Ministry of Justice and Human Rights. After approval is given, the company can seek to be registered on the Company Register at the Ministry of Industry and Trade, and, providing there is no objection, it may then receive a business registration certificate (WB, 2006a, 2007).

Following registration, several important post-registration procedures must be followed. If the company is a non-facility trading company it must obtain a trading license also from the Ministry of Industry and Trade. If the company employs more than 10 employees and/or has a payroll bill of Rp1 million per month, it must next register with the Ministry of Manpower and then subscribe to the social security scheme for its employees (WB, 2007).

According to the World Bank's survey *Doing Business 2006*, the time taken in Indonesia to complete the administrative process described above, is estimated to range from 97 to 151 days. The period needed by the Ministry of Justice and Human Rights to grant approval for the deeds of establishment in itself is estimated at 22 days. The processes of business registration, tax registration, issue of a trading license, and registration with Ministry of Manpower each takes 14–15 days (WB, 2007).

In Vietnam, a start was made in 1999 to reduce bureaucratic procedures in starting a business as a result of the introduction of the Enterprise Law. This in part contributed to a surge in businesses entering the market. However, much remains to be done to fully streamline the business start-up process, despite the creation of the one-stop shop arrangement as discussed later. The World Bank survey *Doing Business 2006*, showed that there were 11 procedures which take on average 50 days with charges levied amounting to 51% of annual income per head. These must be followed sequentially and involve three departments: Department of Planning and Investment, Department of Public Security, and the Tax Department. According to another survey, establishing a business can take anything up to 260 days involving 13 procedures. The survey concluded that "administrative procedures (relating to a business start-up) are still the biggest barriers to an entrepreneur's chances of turning a business idea into a reality" (GTZ-CIEM, 2005; WB, 2006a, p. 13). These views have been repeatedly echoed by the Vietnam Chamber of Commerce and Industry, and local and foreign business managers. Illustrating the time wasted by business owners in meeting their procedural obligations when setting up a business, Van Quang Thinh of the Managing Consulting Group of Vietnam, stated in 2006:

> In some provinces we have worked in, a person starting a business has to visit his local administrative authorities at least 13 times to complete the first three business establishment procedures. In one province, the staff of the relevant administrative agencies spend 27 days over 98 operational steps to process a business establishment application ... As a result business owners have to rum around to fulfil several complicated procedures. (VCCI, 2006b, p. 2)

Reflecting further the frustration of the business community at the impingements of petty officialdom, another business manager, Nguyen Anh Tuan of Bizconsult, referred to the way officials responsible for business registration "refuse to accept an application if minor information is missing. In many cases businesses have to wait seven days to be informed of just one minor mistake" (VCCI, 2006b, p. 2).

Cambodian entrepreneurs when starting a business too suffer from a surfeit of bureaucratic controls, which the government has pledged to eliminate (12 procedures must be followed with costs amounting to 173% of average income) (IMF, 2004a, p. 72). In Laos, when establishing a business nine procedures are mandatory which costs the entrepreneur an amount equivalent to 15% of average income, and are the most protracted in Southeast Asia for business start-ups, extending over 198 days. On a brighter note, the World Bank's 2007 preliminary report on *Doing Business* has indicated the beginning of attempts in Laos to reduce the bureaucratic hurdles to market entry, although further and far-reaching reform is necessary (WB, 2006b, p. 4).

By contrast, in Singapore the number of procedures in starting a business is only six, each taking one day at a cost of US$229, less than 1% of average income. This equates with the average number of procedures in starting a business in OECD countries, which, however, require a longer time span (16 days) and greater cost (5% of average income) (WB, 2006a, p. 150; WB, 2007). The approval of articles of association, and business registration with the Accounting and Corporate Regulatory Authority of Singapore (which was created in 2005 and incorporated the functions of the old Registry of Companies and Businesses) are compounded into one procedure taking about three days and are done online. Under the Companies (Amendment) Act, 2002, and Business Registration (Amendment) Act, 2002, the Registrar of Companies and Businesses no longer undertakes a pre-registration check for similar names. Under the same legislation, the applicant for registration need not submit any hard copy forms, declarations, and affidavits, nor will he/she be issued with a hard copy certificate of registration (Republic of Singapore, 2002a, ss. 8, 11; 2002b, ss. 7, 8, 16, 19, 14). As Lee Hsien Long, the Minister for Finance, in introducing the second reading of the Business Registration (Amendment) Bill stated:

> The proposed amendments in this Bill are expected to benefit business owners in terms of lower costs, more efficient service and greater convenience. It would also align RCB's (Registry of Companies and Businesses) practices with its counterparts in the US, UK and Australia, and allow RCB to provide better service to its customers. (Singapore Parliament [SP], 2002, cols. 55, 65, 66)

This has been made possible by an online facility known as BizFile created in 2002, by which all company submissions, registrations, certifications, and declarations are undertaken electronically. One advantage is to allow businesses, according to Lee Hsien Loong, "same day incorporation, which has become the service standards that businessmen would expect" and "simplifies the filing and incorporation process" (SP, 2002, col. 59).

The post-registration procedures consist only of registering with the Inland Revenue Authority of Singapore (with respect to all taxes levied on the company and its employees) and Central Provident Fund Board, and subscribing to the Workmen's Compensation Insurance. These are undertaken online and each takes only one day. It may be noted that several of the procedures that are mandatory in Indonesia are either eliminated or undertaken simultaneously in Singapore. Retaining only necessary procedures, combining procedures, and using online facilities for every stage of the process in starting an enterprise significantly enhances the efficiency of the process, minimizes the number of days required, and involves little cost.

*External Trade*

Importing and exporting goods in many states is subject to regulation, consisting of restrictions on what goods can be imported and exported (either through prohibition or quota restriction), and customs and other duties levied on them. Accompanying these restrictions are the procedures that must be followed to obtain an import or export permit and to clear customs. Various documents must be submitted identifying and describing the goods, including their volume and value, and specifying countries of origin and destination (WB, 2006a, pp. 53–59). This may require verification through inspections and valuations at the seaport, airport, and border crossing, giving rise to further paperwork and administration. Table 2 shows how much the countries of Southeast Asia have varied in reducing and streamlining administrative requirements relating to the issue of import and export permits and the clearance of customs, and in the consequences in terms of costs and time.

Importers and exporters in Cambodia encounter a high degree of government bureaucracy in relation to trade permits and customs levies and clearance, resulting in serious delays (which are only exceeded in Laos where the situation is distorted by the fact that it is landlocked and extra paperwork and approvals are required for transshipment). In Cambodia, eight documents have to be processed to allow goods to be exported and 12 to allow goods to be imported, necessitating respectively 10 and 18

*Table 2.* Regulatory Process for Importing and Exporting.

|  | Number of Documents to be Submitted for Permit and Customs | | Number of Signatures Needed before Issue of Permit and Customs Clearance | | Time Taken to Obtain Permits and Clearance (Days) | |
| --- | --- | --- | --- | --- | --- | --- |
|  | Export | Import | Export | Import | Export | Import |
| Cambodia | 8 | 12 | 10 | 18 | 43 | 55 |
| Indonesia | 7 | 10 | 3 | 6 | 25 | 30 |
| Laos | 12 | 16 | 17 | 28 | 66 | 78 |
| Malaysia | 6 | 12 | 3 | 5 | 20 | 22 |
| Philippines | 6 | 8 | 5 | 7 | 19 | 22 |
| Singapore | 5 | 6 | 2 | 2 | 6 | 8 |
| Thailand | 9 | 14 | 10 | 10 | 23 | 25 |
| Vietnam | 6 | 9 | 12 | 15 | 35 | 36 |

*Source:* WB (2007).

approvals and taking 43 and 55 days (WB, 2007). The IMF has brought attention to these impediments to the facilitation of trade in Cambodia. In a recent study, it noted that "trade facilitation practices stand out as having high official and unofficial costs," and lead to "delays, uncertainty and discretion for clearance procedures" (IMF, 2004a, p. 49). This has contributed significantly to the "excess transaction costs (in time and money)" which overall Cambodian firms incur in dealing with government agencies. In response, the Cambodian government is currently focusing on reforms "to modernize and streamline customs procedures ... to enhance trade facilitation." The priority is centered on "decreasing the total import and export transaction costs [and] decreasing the overall time it takes to import and export products" (IMF, 2004a, p. 70; IMF, 2004b, p. 24).

Philippines have in recent years significantly streamlined the procedures governing import permits and customs clearance. Contributing to this was the recent introduction of transactional valuations (the price paid by the importer to the exporter plus handling and shipment costs), rather than the valuations undertaken by the customs authorities themselves, the ending of pre-shipment inspections at the country of origin, the use of customs and permit audits of goods on a selective basis and only after they have reached the importer (known as back-end audits). This, together with the adoption of online permit and customs clearance, cuts down the documents that have to be submitted, reduces the delay in securing clearance and costs incurred in obtaining permits (Clarete, 2004).

Singapore is exemplary in having adopted an effective system to facilitate trade, partly attributed to minimizing administrative requirements for imports and exports. Five documents are necessary for imports and six for exports, with two signatures of approval in each case; the entire process taking only 3–6 days. The documents are a bill of lading, cargo manifest, packing list, commercial invoice, certificate of origin (for imports), customs export declaration form, and shipping note (the last two for exports). The administrative process compares favorably with that in OECD countries. The number of documents is similar to the average total needed in foreign trading in OECD countries, but the time taken up for processing is much less and the processing costs are more than a half (WB, 2007; WB, 2006a, p. 150).

## Paying Taxes

Part of the regulatory framework are the tax obligations imposed on businesses, the bulk of which comprise corporate tax, sales and value added taxes withheld from the consumer but paid by businesses, social security contributions, and property tax. The focus here is not on the amount of tax that has to be paid by a business but on the procedural burden that falls on firms in meeting their tax obligations. This is reflected in the total of tax payments a firm is required to make, which is determined both by the number of taxes levied and also the number of times payment must be made during the year. Equally important is the amount of time businesses have to put aside to prepare and file tax returns and to pay (withhold) taxes. Preparation time includes the hours spent to collect all information necessary to compute the tax payable. This includes time spent on keeping separate accounting books for tax purposes, completing all the tax forms, and making all necessary calculations. Payment time is the hours needed to make the payment online or at the tax office, and if the latter the waiting time when visiting a tax office (WB, 2006a, pp. 45–52). The data on the number of tax payments required and time taken to file tax returns in the various countries of Southeast Asia is given in Table 3.

The greatest number of tax payment transactions are recorded in the Philippines and Indonesia (more than 50), with Thailand and Malaysia also requiring large numbers of tax payments from businesses. In terms of hours spent in collecting information and filing returns visiting tax offices, the greatest burden falls on Vietnamese businesses (over 1,000 h per year) followed by Indonesia (just over 570 h). Again Singapore stands out with

*Table 3.* Regulatory Process in Paying Taxes.

|  | Number of Tax Payments | Number of Hours Business Spent in Filing[a] Tax Return |  | Number of Tax Payments | Number of Hours Business Spent in Filing[a] Tax Return |
|---|---|---|---|---|---|
| Cambodia | 27 | 121 | Philippines | 59 | 94 |
| Indonesia | 52 | 576 | Singapore | 16 | 30 |
| Laos | 31 | 180 | Thailand | 46 | 104 |
| Malaysia | 35 | 190 | Vietnam | 32 | 1,050 |

*Source:* WB (2007).

relatively few tax payments (16), necessitating only 30 h to be spent in collecting information and filing returns. The more streamlined procedure and less time-consuming the task in filing tax returns and making payments is partly the product of a simplified business tax system and the extensive provision of online filing of tax returns and payment of tax liabilities. The procedural requirements for tax payment by businesses in Singapore is just slightly above the average for OECD countries with 15 procedures taking 203 h (WB, 2006a, pp. 129, 137, 146, 150, 155, 160).

In such countries as Indonesia, the Philippines, and Vietnam, the administrative burden in making several tax payments even for the same tax, and in spending time in collecting records and completing returns, falls heaviest on small and medium enterprises, which may not be conversant with all the minutiae of tax regulations and not able to hire tax accountants or employ finance officers.

### *Procedural Regulations in Constructing a Commercial Building*

The construction industry is a sector of the economy where regulation is an obvious necessity. This is to ensure that a building is sound and durable and therefore is safe to occupy and use, does not utilize excessive land space (where land is scarce), and conforms with land zoning and environmental stipulations. As with other substantive regulations, bureaucratic procedures must be followed to ensure or determine compliance (WB, 2006a, pp. 15–20). As shown in Table 4, significant variations exist across Southeast Asia in relation to the number and complexity of administrative procedures imposed on the construction industry and the resultant transactional costs and expenditure of time.

*Table 4.* Regulatory Process in Constructing a Commercial Building.

|  | Procedures | Time (Days) | Cost (% of Income per Capita) |
|---|---|---|---|
| Cambodia | 28 | 181 | 1,640 |
| Indonesia | 19 | 224 | 311 |
| Laos | 24 | 192 | 204 |
| Malaysia | 25 | 281 | 78 |
| Philippines | 23 | 197 | 113 |
| Singapore | 11 | 129 | 22 |
| Thailand | 9 | 127 | 11 |
| Vietnam | 14 | 133 | 56 |

*Source:* WB (2007).

The most numerous and tortuous procedures are recorded in Cambodia. Here 28 procedures must be completed before a building can become fully operational. To acquire a building permit from the municipal authority (for a smaller building), and the Ministry of Land Management, Urban Planning, and Construction (for a larger one) entails the submission, review, and approval of 11 documents at the commune (sangkat), district, municipal, and in some cases central government levels. Nine of these are the building plans for the different facets of the building and site. Once a permit has been granted, the company must notify the district and sangkat authorities. At the completion of the different stages in the process of construction, the company must inform the Ministry so that an inspection can be undertaken (e.g. when the foundation works are completed or the walls erected). Altogether seven inspections are carried out. Three further inspections must be undertaken before each of the main utility services is provided. The time taken to process the documents and give approvals is estimated at 181 days. It takes on an average 30 days to obtain a certificate from the district governor prior to applying for a building permit, and another 30 days to obtain the permit from the municipal authority or from the Ministry. A further 56 days should be allowed before electricity and other utility connections are made. What's more the transactional costs incurred are just over US$6,230 (most of which is the cost of acquiring the building permit), more than 16 times average income per capita. This is no small sum for a small construction contractor struggling to get on his feet.

In several other Southeast Asian countries, a lengthy and similar sequence of bureaucratic procedures has to be followed in the construction of a commercial building – in Laos, Malaysia, Philippines, and Indonesia, the number of procedures range between 19 and 25. The time taken to complete these procedures ranges between 192 days (Laos) and 281 days (Malaysia).

In Singapore and Thailand, the bureaucratic system regulating the construction industry is much less complex, more expeditious, and significantly less costly. In Thailand, nine procedures have to be followed in the construction of a commercial building, extending over 123 days with a cost of only 11% of average income, whilst in Singapore there are 11 procedures taking 129 days at a cost of 22% of average income. These figures are even slightly below the OECD average of 14 procedures in constructing a commercial building taking 150 hours (WB, 2006a, pp. 150, 155; 2007).

The difference between these two countries and Cambodia and other countries characterized by complex, drawn out, and costly procedures in the construction sector is the minimal involvement or non-involvement of subnational entities, and the absence of repeat inspections at the different stages in the process of construction. In fact, once a building permit has been granted, there is no inspection until the building is complete. In other words, the government agencies in Singapore and Thailand responsible for construction matters do not engage in undue interference in a building project once it is underway (although in Singapore more emphasis is now given to work safety checks).

*The Overall Scale of Administrative Regulations for Business Activities in Southeast Asian States*

The countries of the region may be divided into two groups in the extent to which bureaucratic procedures impinge upon business activity. This may be adduced from the World Bank's governance indicator on regulatory quality, in part reflecting procedural regulations, and the measure of red tape provided by Forbes Media. Both measures are available as percentile rankings within a list that covers nearly all countries, which are given in Table 5.

In one group, consisting of Singapore, Malaysia, Thailand, and Brunei, bureaucratic procedures and red tape have been significantly streamlined with a resultant reduction of transaction costs and minimizing of delays, as well as restricting opportunities for arbitrary decisions by officials. In the other group, comprising Cambodia, Indonesia, Laos, Myanmar, Philippines, and Vietnam, administrative regulations remain numerous and burdensome, although limited and incipient efforts have been made to

**Table 5.** Red Tape and Regulatory Quality.

|  | Red Tape: Percentile Score in 2006 | Regulatory Quality: Percentile Score in 2005 |  | Red Tape: Percentile Score in 2006 | Regulatory Quality Percentile Score in 2005 |
|---|---|---|---|---|---|
| Brunei | N/A | 77 | Myanmar | N/A | 2 |
| Cambodia | 11 | 27 | Philippines | 34 | 52 |
| Indonesia | 4 | 37 | Singapore | 95 | 99 |
| Laos | 1 | 11 | Thailand | 65 | 64 |
| Malaysia | 71 | 67 | Vietnam | 31 | 26 |

*Source:* WB (2006c) and Forbes Media (2006).

reduce bureaucratic requirements on businesses. The worst examples are Myanmar with a regulatory quality measure at the 2nd percentile and Laos with a red tape measure ranking at the 1st percentile. In Cambodia which has a percentile rank of 11 for red tape, the World Bank has reported that "the formal private sector faces a myriad transaction costs and barriers to establishment and operation" (IMF, 2004a, pp. 49, 69). In Vietnam, which has higher percentile scores for both red tape and regulatory quality, bureaucratic procedures continue to seriously hamper private firms, despite the implementation of the one-stop shop arrangement, as discussed later. According to the Vietnam Chamber of Commerce and Industry in 2006, "the business community considers the widespread use of increasing business licenses and conditions to be a major barrier to doing business, increasing entry and operational costs as well as the freedom to do business. Although many business licenses have been abolished, a number of new licenses have been issued and many abolished licenses reintroduced in a different form" (VCCI, 2006a, p. 1). These together with "a large volume of unwritten conditions" have imposed "heavy burdens on businesses" (VCCI, 2006a, p. 1). The tendency to reintroduce regulations has been noted too in a recent IMF survey of Vietnam (IMF, 2006a, p. 66). Even in the Philippines, with higher red tape and regulatory quality percentile rankings than the countries mentioned above, the investment climate is considered by the IMF as being undermined by excessive bureaucracy, and the need to address this issue through simplifying procedures has been highlighted in the Medium-Term Philippine Development Plan, 2004–2010 (IMF, 2004c, pp. 15, 20).

## REASONS FOR THE FAILURE TO REFORM ADMINISTRATIVE REGULATIONS

It is noticeable that in most countries of Southeast Asia market reforms have been implemented to liberalize their economies, providing more opportunities for the private sector to expand. This has entailed, amongst other things, removing restrictions on enterprise formation, especially in sectors where government monopolies had existed, lessening controls over property acquisition, reducing impediments to foreign investment, and lowering trade barriers. Yet economic reform has in some cases not been accompanied by a commensurate degree of reform of bureaucratic procedures entailing reducing and simplifying procedures and making them more precise and transparent.

Various reasons may be posited why reform of administrative regulations has not kept in step with economic deregulation. The most significant is bureaucratic self-interest, measured in terms of power, private remuneration, agency budgets, and jobs or career opportunities (Baldwin & Cave, 1999, pp. 5–7). Whilst the policy to lessen or abolish direct economic restrictions over business is one decided by the government itself, bureaucratic procedures to which business must adhere, are a matter for government administrators. The liberalization of the economy allowing the private sector to expand and generate more wealth represents a shift in the balance of power within the society. The power of bureaucratic elites is, therefore, increasingly rivaled by the rising influence of independent and wealthy business leaders. The continuation or creation of complex and ill-defined procedures entailing multiple approvals and inspections, and allowing scope for arbitrary decisions, helps bureaucratic elites to retain some of their power and status.

A further advantage to the bureaucrat is the opportunity for rent seeking. To expedite otherwise protracted procedures, and to obtain a registration, license or permit, or to pass an inspection test (which could be refused or failed for a purely technical or minor reason), a private business may have little choice but to resort to bribery. It is noticeable how many procedures, identified in the World Bank survey *Doing Business*, mentioned above, necessitated "unofficial" payments, often determined by "negotiation." This occurred either when no official charge was levied or as an addition to an existing charge. Moreover, when official charges were levied, part of the revenue generated could be readily embezzled. For this reason, it was financially rewarding to the bureaucracy to retain as many bureaucratic steps as possible in regulating different aspects of a business activity.

Indonesia is an example, where illegal taxes and charges have to be paid to secure both central and local government approvals. The IMF has observed that "illegal fees are a major problem of doing business in Indonesia and decentralization has exacerbated this problem." Moreover, "extortion by customs and tax officials is increasingly cited as a problem" (IMF, 2006b, p. 4; 2004d, p. 19).

Besides, a plethora of procedures necessitating a good deal of time-consuming work in processing documents, verifying records, conducting inspections and valuations, issuing licenses, permits and certificates, hearing appeals, etc., safeguards employment in government administration. The need for a management structure to supervise and direct such work and provide policy input, ensures possibilities of career advancement. In addition, the manpower and resources needed to undertake the procedures mentioned above enables agencies to maximize their budgets (Niskanen, 1971).

Another reason for the failure to reform regulatory procedures is the continuance of a traditional bureaucratic culture in several countries of Southeast Asia, which espouses rules, procedures and paperwork, hierarchical control, and rigid divisions of responsibility. Such a traditional mindset in ministries and other agencies of the state bureaucracy responsible for regulation and licensing is often accompanied by their ability to pursue their own policies, independently of the executive and legislature, as well as the sovereign law. The upshot is that progress in lightening the regulatory burden upon business is frustrated despite the good intentions of government leaders. An example is the Task Force set up by the Vietnamese government in 2000 with the remit to radically reduce bureaucratic control of the business sector. According to one member:

> The Task Force had to discuss the details of each and every term in the licenses with all of the Ministries and try to convince them to cancel some terms, but in the end, most of the Ministries did not agree. Ministries have great power and if they do not approve the cancellation of licenses, ultimately the Task Force cannot do anything. (VCCI, 2006a, p. 3)

The failure to streamline and reduce unnecessary and cumbersome procedures that regulate businesses may also be attributed to a lack of coordination and information sharing amongst government agencies, especially in the case of separate procedures which require the same or overlapping information. This has meant that such procedures have to be repeated time and again, which otherwise could be compounded into a single procedure (de Sa, 2005, pp. 13–16). An example are the various procedures required in a business start-up, the main ones being the approval of the articles of association, the registration of the business, tax registration and issue of a tax code number, and incorporation into employees' social security scheme, all of which can be consolidated into one procedure, as pointed out later (WB, 2006a, pp. 9–14). Of course, it can be argued that the impediment to coordination and information sharing is bureaucratic self-interest mentioned earlier, since the number of tasks involved would decrease and with it the opportunities for rent seeking, the exercise of arbitrary power, and the reason to retain jobs which otherwise would not be needed.

The lack of reform of regulatory procedures affecting business can also be attributed to the decentralization of administration. In countries such as Cambodia, Indonesia, Philippines, and Laos, regional, district, and village authorities have become part of the chain of the procedures, partly as a way of assigning to them a role in matters affecting local interests and the local economy. But if two, or as in some cases three levels of government are involved, the number of procedures is multiplied. In Cambodia, three levels of government play a role in the building approval process significantly extending the chain of procedures. In Indonesia, 21 regulations related to the hiring of labor, administered by regional governments, have been recently revoked by the Minister for Internal Affairs because of the impediments to hiring they had created (IMF, 2004e, p. 4).

# THE LINK BETWEEN REFORM OF ADMINISTRATIVE REGULATIONS AND ECONOMIC AND SOCIAL DEVELOPMENT

By comparing the foregoing tables and Table 6, it can be adduced that the extent of administrative regulation imposed on businesses, or conversely the extent of reform to reduce and simplify such regulation, varies according to the level of economic and social development of a country measured by the Human Development Index score, and GDP per head at purchasing power parity (PPP). The region can be divided into two groups according to these measures. As shown in Table 6, in the more developed group (comprising Thailand, Malaysia, Brunei, and Singapore), the HDI score is above .75 out of 1, and the GDP per head is above US$8,000, with global rankings for each country with respect to both measures within the first 75 out of 177 countries. In these countries, regulatory reform has been noticeable and

**Table 6.** Measures of Social and Economic Development of Southeast Asian States.

|  | HDI in 2006 | | GDP per Head in 2006 | |
| --- | --- | --- | --- | --- |
|  | Score (0–1) | Ranking (out of 177 Countries)[a] | US$ at PPP | Ranking (out of 177 Countries)[a] |
| Brunei | .871 | 34 | 19,210 | 36 |
| Cambodia | .583 | 129 | 2,423 | 122 |
| Indonesia | .711 | 108 | 3,609 | 113 |
| Laos | .553 | 133 | 1,954 | 134 |
| Malaysia | .805 | 61 | 10,276 | 57 |
| Myanmar | .581 | 130 | 1,027 | 158 |
| Philippines | .763 | 84 | 4,614 | 100 |
| Singapore | .916 | 25 | 28,077 | 21 |
| Thailand | .784 | 74 | 8,090 | 65 |
| Vietnam | .709 | 109 | 2,745 | 118 |

*Source:* UNDP (2007).
[a]The ranking is in descending order so that the highest ranked country is 1 and the lowest is 177.

administrative regulations impose at most limited obstacles to business activity. The second and less developed group in the region (comprising Myanmar, Laos, Vietnam, Cambodia, Indonesia, and the Philippines) is marked by HDI scores and GDP per head below (in some cases well below) the thresholds indicated above. Here, business continues to be heavily regulated by bureaucratic procedures with only limited and halting progress in implementing reform. The distinction applies to both administrative regulation of specific aspects of business activity, as shown in Tables 1–4 (e.g., forming a business and trading), and the overall level of administrative regulation and red tape as shown in Table 5.

Given the correspondence between the level of development and the reform of the regulatory system which minimizes bureaucratic restrictions on business, the question arises whether the former is the determinant or consequence of the latter. The answer is probably both.

On the one hand, regulatory reform removes many of the bureaucratic impediments to engaging in business activity and doing what is necessary to enable companies to grow and become profitable. Owners and managers are no longer faced with the difficulties of dealing with numerous, complex, and opaque procedures. Furthermore, onerous transactional costs and protracted delays are avoided with less opportunity for bureaucrats to make arbitrary decisions that frustrate what businesses can do. This ensures an environment much more conducive to business growth, employment creation, and a wider public revenue base, leading to improved living standards and public services.

On the other hand, it could be argued that regulatory reform that reduces bureaucratic impediments is a consequence (and not just a determinant) of social and economic development. In the group of countries with a higher HDI index score and GDP per head, the business sector is already well established. Business leaders, occupying positions of influence, may more effectively lobby policy-makers to implement measures that reduce and simplify administrative regulations. Moreover, policy-makers themselves may pursue opportunities to build up their own business interests as owners, shareholders, and partners, and therefore may become more sympathetic to calls for deregulation. Besides, the capital resources and greater technical expertise generated by economic development facilitates the adoption and use of IT systems providing online services which play an important role in reducing and simplifying procedures, an example being the on-line one-stop shop.

## CONCLUSION – SCOPE FOR REFORM

The foregoing analysis shows significant variation in the burdens on the businesses sector imposed by bureaucratic procedural regulations within Southeast Asia. In some countries, the burden is light, viz. Singapore followed by Thailand and Malaysia. In other countries (Laos, Vietnam, Cambodia, Indonesia, and to some extent the Philippines), bureaucratic procedures continue to weigh heavily upon private firms and impede business activity. The former group of countries provide examples of what can be done to reform bureaucratic procedures, which can provide precedents for the others to follow.

One reform is to identify different regulatory procedures which draw upon a large amount of identical information. As mentioned earlier, the procedures could then be conjoined either through the amalgamation of the administrative units responsible for the procedures or by the automatic dissemination of such information once received to the other responsible agencies. This could be achieved by the creation of a central processing agency based on the one-stop shop (sometimes called one-stop one stamp or single access point) concept (de Sa, 2005, pp. 15–16). Such an agency could itself be responsible for issuing a range of related licenses, permits, and registrations, or by combining the separate procedures where feasible, granting simply one umbrella approval subsuming different requirements. Alternatively it could disseminate the information it receives to other relevant agencies for the granting of permits, licenses, and registrations, and so act as a single access point feeding other agencies. The various procedures could be then undertaken simultaneously (IMF, 2004e, pp. 13–14).

The one-stop shop concept has been applied in Singapore with the BizFile online facility mentioned earlier. Even amongst the countries in which the regulatory burden is still excessive, the idea has found favor. In Vietnam it has been applied to tax administration and to most central government agencies at the provincial levels. In Laos and Indonesia, new or proposed investment and enterprise laws have provided a framework for the one-stop shop arrangement, whilst in Cambodia, it is envisaged that the Council for the Development of Cambodia that oversees investment will assume such a role (WB, 2004, pp. 63, 79).

To create an effective one-stop shop system depends on a thorough analysis to identify in what procedures there is a duplication and correspondence of information, and no less, a willingness of different agencies to overcome institutional rivalry and self-protection, permitting the merging of functions and sharing of information. It is also necessary to ensure that staff in the central processing agency is competent enough and see themselves as having the authority to make decisions in relation to various business functions (de Sa, 2005, pp. 18–19). These requirements though have hindered the further development of the one-stop shop system in Vietnam. One businessman in Vietnam has stated that despite the implementation of the one-stop shop system, "businesses still have to go through too many doors" and that staff responsible in provincial agencies practicing the one-stop shop approach "lack sufficient competence to provide businesses with the appropriate guidance [and] tend to be rigid when dealing with businesses" (VCCI, 2006a, p. 1; VCCI, 2006b, p. 2).

Equally important in reducing the burden imposed by bureaucratic procedures on private firms is the introduction of online applications, processing, and clearance. In consequence, applications and information can be readily submitted by firms to regulatory and licensing authorities, and clarification sought on how a procedure should be followed. With the relevant software, applications can be quickly processed, and the checks, verification, categorization, and calculations can be done accurately with the minimum of effort and time. A related benefit of an online system is to allow large amounts of data to be stored and retrieved. This is invaluable in enabling not only checks and verification, but in allowing the merger of procedures which draw upon similar or overlapping information and in automatically disseminating information to other agencies to enable them to undertake procedures for which they are responsible simultaneously without further action by the firm. Thus online systems are particularly useful in establishing the one-stop shop and single access point arrangement, and in minimizing inconvenience, delays, costs, and arbitrary controls suffered by private business in dealing with the public bureaucracy.

A key constraint impeding the advancement of online systems is the deficiency in technical know-how and hardware capacity in the less developed countries of the region (de Sa, 2005, p. 18). In 2004, the Cambodian government announced its intention to adopt an online system for customs clearance and trade data gathering, based on a single interface between importers and customs officials, known as the Automated System of Customs Data (ASYCUDA). As yet it has not been able to implement it, perhaps due to a lack of technical know-how and appropriate hardware capacity (UNCTAD, 2007). Equally important is a commitment to make best use of online systems, when fully operational, to reduce bureaucratic obstacles. Vietnam for example has used a variant of ASYCUDA for several years, yet its trade facilitation system is still characterized by a maze of procedures, delays in clearances and the issue of permits, and substantial transactional costs for importers and exporters (see Table 2) (UNCTAD, 2007). Lack of commitment may further explain Cambodia's delay in implementing ASYCUDA since the minimizing of contact between importers and officials reduces the opportunity for rent seeking.

Even without a one-stop shop system, single access point and online processes, much time could be saved by the simple expedient of switching from a sequential to a simultaneous ordering of procedures wherever possible, especially when they are not inter-dependent. Sequential ordering of procedures has significantly contributed to the protraction of time in meeting bureaucratic requirements.

Another reform to lighten the bureaucratic load upon business is to change where appropriate from ex ante to ex post controls. The business activity, instead of being stalled until all processes have been complete, may be allowed on a provisional basis, during which time the firm concerned will be subject to the necessary procedures, checks, and inspections leading to final approval or clearance (de Sa, 2005, p. 15). This is exemplified by the ex post or back-end customs clearance used by the Philippines customs authority mentioned earlier.

Also necessary in many of the countries of Southeast Asia is a regulatory watchdog or overseeing body which has the power to vet each new regulation and procedure in terms of the extra burdens imposed on business balanced against benefits to the community and economy. The essential value of such a body would depend on its power to veto a proposed regulation or procedure where it has not been demonstrated that the potential benefits outweigh the additional burdens. This prompted one Vietnamese business leader to propose "an independent committee" before which "regulators are required to prove the need and effectiveness of their regulations, [and] if they fail, those regulations should be abolished" (VCCI, 2006a, p. 4). In fact, in Vietnam one of the implementing decrees currently being drafted under the Enterprise Law of 2005, on state management of business licenses, proposes to create two regulatory overseeing bodies: National Council for Business Licenses, based on one already established in South Korea, and the Registration Office for Business Licenses. The first of these bodies will "oversee the procedures for businesses license issuance and to control the quality of the licenses to ensure they are justified and effective." The second body "would be responsible for ensuring that information on businesses licenses and conditions is transparent and easily accessible to businesses and the public." Within this remit will be the power "to review the current stock of businesses licenses and to control the flow of new ones" (VCCI, 2006a, p. 4; de Sa, 2005, p. 19).

Equally important would be the creation of an appeals system. This would enable businesses collectively through their various associations to appeal against a new but potentially burdensome and inconvenient regulatory procedure. Within such an appeals system there would exist opportunities for individual firms to seek redress in the face of adverse decisions, undue delay, and additional and unnecessary costs. The power to adjudicate in both cases could be vested in the regulatory overlord mentioned earlier.

# REFERENCES

Baldwin, R., & Cave, M. (1999). *Understanding regulation: Theory, strategy, and practice.* Oxford: Oxford University Press.

Clarete, R. (2004). *Customs valuation reform in the Philippines.* Manila: World Bank.

de Sa, L. (2005). *Business registration start-up: A concept note.* Washington: World Bank.

Djankov, S., La Porta, R., de Silanes, F., & Shleifer, A. (2002). Regulation of entry. *Quarterly Journal of Economics, 117*(1), 1–37.

Fonesca, R., Lopez-Garcia, P., & Pisarides, C. (2001). Entrepreneurship, start-up costs and employment. *European Economic Review, 45*(4–6), 692–705.

Forbes Media. (2006). The Capital Hospitality Index. New York: Forbes Media. Available at http://www.forbes.com/2006/01/20/capital-hospitality-index.

GTZ-CIEM. (2005). *From business ideas to reality: Still a long and costly journey.* Hanoi: GTZ-CIEM.
Hafeez, S. (2003). *The efficacy of regulation in developing countries.* New York: United Nations Department of Economic and Social Affairs.
Hopkins, T. (1992). *Costs of regulation: Filling the gaps.* Washington: Regulatory Information Service Centre.
IMF. (2004a). *Cambodia: Poverty reduction strategy paper progress report.* IMF Country Report 04/333. Washington: IMF.
IMF. (2004b). *Cambodia: Ex post assessment of longer-term program engagement.* IMF Country Report 04/324. Washington: IMF.
IMF. (2004c). *Philippines: 2004 Article IV consultation and post-program monitoring discussions – Staff report.* IMF Country Report No. 05/105. IMF: Washington.
IMF. (2004d). *Indonesia: 2004 Article IV consultation and monitoring discussions – Staff report.* IMF Country Report No. 04/188. Washington: IMF.
IMF. (2004e). *Indonesia: Post-program monitoring discussions – Staff report.* Country Report No. 05/108. Washington: IMF.
IMF. (2006a). *Vietnam: Poverty reduction strategy paper: Annual progress report.* IMF Country Report No. 06/70. Washington: IMF.
IMF. (2006b). *Indonesia: 2006 Article IV consultation and fifth post-program monitoring discussions – Staff report.* IMF Country Report No. 06/319. Washington: IMF.
Khan, R. (2000). *Reviving regulatory reform: A global perspective.* Washington: AEI-Brookings Joint Center for Regulatory Studies.
Niskanen, W. A. (1971). *Bureaucracy and representative government.* Chicago: Aldine-Atherton.
OECD. (1997). *The OECD report on regulatory reform: Synthesis.* Paris: OECD.
Republic of Singapore. (2002a). Business Registration (Amendment) Act, 2002, Chapter 30. Singapore: Attorney-General's Office. Available at http://statutes.agc.gov.sg/.
Republic of Singapore. (2002b). Companies (Amendment) Act, 2002, Chapter 50. Singapore: Attorney-General's Office. Available at http://statutes.agc.gov.sg/.
Singapore Parliament. (2002). Reports, 75 (July 8). Singapore: Singapore: Parliament.
UNCTAD. (2007). ASYCUDA. Geneva: UNCTAD. Available at http://www.asycuda.org/.
UNDP. (2007). *Human Development Report, 2006: Beyond scarcity: Power, poverty and the global water crisis.* New York: UNDP. Available at http://hdr.undorg/hdr2006/statistics.
Vietnam Chamber of Commerce and Industry. (2006a). *Business Issues Bulletin,* June 17.
Vietnam Chamber of Commerce and Industry. (2006b). *Business Issues Bulletin,* August 18.
World Bank. (2004). *Cambodia: Seizing the opportunity: Investment climate assessment and reform strategy for Cambodia.* Report no. 27925-KH. Washington: World Bank.
World Bank. (2006a). *Doing business in 2006: Creating jobs.* Washington: World Bank.
World Bank. (2006b). *Doing business 2007: How to reform.* Washington: World Bank.
World Bank. (2006c). *Governance indicators: 1996–2004.* Washington, DC: World Bank. Available at www.worldbank.org/wbi/ governance/govdata.
World Bank. (2007). Doing business: Benchmarking business regulations: Singapore; Cambodia; Thailand; Indonesia. Available at http://www.doingbusness.org.

# A PRELIMINARY ASSESSMENT OF PUBLIC MANAGEMENT REFORM IN TAIWAN'S LOCAL GOVERNMENT

Milan Tung-Wen Sun

## ABSTRACT

*Although the "Administrative Reform Program" was initiated by former Premier Lian Chain in 1993, the comprehensive "Government Reinvention" programs which emphasized the notion of entrepreneurial government were proposed and implemented by former Premier Vincent Shiew in 1998, and similar reform strategies and designs have been followed by the DPP administration since 2000. Despite the continuity in reform efforts, full-scale reform assessment based on concrete empirical evidences is still difficult to be found. The proposed study attempts to evaluate the results of government reform in Taiwan's local government by focusing on one major question: Have local governments in Taiwan become "smaller and better"? This question will be addressed by looking at indicators in three areas: changes in the size of local government in terms of human and financial resources, changes in the level of corruption, and changes in citizen's evaluation of the performance of local government. It is argued that the progress of government reform at the local level is slow, and the tentative evaluation show warning signals.*

## INTRODUCTION

Nowadays, few governments in the world have been isolate from the wave of reform over the past several decades. Given the different contexts and problems faced by each nation, every government has taken divergent strategies or structural adjustments to achieve reform objectives. However, the situations have been criticized as lack of "clear visions and integrated strategies" (Peters, 1994, p. 299), and the results have tended to be dissatisfied by many advocates of reform (Caiden, 1990). Several alternatives to the traditional model of governance have been proposed and practiced, the most familiar one is that of market model of administration and the related "New Public Management" movement, there are ample examples form the experiences in the United Kingdom and New Zealand (Peters, 1994). A different version of the market model has been practiced in the United States – the "reinventing government" – which emphasizes the notion of "entrepreneurial government" (Osborne & Gaebler, 1992).

Although the reform has generally focused on the central government, but eventually all politics are local. In the era of globalization, the deterritorization of public problems demands both global frameworks and local implementations together to address these issues. In the age of reform, devolution is pivotal for the transformation of the role and function of the state. Therefore, any assessment of reform efforts also has to evaluate the results of local government transformation.

The wave of reform also swept through Asian countries, including the Republic of China (Taiwan), over the past two decades. The history of administrative reform in Taiwan can be traced back to 1949, when the Nationalist government was defeated and moved to Taiwan. Since 1949, administrative reforms in Taiwan can be divided into three phases: 1949–1987, 1987–1998, and 1998 to present (Research, Development and Evaluation Commission (RDEC), 2003). Although the current phase of reform can be described as from government to governance, the notion of "entrepreneurial government" which characterized the second phase (RDEC, 2003, p. 12) still prevails on all fronts of current reform efforts.

Despite the continuity in reform efforts, full-scale reform assessment based on concrete empirical evidences is still difficult to be found in Taiwan, and few studies are devoted to analyze the results of local reforms in Taiwan. This study attempts to address the research issue by concentrating on one major question: Have local governments in Taiwan become "smaller and better"? This question will be addressed by looking at indicators in three areas: changes in the size of local government in terms of human and financial resources, changes in the level of corruption, and citizen's evaluation of the performance of local government. In the following sections, the evolution of local governance in Taiwan is discussed first; then, an assessment of the results of local reform on the basis of empirical evidences is made; it is followed by a brief conclusion in the last section.

## THE TRANSFORMATION OF LOCAL GOVERNANCE IN TAIWAN

Many scholars have analyzed the development of local self-governance in Taiwan by dividing it into different phases (Hwang, 2000; Chi, 1999; Chen, 1999; Lee, 1999). On the basis of these studies, it is proposed that the evolution of local governance in Taiwan can be distinguished into four phases (Chiang, 2006). These "punctuated equilibriums" are separated by three very important events in the development of local governance in Taiwan, namely, the abolishment of martial law in 1987, the passage of *Self-Governance Act for Provincial Government* and *Self-Governance Act for Special Municipality*[1] in 1994, and the designated date for the downsizing of Taiwan Provincial government in 1999.

### *The Authoritarian Government Phase (1949–1987)*

The Constitution of the Republic of China[2] went into effect on December 25, 1947, but it was suspended in 1948 due to civil war. After the Nationalist (Kuomintang (KMT)) government retreated to Taiwan in 1949, the island remained under martial law until 1987. During this period of time, much of the Constitution provisions were not in effect and most of the local government policies were implemented by the means of administrative regulations.

In the Constitution, Chapter 10 (Article 107–111) is designed to specify the central-local relations, and Chapter 11 is about the arrangements and provisions of the Provincial government (Article 112–120) and County government (Article 121–128). According to the Constitution, the autonomy of the Provincial (Article 112) and County (Article 121) governments are contingent upon the passage of the *General Self-Governance Principles for Provincial and County Governments* by Legislative Yuan, but such a law never existed. As a result, local self-governance in Taiwan after 1949 was functioning on the basis of several administrative regulations issued by the Executive Yuan and the Provincial government. The latter had served as an arm-length agency of the Central government in supervising and monitoring local governance. Among these regulations, the *Guidelines for Implementing Local Self-Governance Among County Governments*, issued by the Taiwan Provincial government, had served as the most important legal foundation for the operations of local governments in Taiwan until 1994.

In this phase, power and financial resources were highly centralized in the Central government. It was criticized as a "guardian local self-governance" in which the Central government dominated the intergovernmental relations extensively. It had also been described as a "semi-autonomy" in which the Governor of Taiwan Provincial government and the Mayors of the Special Municipalities[3] (Taipei and Kaohsiung) were appointed by the Executive Yuan rather than directly elected by their citizens. The central-local relations during this phase emphasized national norms and the power of the Central government to monitor the operations of local governments; the Central government had monopolized the powers in every aspect of local self-governance, including local legislation, financial and personnel administrations, organization structuring, etc.; the Central government could revoke or repeal any administrative act made by local government; the Central government could discipline any local official, including the elected one, for misconducts or negligence.

*The Legalization of Local Self-Governance Phase (1987–1994)*

Since the lifting of martial law, Taiwan has undergone a drastic process of democratization and reform, Tien (1989) describes the magnitude of the reforms as a "great transformation." On the basis of nationalism, the rise of civil society in Taiwan had forced the authoritarian regime to transform itself toward a system of democratic governance (Shiau, 1995; Sun, 2003). To reconstruct the local self-governance system on formal legal basis was one important project for constitutional reform during this period of time (Hwang, 1995).

Actually, to legalize local self-governance was already on the ruling party's (KMT) reform agenda before lifting the martial law. The demand for direct election of the Governor of Provincial government was very popular during that time. However, considering the fact that the territories of Provincial government and that of Central government were highly overlapped geographically, and the President was not elected directly by the citizens yet, a compromised solution had been tried by the Kuomintang Party by drafting an *Organic Act of Provincial Government* in which the Governor would be nominated by the Premier and then ratified by the Provincial Assembly. The effort was challenged by members of the Legislative Yuan as unconstitutional and was petitioned for constitutional interpretation, the Council of Grand Justices then made the influential No. 260 Interpretation (Wu, 2003, pp. 48–49) on March 19, 1990:

> According to (Constitutional) provisions, the Central Government has no authority to enact individual laws for specified provincial assemblies and the organization of the provincial government. The established provincial representative bodies have no legislative power either. When applying the Constitution, if matters that have not been contemplated at the time of drafting arise, the central government shall respond by balancing the needs of the nation, taking into consideration the special circumstances of the regions, and promptly resolve the matters pursuant to the constitutional procedures. Prior to resolution under the constitutional procedures, the self-governance and administration of provincial and county governments cannot be suspended.[4]

The compromised effort had failed. However, on the basis of No. 260 Interpretation and the bi-partisan consensus reached on the National Affairs Conference in 1990, the Second Constitutional Amendment in 1992 was made possible. There were eight amended articles passed by the National Assembly on May 27, 1992, and promulgated by the President on May 28. One of the key points of these amended articles was that local self-governance ought to be granted a legal basis and the provincial governor and municipal mayors should be elected by popular vote.[5] In July 1994, the *Self-Governance Act for Provinces and Counties* and the *Self-Governance Act for Special Municipalities* were signed by the President and elections for the Governor of Taiwan Provincial government and Mayors for the Taipei and Kaohsiung cities were held, respectively, for the first time in the same year.

Although the local self-governance was in a process of legalization during this period of time and substantial improvements had been made, intergovernmental problems and conflicts between Central and local governments in Taiwan had been intensified and incandesced after the Governor and the Mayors were directly elected. For example, Taipei City Council had asked for more authorities for local self-governance relentlessly, some of the requests and petitions had resulted in Constitution Interpretation No. 234 (regarding General Revenue Sharing, 1989/3/3), 235 (regarding the authority of National Auditing Office to audit the finances of the Provincial and Municipality governments, 1989/3/17), 279 (regarding premium subsidy provided by the Provincial or Municipality government to different categories of workers insured with labor insurance according to

*Labor Insurance Act*, 1991/5/17), and 307 (relating to whether the Provincial or County governments can set expenditure budgets for matters of police administration, 1992/10/30). In these Interpretations, although the Council of Grand Justices had upheld the Central government's positions that the related laws were not unconstitutional, they nevertheless had created tremendous pressures for more and faster reforms in local government system.

## The Downsizing of Provincial Government Phase (1994-1999)

The quests for the legalization of local self-governance had resulted in the passage of the *Self-Governance Act for Provincial Government* and *Self-Governance Act for Special Municipality* in July 1994. On the basis of the former, the Governor was able to be elected directly by the citizens of Taiwan Province for the first time in 1994. Although these two Acts had partially achieved the goals of legalizing the local self-governance, their contents had been criticized as failed to taking into consideration structural problems associated with the "guardian self-governance." The crucial problem was the ambigous allocation of power between the Central and Provincial governments, particularly the four-level government structure in which the status of Provincial government and Spacial Municipalities had not been changed (Hwang, 1995, pp. 19-33). After the Governor was inaugurated in 1995, many events had occurred in which the Provincial government challenged the authorities of the Central government from time to time, the conflicting central-local relations had been intensified (Chao, 1998).

In March 1996, the first presidential election in the history of political development in Taiwan was over. A National Development Conference was held later that year in which another constitutional reform consensus was reached among the participated political elites. On issues related to local governance reform, they agreed to downsize the functions and organizations of the Provincial government, and to freeze the gubernatorial election in the next term. In July 1997, decisions such as the terms for the Governor and members of Provincial Assembly should be ended on December 20, 1998, and the respective elections should be terminated accordingly were made during the fourth round of Constitutional amendment. Consequentially, the Legislative Yuan passed the *Regulations Governing the Adjustments of Taiwan Provincial Government's Functions, Business and Organization* in October 1998 to set objectives and schedule to downsize the Provincial government. Basically, the Provincial government would remain as a legal entity, but its status as a local self-governance organization was no longer valid. As originally scheduled, the *Self-Governance Act for Provincial Government* was formerly replaced by the *Local Government System Act* in January 1999. To a certain extent, the once powerful Taiwan Provincial government was history thereafter.[6]

The downsizing of the Provincial government could be attributed to the dysfunction of the four-level government structure. According to Wei (2000, pp. 82–84), the former Minister of RDEC (July 1999–May 2000), the four-level government structure had not only created red tape, but also reduced administrative efficiency and quality. The expected results of downsizing the Provincial government included: to reduce the number of overlapping agencies, civil servants, laws and regulations; to improve fiscal conditions; to enhance local autonomy and administrative quality; and to reengineer administrative process (Wei, 2000, pp. 89–99).

Another reason for this Provincial level reform was the potential power conflicts between the President and the Governor. According to the Constitutional Amendment passed on May 28, 1992, the President of the Republic of China (Taiwan) would be elected by popular sovereignty for the first time in 1996. However, between 1994 and 1996, former President Teng-hui Lee was not elected directly. Compared to former Governor James Song who had been elected by several million of voters in Taiwan, although both of them were from the same party, President Lee was facing a legitimacy crisis. Even if the President was also directly elected, since the populations and territories of the Taiwan Province and the Central government overlapped for more than 80%, the potential political tensions and conflicts between the Governor and the President were almost inevitable. It had been speculated that these so-called "Yeltsin's Effects" might have induced the reform of downsizing the Provincial government.[7]

## The "Local Government Systems Act" Phase (1999–present)

The previous phase might be described as the most turbulent one in the evolution of local governance in Taiwan, but the passage of *Local Government System Act* does not imply that local governance reform has been completed. Downsizing the Provincial government might solve one structural problem for local governance, there are other reform issues needed to be dealt with, such as how to accomplish one of the ultimate goals of local governance reform in Taiwan – to become a two-level (Central and

County) government structure? Should County government be allowed to be upgraded into a special municipality? How to redraw the administrative boundaries of local governments? Should the executive leaders at township level be appointed by county magistrate rather than be elected? How to mutually adjust the functions of village level government and the community development systems (Hwang, 2000; Liu, 2003)?

On the other hand, although the *Act Governing the Allocation of Government Revenues and Expenditures* has been modified in accordance with the *Local Government Systems Act*, the newly emerged "party turnover" effects[8] have intensified the competitions for intergovernmental resources. Thus, the rationalizations of mechanisms for monitoring and supervising local self-governance and for allocating intergovernmental revenues are the two very important issues in this phase. No. 498 and No. 550 Interpretations are directly related to the issue of intergovernmental revenue, and the results have given the local governments more equal position in dealing with the Central government than before. Both of them can be understood as passive protections for local governments, but they ought to be defined together as a basis upon which central-local partnership can be developed initially.

As for the matters of supervising local governance, the Grand Justices have made their positions clear in No. 527 (June 15, 2001) and No. 553 (December 20, 2002) Interpretations. They explain various aspects of the *Local Government Systems Act* in terms of its norms and underlying principles regarding local self-governance. The Grand Justices explicitly identify the rights for the local self-governing body to file petition for constitutional interpretation to against any perceived unlawful supervision from the Central government in these two cases, and they try to direct the attentions of the parties involved to resolve their conflicts through due process of administrative litigation. These two Interpretations ought to be able to reduce unnecessary vertical intergovernmental conflict and potential petition for constitutional interpretation.

In general, these four phases provide a brief historical background upon which local government reforms in Taiwan can be assessed. As in any other unitary state, the power to design government architecture is always concentrated in Taiwan's Central government. Despite the efforts of the local governments, local governance reforms have been packaged by the Central government as a part of its grand "Government Reinvention" program. That is to say, local government reforms are structured and implemented according to the same reform framework and strategies that are designed for the transformation of Central government in Taiwan.

## A SMALLER AND CAPABLE LOCAL GOVERNMENT?

On the basis of the conclusions reached in the National Development Conference in 1996, the notion of "entrepreneurial government" has been widely accepted among public administration scholars and practitioners in Taiwan as the dominant model of the "Government Reinvention" programs. To support the Conference's conclusions and to respond to a suggestion made by the Economic Development Advisory Committee at a meeting convened in 2001, the Office of the President set up a Committee of Government Reform charged with the task of promoting and restructuring "an energetic government that is globally competitive." The spirits of the proposed reform include "customer-oriented, elastic and innovative partnership, accountable politics, and honest and capable government"; and its visions are "to establish an innovative and service-oriented mechanism; to streamline the administrative organizations; to create a professional and efficient personnel system; to develop an autonomous and coordinated governmental structure; and to arrive at a reformed Legislative Yuan that abides by people's opinion" (RDEC, 2003, p. 14). Fig. 1 presents the comprehensive framework for designing the current government restructuring programs in Taiwan.

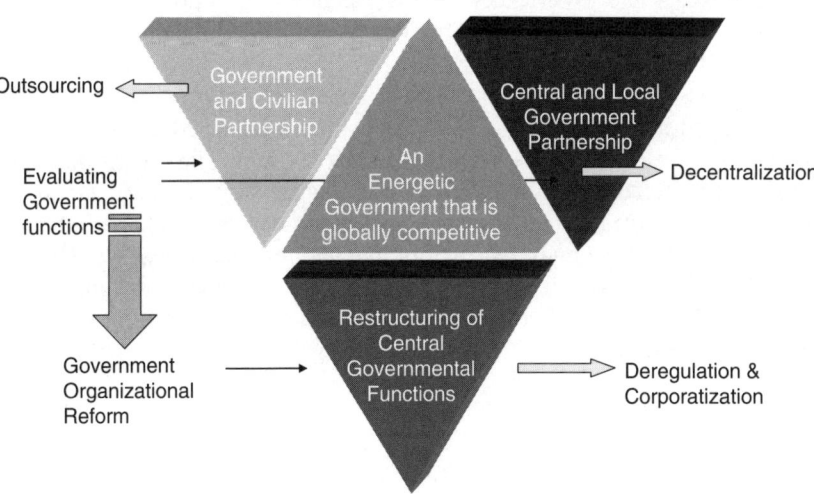

Data Source: Modified and translated from
http://reform.rdec.gov.tw/public/Attachment/5691015571.ppt.

*Fig. 1.* Framework for Government Organization Reform.

Although it can be argued that the design of "Government Reinvention" program in Taiwan actually embraces many types of reform ideas, such as market mechanism for better service delivery and managerialism for more flexible tools for the managers, "entrepreneurial government" is officially used by RDEC (2003, p. 12) as the dominant theme of reform.

As suggested by Kellough (1998, p. 8), "reinvention is, quite frankly, a set of proposed reforms aimed at solving persistent problems in government by promising that we can do more with less." The notion of "a smaller and capable government" has also prevailed in the organization reform (Central as well as local governments) framework in Taiwan (Wei, 2000, pp. 55–58). In addition to downsizing the Provincial government, the efforts to restructure government functions and organizations by incorporating market mechanism and voluntary organizations (i.e., deregulation, corporatization, and outsourcing) into public service delivery system are to make Central and local governments in Taiwan smaller. On the other hand, the devolution of functions and authorities to the local governments is made by emphasizing the importance of enhancing local capacities in decision-making and implementation.

Despite all these efforts, questions can be raised regarding the results of government reform in Taiwan in general, and its impacts on the local government in particular. On the one hand, there are conflicting evidences indicating that the experiences of government reinvention in the United States are controversial at best (Durst & Newell, 1999; Brudney, Hebert, & Wright, 1999; Gargan, 1997; Kellough, 1998). On the other hand, an empirical assessment of the Central government reform programs in Taiwan suggests that its implementation has not achieved the desired objectives due to lack of political supports from the President (Sun, 2006). Thus, have the reinvention efforts been successful at the local level in Taiwan? Or, to be more specific, have local governments in Taiwan become smaller and better? This question will be analyzed by looking at three related aspects: Has the size of local government in terms of employee and financial figures been smaller? Has the level of corruption been lower? and, how do local citizens evaluate the performance of their own local government?

## The Size of Local Government

Local governments in Taiwan consist of two Provincial governments (Taiwan and Fujian), two Special Municipalities (Taipei and Kaohsiung), sixteen County governments, and five City governments. Due to the effects of downsizing the Provincial government, and the special status of the Special Municipality, they are excluded from the following analysis.

Table 1 presents the personnel statistics of County and City governments[9] in Taiwan between 2000 and 2005. Due to changes in the reporting format, no data regarding the official (budget-allocated) positions before 2003 is available, but it is clear that the number has increased from 104,290 positions in 2003 to 106,565 in 2005. Not only the budget-allocated positions have been increased, the actual number of employees has also increased from 114,370 in 2000 to 158,949 in 2005. The difference between the budget-allocated positions and the actual number of employees over the three-year period (2003–2005) is more than 50 thousand people in each year. The difference is partially attributed to the contracted temporary employees, ranged from 36,526 in 2005 to 48,621 in 2003, but the reason for the remaining "extra" employees is not clear. Some of the temporary employees are on contract basis due to special projects (mandates) initiated by the Central government, they are paid by contract grants provided by the Central government. However, many of these temporary employees are hired on the basis of favoritism rather than merit principle, and they tend to stay in office even after the Central government projects are over.

Given that outsourcing is encouraged by the Central government as a strategy of government reform, these temporary employees do not constitute what Light (1999) has termed the "shadow government." Although there is a tendency to decrease over the past several years, they still occupy more than 20% of Taiwan local government's work force.

*Table 1.* Personnel Statistics: County/City Governments (2000–2005).

| Year | Officially Allocated Positions (A) | Actual Number of Employees (B) | Difference (B)–(A) | Regular Full-Time Employees (%) | Temporary (Contracted) Employees (%) |
|---|---|---|---|---|---|
| 2000 | – | 114,370 | – | 88,671 (77.53) | 25,699 (22.47) |
| 2001 | – | 122,371 | – | 96,673 (79.00) | 25,698 (21.00) |
| 2002 | – | 125,983 | – | 100,875 (80.07) | 25,108 (19.93) |
| 2003 | 104,290 | 157,655 | 53,365 | 109,034 (69.16) | 48,621 (30.84) |
| 2004 | 106,082 | 161,029 | 54,947 | 122,930 (76.34) | 38,099 (23.66) |
| 2005 | 106,565 | 158,949 | 52,384 | 122,423 (77.02) | 36,526 (22.98) |

*Sources:* Combined from personnel yearly report, various years, Central Personnel Administration (http://www.tpgpd.gov.tw/statistic/index.htm).

Another way of evaluating the size of local government in Taiwan is to examine the amount of expenditures spent on civil servants' salary and related benefits (Table 2). On average, personnel-related expenditures constitute about 55% of local government's total expenditures. Moreover, personnel-related expenditures in local government is 106.75% of its own revenue (local taxes plus General Revenue Sharing), and it is 145.34% of its self revenue (local taxes only) in 2004. Although the descending trend is encouraging, the sheer size of local government employees is large enough that its expenditures cannot be covered by pooling local taxes and General Revenue Sharing together.

From the financial aspect, the total local government expenditure is about 511.25 billion NT dollars in 2004. Using the figure in 2000 as the baseline, local government expenditure has been increased by 5.64%. Together, grants, mandate revenue and General Revenue Sharing that were provided by the Central government occupied more than 40% (41.61%) of total local government expenditures in 2004, and it has increased about 10% since 2001.

To make the financial situation of Taiwan's local government even worse, public debts are about 59.34% of total expenditures in 2004, which is much higher than what is allowed according to the *Public Debt Act* (the maximum limit is set at 45%),[10] and the percentage has increased by 55.86% over a four-year period (from 2001 to 2004) (Table 3). Local governments in Taiwan can barely survive if they cannot borrow money from the private sector.

*Table 2.* Personnel Expenditures: Country/City Governments (2001–2004).

| Year | Total Personnel Expenditure (NT$ 1,000) (A) | Total Local Government Expenditure (NT$ 1,000) (B) | (A)/(B) % | Own Revenue (NT$ 1,000) (C) | Self Revenue (NT$ 1,000) (D) | (A)/(C) % | (A)/(D) % |
|---|---|---|---|---|---|---|---|
| 2001 | 254,971,979 | 483,947,222 | 52.69 | 212,697,364 | 151,209,136 | 119.88 | 168.62 |
| 2002 | 266,022,763 | 456,469,296 | 58.28 | 226,146,357 | 156,605,793 | 117.63 | 169.87 |
| 2003 | 272,142,635 | 478,622,846 | 56.86 | 237,746,129 | 172,423,658 | 114.47 | 157.83 |
| 2004 | 281,022,351 | 511,245,365 | 54.97 | 263,242,373 | 193,349,866 | 106.75 | 145.34 |

*Notes:*

1. Personnel expenditures do not include that of township governments.
2. Own revenue includes General Revenue Sharing, self revenue does not.

*Sources:* Combined from Statistics Yearly Reports, Ministry of Audit (http://www.audit.gov.tw/Doc/DocList.aspx?MenuId = Fin).

**Table 3.** Financial Statistics: County/City Governments (2001–2004).

| Year | Total Expenditure (NT$ 1,000) (A) | Increase Ratio[a] | Grants and Mandates Revenues (NT$ 1,000) (B) | (B)/(A) % | Increase Ratio[a] | Public Debts (NT$ 1,000) (C) | (C)/(A) % | Increase Ratio[a] |
|---|---|---|---|---|---|---|---|---|
| 2001 | 483,947,222 | 100 | 192,709,045 | 39.82 | 100 | 194,633,688 | 40.22 | 100 |
| 2002 | 456,469,296 | 94.32 | 170,015,326 | 37.25 | 88.22 | 238,647,688 | 52.28 | 122.61 |
| 2003 | 478,622,846 | 98.90 | 204,212,010 | 42.67 | 105.97 | 281,518,123 | 58.82 | 144.64 |
| 2004 | 511,245,365 | 105.64 | 212,752,881 | 41.61 | 110.40 | 303,354,346 | 59.34 | 155.86 |

*Sources:* Combined from statistics yearly reports, Ministry of Audit (http://www.audit.gov.tw/Doc/DocList.aspx?MenuId = Fin).
[a]2001 is the base year to calculate the increase ratios.

In sum, there is no illusion of smallness in terms of the size of local government in Taiwan. Since former Premier Vincent Shiew proposed the "Government Reinvention" programs in 1998, government reform efforts have not substantially reduced the number of local government employees and expenditures after all these years.

## Corruption

But, is local government in Taiwan now better? There is no data available regarding the capacity of local government in Taiwan, the level of corruption is adopted as the variable to examine the issue from a slightly different perspective instead. Anti-corruption is one major objective for government reform in Taiwan. The current administration has started an "Anti-corruption Action Plan" on July 1, 2000, a total of 3,467 cases and 8,720 people have been prosecuted for corruption over the past six-year period (from July, 2000 to December, 2006), and the total money involved is 2.8 billion NT dollars (Table 4).

Comparing the figures to that of the six-year period before the plan was started (3,781 cases, 8,924 people, and 3.2 billion NT dollars, 1994–2000), data indicate that the level of corruption at the local level has been controlled to a certain degree (decreased about 8.3%, 2.29%, and 13.1%, respectively). However, among those people who have been charged for corruption, more high level civil servants and general public are involved (increased by 10.93% and 25.14%, respectively after the 2000), but there is a substantial improvement for the low level government employee (decreased by 20.92%). Seemingly, while the integrity of local civil servants has been improved, it is the middle and low level public employees who can better control their greed.

*Table 4.* Corruption Statistics: Before and After the "Anti-Corruption Action Plan."

| | Number of Cases Involved | Number of Persons Involved | Categories of Suspects | | | | | Total $ Involved (NT$) |
|---|---|---|---|---|---|---|---|---|
| | | | High level | | Middle level | Low level | GP | |
| | | | CS | R | | | | |
| 6 years before | 3,781 | 8,924 | 421 | 609 | 1,745 | 3,384 | 2,765 | 32,738,410,431 |
| 6 years after | 3,467 | 8,720 | 467 | 542 | 1,575 | 2,676 | 3,460 | 28,450,833,238 |
| Increase/ decrease % | −8.30 | −2.29 | 10.93 | −11.00 | −9.74 | −20.92 | 25.14 | −13.10 |

*Notes:* CS, civil servants; R, representatives; GP, general public.
*Sources:* Ministry of Justice, based on figures provided by District Courts and District Prosecutors Offices (http://www.moj.gov.tw/public/Attachment/61059511175.pdf).

If more high level civil servants in local governments are involved in corruption, it is assumed that these cases tend to be larger scandals.

According to a survey recently conducted by the *Common Wealth* magazine during the period from August 30 to September 12, 2006, when the respondents were asked about do they think their local chief executive (magistrate or mayor) is honest, only four magistrates (Taoyuan, Kaohsiung, Hualien, Penghu County) and 3 mayors (Hsinchu, Taichung, Chiayi City) have been approved (honest or very honest) by more than 50% of the respondents (Table 5, Column C). When they were asked to evaluate the integrity of their local civil servants or representatives, only the Penghu County has more than 40% of the respondents (45.5%) saying that their civil servants and representatives are not seriously corrupted (Table 5, Column D), and only six other local governments (Yilan, Taoyuan, Taitung County and Hualien, Hsinchu, Chiayi City) have more than 30% of the respondents in these Counties or Cities saying so.

Although corruption at the local level in Taiwan might have been seemingly improved in terms of objective indicators (the number of cases and people involved, see Table 4), local citizens do not have high confidence in the integrity of their civil servants and representatives subjectively.

*Performance Assessments*

Performance assessment is another aspect to evaluate the capacity of local governments in Taiwan. There are two types of questions that can be used to

**Table 5.** Performance Assessments of County (Magistrate)/City (Mayor).

| | Are You Proud of Your County/City? (% of Proud) (2005) | After Three and a Half Years, do You Think Your County/City Has Made Substantial Progress? (% of Yes) (2005) | Do You Think Your Magistrate/Mayor is Honest? (% of Very Honest and Honest) | Do You Think Civil Servants and Representatives of Your County Are Acute Corrupted? (% of Not Serious and Very Not Serious) | Are You Satisfied about the Overall Performance of Your Magistrate/ Mayor? (% of Very Satisfied and Satisfied) | Magistrate/ Mayor's Performance Assessment (Total = 100 Points) |
|---|---|---|---|---|---|---|
| | (A) | (B) | (C) | (D) | (E) | (F) |
| *County* | | | | | | |
| Taipei | 65.1 | 69.1 | 35.9 | 15.9 | 38.9 | 36 |
| Yilan | 76.8 | 58.5 | 46.0 | 34.8 | 48.3 | 45 |
| Taoyuan | 74.4 | 63.7 | 60.2 | 32.7 | 71.5 | 68 |
| Hsinchu | 80.9 | 64.3 | 41.0 | 29.4 | 70.6 | 64 |
| Miaoli | 65.6 | 60.9 | 38.5 | 24.4 | 44.9 | 48 |
| Taichung | 75.0 | 66.4 | 42.5 | 22.3 | 60.5 | 60 |
| Changhua | 69.2 | 51.2 | 41.6 | 23.9 | 46.0 | 51 |
| Nantou | 67.1 | 41.6 | 40.5 | 23.9 | 43.2 | 47 |
| Yunlin | 52.0 | 38.8 | 37.1 | 18.0 | 39.5 | 48 |
| Chiayi | 70.3 | 65.0 | 35.6 | 22.9 | 64.4 | 62 |
| Tainan | 70.9 | 50.2 | 33.1 | 16.1 | 46.4 | 42 |
| Kaohsiung | 66.2 | 65.7 | 61.1 | 24.4 | 69.2 | 62 |
| Pingtung | 68.5 | 52.7 | 44.5 | 24.0 | 41.8 | 43 |
| Taitung | 74.0 | 63.0 | 31.4 | 30.9 | 38.2 | 38 |
| Hualien | 79.2 | 65.9 | 54.8 | 33.0 | 66.8 | 57 |
| Penghu | 80.9 | 77.2 | 51.7 | 45.5 | 52.7 | 52 |
| *City* | | | | | | |
| Keelung | 52.6 | 41.4 | 13.0 | 19.0 | 27.8 | 27 |
| Hsinchu | 76.9 | 68.0 | 53.8 | 36.4 | 70.9 | 70 |
| Taichung | 75.4 | 57.4 | 63.2 | 23.9 | 60.0 | 67 |
| Chiayi | 64.3 | 49.4 | 50.4 | 30.1 | 49.9 | 51 |
| Tainan | 77.1 | 62.3 | 38.3 | 23.4 | 65.6 | 53 |

*Notes:* Columns A and B are based on a survey conducted by the *United Daily News* on November 11, 2006; Columns C and D are based on a survey conducted by the *Common Wealth* magazine, No. 354 (August 30–September 12, 2006); Columns E and F are based on a survey conducted by the *Global Views Monthly*, No. 229 (July, 2005).

assess the performance of individual local government, one is concerning local identity (i.e., the sense of "proud") and improvement in government services, the other is about the performance of local chief executive (Magistrate or Mayor).

The magazine of *Global Views Monthly* had conducted a survey regarding the performance of Taiwan's local governments in 2005. One question asked the respondents to indicate whether they are proud of their own local government, another question asked the respondents to reflect their opinions as whether their own County or City government had made substantial improvement.[11] There are only 12 local governments in which over 70% of the respective respondents indicated that they are proud of their home County or City (Table 5, Column A). The benchmark (over 70%) is presumably not a very high standard. And using 60% as the benchmark, there are only 12 local governments which are believed by the respondents as making good progress (Table 5, Column B). Again, the record of evaluation has not been very impressive.

In another survey which was conducted by the *United Daily News* on November 11, 2006, respondents were asked to answer the following question: "Are you satisfied about the overall performance of your magistrate/mayor?" There are only nine local chief executives, out of the total of 21 local governments included in this study, been evaluated by more than 50% of the respondents in these Counties or Cities respectively as satisfied or very satisfied (see Table 5, Column E). Taoyuan County Magistrate has the highest approval rating (71.5%), and the Mayor of Keelung City has the lowest one (27.8%).

If the evaluation is made on a 100-points scale, only seven magistrates or mayors passed the 60 points benchmark of the performance assessment (Table 5, Column F). There are one Magistrate (Hualien County) and one Mayor (Tainan City) who have good approval ratings (66.8% and 65.6%, respectively) but have failed the performance assessment (57 and 53 points, respectively).

## DISCUSSIONS

Has local government in Taiwan become smaller and better as the results of Government Reinvention programs? The answer to this question has to be a qualified "no." The strategies and visions of Taiwan's government reform are designed according to the model of entrepreneurial government which emphasizes the notion of "smaller and better" in government structure and function. The same design and strategies have also been applied to reform the local government. However, data has indicated that the size of local government in Taiwan has not been smaller in terms of personnel and financial indicators; the level of corruption has been improved but more high level local civil servants have involved in corruption cases; and citizen's assessments of the performance of local governments and their chief executives have been relatively unsatisfactory.

There can be several potential reasons for explaining the results: (1) the fierce competition between political parties might have consumed too many energies and resources which ought to be concentrated on implementing the reform programs; (2) there might be a gap between the comprehensiveness in the design of reform and the feasibility of implementing the reform; (3) the newly emerged party turnover effects might have discouraged public administrators to faithfully carry out the reform programs; (4) political correct might have replaced professionalism as the basis for government operation; (5) civil servants in the local governments might not have sufficient capabilities to fulfil the reform objectives; (6) local governments might not have adequate human and financial resources to carry out the reform programs; (7) the efforts of Central and local governments might not have been well coordinated; and (8) the concept of entrepreneurial government and the notion of "smaller and better" government might not fit the political, social and economic conditions in Taiwan, either culturally or contextually. These hypothetical explanations require careful examinations in the future.

In addition, three observations can be made regarding the evolution of local governance in Taiwan. First, Taiwan is still muddling through in the process of authoritarian transition. Although the records of democratic development are outstanding, government structure and the allocation of power remain unstable in Taiwan. Second, the direction of further decentralization is clear in the evolution of local governance in Taiwan. In the pursuit of decentralization, institutionalization and legalization are two pillars for the success of future reforms.

Third, local government and the Justices of Constitutional Court have played very important roles in local governance reform in Taiwan. There have been a total of 30 intergovernmental-relations related Constitution Interpretations; their distributions are 11, 10, 4, and 5, in the respective phases as mentioned previously. The descending numbers may suggest the stabilization of central-local conflicts in Taiwan, but it also indicates that the Justices of Constitutional Court has contributed significantly in solving local governance related Constitutional crisis. On the other hand, among these 30 cases, 18 are filed by individual local governments, only 6 are initiated by the Central government (Chiang, 2006, p. 65). It is the local governments relentless struggles against the Central government that have stimulated the process of local governance reform in Taiwan.

## CONCLUSION

Doherty and Stone (1999, p. 157) have described the practice in U.S. local government as experiencing the difficulties of "increasingly fragmented, fiscal strained, and subject to broad public disenchantment." These difficulties tend to be amplified in the contexts of authoritarian transition in Taiwan. The urging demands for better government structure and more democratic governance in the globalization era have pushed Taiwan into a new phase of local governance transformation. If a smaller and capable local government is truly desirable in Taiwan, more attentions ought to be focused on the implementation of government reform programs. Otherwise, a new and more holistic perspective is needed for building an energetic government that is globally competitive in Taiwan.

## NOTES

1. The English translations of laws and regulations in Taiwan are based on translations provided by Judicial Yuan. Information source: http://www.judicial.gov.tw/QnA/bilingual.asp.

2. The Constitution consists of 14 chapters and a total of 175 articles. It was amended seven times from 1991 to 2004.

3. There are four government layers in Taiwan – Central, Provincial and Special Municipality, County, and Township governments. Due to the effect of downsizing, the Provincial government no longer serves as a local self-governance entity. However, it still constitutes one government layer, and the Special Municipality is equivalent in status to the Provincial government.

4. Information source: www.judicial.gov.tw/constitutionalcourt/EN/p03_01.asp? expno = 260.

5. Information source: english.www.gov.tw/Yearbook/index.jsp?categid = 22& recordid = 52746.

6. The Taiwan Provincial Government has not been abolished. The Governor was appointed by the Executive Yuan, and it was gradually reduced to a minimum of 200 employees with very limited functions over the past some seven years. Since 2006, the Executive Yuan appointed no one to the post.

7. Taking into consideration of the scenario regarding the former Soviet leader Mikhail Gorbachev and Boris Yeltsin, this type of potential conflicts were referred as the "Yeltsin Effects" in Taiwan.

8. Although party competitions were very high at the local level, KMT had swept elections at the national level throughout the years. But the Democratic Progressive Party (DPP) had won the Presidential election for the first time in 2000, and President Cheng was re-elected in 2004. There are many evidences indicating that the transition has not been smooth. In the foreseeable future, party turnover effects tend to disturb government operations at every level in Taiwan.

9. Data include civil servants employed by the County/City and township governments. However, principles and teachers working at high, junior high and elementary schools are excluded.

10. See *Public Debt Act*, www.tccg.gov.tw/site/3fd694a1/3fd6bc0f/44f90782/4541a172/files/law-7.doc

11. 2005 is the last year of the four-year term for the previous Magistrate or Mayor (2001–2005). Therefore, the survey question was designed as "After three and a half years, do you think your County/City has made substantial progress?" (see Table 5, Column B).

# REFERENCES

Brudney, J. L., Hebert, F. T., & Wright, D. S. (1999). Reinventing government in the American states: Measuring and explaining administrative reform. *Public Administration Review*, 59(1), 19–30.

Caiden, G. F. (1990). *Administrative reform comes of age*. Berlin: Aldine de Gruyter.

Chao, Y. M. (1998). *Decentralization and the executive–legislative relations in local governments: A case study* (in Chinese). Taipei: Research, Development, and Evaluation Commission.

Chen, L. K. (1999). A Comparative study of intergovernmental relations on either side of the Taiwan Strait. In: W. C. Chen (Ed.), *Local governments and politics on either side of the Taiwan Strait* (pp. 147–163). Kaohsiung City: Department of Political Science, National Sun Yat-sen University (in Chinese).

Chi, C. C. (1999). *The downsizing of provincial government and the new political system: Origins, designs, and development* (in Chinese). Taipei: The Chinese Association of Local Self-Government, Shih-Ying Publishers.

Chiang, T. S. (2006). *Approaching local governance: Issues, theories, and practices* (in Chinese). Taipei: Angel Publishers.

Doherty, K. M., & Stone, C. N. (1999). Local practice in transition: From government to governance. In: D. Martha (Ed.), *Dilemmas of scale in America's federal democracy* (pp. 154–186). London: Cambridge University Press.

Durst, S., & Newell, C. (1999). Better, faster, stronger: Government reinvention in the 1990s. *American Review of Public Administration*, 29(1), 61–76.

Gargan, J. J. (1997). Reinventing government and reformulating public administration. *International Journal of Public Administration*, 20(1), 221–247.

Hwang, G. T. (1995). *Problems for the legalization of local self-governance* (in Chinese). Taipei: Moonsun Publishers.

Hwang, G. T. (2000). *The fundamental problems of Local Government Systems Act* (in Chinese). Taipei: Hanlu Books Company.

Kellough, J. E. (1998). The reinventing government movement: A review and critique. *Public Administration Quarterly, 22*(1), 6–20.

Lee, C. Y. (1999). *Intergovernmental relations between Central and Local Governments in Taiwan: The British experiences*. Ph.D. dissertation of the Department of Public Administration, National ChengChi University, Taipei, Taiwan (in Chinese).

Light, P. C. (1999). *The true size of government*. Washington, DC: Brookings Institution Press.

Liu, W. S. (2003). *The constitutional foundation and problems of local government reform*. Taipei: Sharing Cultural Enterprise Co., Ltd.

Osborne, D., & Gaebler, T. (1992). *Reinventing government: How the entrepreneurial spirit is transforming the public sector from schoolhouse to statehouse, City Hall to the Pentagon*. Reading, MA: Addison-Wesley.

Peters, B. G. (1994). New visions of government and the public services. In: P. W. Ingraham & S. R. Barbara (Eds), *New paradigms for government* (pp. 295–321). San Francisco, CA: Jossey-Bass.

Research, Development, and Evaluation Council (RDEC). (2003). *Government reform* (in Chinese). Taipei: RDEC.

Shiau, C. J. (1995). *Taiwan's new ideology: Nationalism* (in Chinese). Taipei: Shih-Ying Publishers.

Sun, T. W. (2003). *From authoritarian government to democratic governance*. Taipei: Angle Publishing Co., Ltd.

Sun, T. W. (2006). The transformation of governance in Taiwan: A critical assessment. Paper presented in the Third East Asian Social Policy Research Network International Conference on "GDPism and Risk: Challenges for Social Development and Governance in East Asia", July 12–13, organized by Centre for East Asian Studies, Bristol University, Bristol, UK.

Tien, H. M. (1989). *The great transformation: Political and social change in the Republic of China*. Standford, CA: Hoover Institution Press, Standford University.

Wei, C. L. (2000). *Government reinvention* (in Chinese). Taipei: Morning Star.

Wu, G. (2003). *The interpretations and applications of the constitution* (in Chinese). Taipei: Geng Wu.

# BUILDING NATIONAL INTEGRITY THROUGH CORRUPTION ERADICATION IN SOUTH KOREA

Pan Suk Kim

### ABSTRACT

*Since South Korea gained a substantial degree of political and economic development, the South Korean government has tried to eradicate corruption by introducing institutional frameworks in addition to a number of new laws and institutions. As a matter of fact, the Transparency International's Corruption Perceptions Index score of South Korea is improving over time, but it still far behind other leading countries. The purpose of this chapter is to review the South Korean government's efforts at curbing corruption. This chapter first reviews the development of major anti-corruption infrastructure such as the anti-corruption legislation and the South Korean government's independent agency for anti-corruption, followed by discussion of the development of major anti-corruption measures, the international evaluation on corruption, and the role of civil society in curbing corruption. After that, there is a discussion of policy implications and the conclusion.*

## INTRODUCTION

According to public-office-centered definitions of corruption,[1] corruption in government is defined as the abuse or misuse of public office or authority for private gains and benefits that occurs at the interface of the public and private sectors.[2] Whenever a public official has discretionary power over the distribution of benefits or costs to the private sector, incentives for bribery are created (Rose-Ackerman, 1978, 1997). Klitgaard (1988) asserts that illicit behavior flourishes when agents have monopoly power over clients, when agents have great discretion, and when accountability of agents to the principal is weak. Corruption poses serious challenges to development: it undermines democracy and good governance by subverting formal processes, it reduces accountability and representation in policymaking, it suspends the rule of law, it results in the unequal provision of services, and it erodes the institutional capacity of government as procedures are disregarded (Dininio, Kpundeh, & Leiken, 1998).

The public sector increasingly recognizes that good governance requires the highest standards of public integrity, openness, and transparency, as well as a sound criminal justice system. This can be illustrated by the pervasive effects these factors have on government performance, the use of public resources, the general morale in public services, the legitimacy of the state, and the rule of law. Launching programs to deal with corruption are a precondition for overall public sector reform, and progress in curbing corruption is considered evidence of will and commitment to good governance (World Bank, 1994; Rhodes, 1997; Kooiman, 2003; IMD, 2006).

For decades, the South Korean government has stressed the significance of curbing corruption. The South Korean public had a particular antipathy toward political instability, which can be attributed to prevailing political corruption and serious political scandals in the past. The corrupt practices of politicians and high officials have generated an atmosphere of resentment, frustration, and distrust for many years. Previous authoritarian administrations, however, tended to consider anti-corruption initiatives merely as a means to soothe public outrage over the unfairness of corrupt public service and public officials. Moreover, authoritarian regimes used anti-corruption initiatives as a means for removing key political opponents from the political arena.

When authoritarian regimes were over, however, the South Korean government was concerned with more than the political aspects of corruption. It perceived the collusion of bureaucrat and business as one of the most crucial obstacles to a free market economy and good governance. Such collusion contributed to South Korea's economic crisis in the past. Corruption undermines economic development by causing considerable distortion and inefficiency. Corruption increases the cost of business through the price of illicit payments themselves, the management cost of negotiating with officials, and the risk of breached agreements or detection (Dininio et al., 1998).

Various anti-corruption initiatives had taken place by various administrations, but substantial changes appeared during early 1990s. During the Kim Young-sam Administration (1993–1998), the Real Name Financial Transactions System was executed by the Presidential Emergency Order for national finance and economy in 1993. It was a significant step toward financial transparency in banning the use of anonymous financial accounts. Later, the Act on Real Name Financial Transactions and Guarantee of Secrecy was enacted in 1997 in order to solve partial defects, such as inconveniences in financial transactions following verification of real names and the anxieties about tax investigations under the Presidential Emergency Order. President Kim Young-sam also strengthened the role of the Board of Audit and Inspection (BAI) as a de jure anti-corruption agency[3] and established the Corruption Prevention Committee (CPC) as an advisory body of the BAI's chairman in the task of fighting corruption (Quah, 1999, p. 181). In addition, he seriously pursued regulatory reforms through activities of the Administrative Reform Committee, and such deregulation contributed to the reduction of corrupt practices in government.

However, much more salient transformations took place during the Kim Dae-jung Administration in modern South Korean history. President Kim requested the Office of the Prime Minister (OPM) to develop more systematic anti-corruption programs.[4] In 1999, the OPM announced comprehensive programs including the following five issues: (1) the establishment of a special committee on anti-corruption; (2) promulgation of a basic law on the prevention of corruption; (3) the development of a public awareness campaign; (4) the development of a campaign encouraging citizen participation in corruption detection; and (5) administrative reforms in corruption-prone areas. This plan brought a significant development on corruption eradication and the author labeled it here as the "Kim Dae-jung Plan of 1999" on anti-corruption. Furthermore, President Kim formed the Regulatory Reform Committee (RRC) based on the Basic Law on Administrative Regulations of 1998 in order to intensively review existing regulations and screen regulations to be introduced or deregulated.[5]

Current Administration (Roh Moo-hyun Administration: 2003–2008) revised the Public Office Election Act to minimize corrupt practices in the process of the public office election and renamed the Korea Independent Commission Against Corruption (KICAC) to the National Integrity Commission in order to encourage a full-scale national integrity instead of curbing narrowly focused anti-corruption.[6] In accordance with the Article 8 of the Anti-Corruption Act, the Code of Conduct for Public Officials (CCPO) went into force on May 19, 2003, to lay down behavioral guidelines for public officials in their private and public life.[7] Furthermore, applications of information and communication technology (ICT) in public service delivery reduced opportunities of corrupt practices in government.[8] The E-Government Readiness Index of Korea was in the 5th place among the UN member states in 2004 and 2005, following USA, Denmark, Sweden, and UK (UN/DESA, 2005).

South Korean government's anti-corruption efforts were somewhat political, symbolic, or limited in its nature before the 1990s. Since the 1990s, however, realistic and practical measures for corruption eradication have been developed. Such development might be correlated with political and economic developments in South Korea. Accordingly, it would be interesting to see how the South Korean government's anti-corruption measures have been developed and what measures are taking place; where and in what ways. It would be also interesting to see the evaluation of South Korean government's anti-corruption efforts from a professional international organization. Thus, this chapter first reviews the development of major anti-corruption infrastructure such as the anti-corruption legislation and the independent agency for anti-corruption in the South Korean government, followed by discussion of the development of major anti-corruption measures, the international evaluation on corruption, and the role of civil society for curbing corruption. After that, policy implications and conclusion follow.

# THE DEVELOPMENT OF MAJOR ANTI-CORRUPTION INFRASTRUCTURE: ANTI-CORRUPTION ACT AND THE INDEPENDENT AGENCY FOR ANTI-CORRUPTION

In 1999, the Special Commission on Anti-Corruption (SCAC) was established by President Kim Dae-jung to promote anti-corruption measures. However, the SCAC was found to be ineffective in curbing corruption because it was just an advisory body of the President without substantial administrative backup machinery; and all members of the commission are non-standing members. Consequently, there was a growing demand in government and society to restructure a special body for combating corruption along with the anti-corruption legislation.

The Citizens' Coalition for Promulgating a Corruption Prevention Law (composed of 38 NGOs in South Korea) was established in early 2000 and it requested the National Assembly and major political parties to make a new law for corruption prevention. After that, both the then ruling, and opposition parties, prepared a bill on anti-corruption in late 2000 and then enacted the Anti-Corruption Act on July 24, 2001. The purpose of this Act is to serve to create the clean climate of the civil service and society by preventing and efficiently regulating the acts of corruption.[9] In 2001, the Money Laundering Prevention Act was also enacted. Furthermore, the Code of Conduct for Maintaining the Integrity of Public Officials (Presidential Decree Number 17906) was enacted on February 18, 2003, and it went into force on May 19, 2003 at central and local administrative organs and autonomous education authorities for integration with existing regulations.[10] Thus it is fair to say that major basic pillars of the anti-corruption infrastructures have been established during the Kim Dae-jung Administration (1998–2003).[11]

In accordance with Article 10 of the Anti-Corruption Act enacted in 2001, the KICAC was established on January 25, 2002. During the establishment process, however, there was a serious struggle among key stakeholders such as the prosecutors and the police, although it was overruled by the President and public opinion. At one time, the central government was considering creating the Bureau of Investigation of Public Officials' Corruption as a quasi-autonomous body in the Pubic Prosecutor's Office because the prosecutors strongly demanded to have it within their territory. In addition, the police also lobbied to have such a function within the National Policy Agency. Moreover, many lawyers among members of the National Assembly and lawyers of the legal policy community did not fully support the establishment of KICAC because of the different sectoral group interests. Accordingly, KICAC's functions have not been fully equipped as compared with Singapore and Hong Kong. This is a classic example of conflict of interests among key stakeholders.

In comparison, South Korea is a latecomer in Asia in establishing a specialized independent anti-corruption agency: Singapore established the Corrupt Practidces Investigation Bureau (CPIB) in 1952[12]; Malaysia organized the Anti-Corruption Agency (ACA) in 1967[13]; Hong Kong made the Independent Commission Against Corruption (ICAC) in 1974[14];

Thailand established the National Counter Corruption Commission (NCCC) in 1999[15]; and Indonesia organized the Corruption Eradication Commission (CEC) in 2003.[16] As a matter of fact, there are three different patterns of corruption control around the world: (1) anti-corruption laws without specific agency to implement these laws; (2) the combination of anti-corruption laws and several anti-corruption agencies; and (3) the impartial implementation of comprehensive anti-corruption laws by a specific anti-corruption agency (Quah, 2003, p. 16). Asian countries mentioned previously use the third pattern of corruption control.[17]

KICAC is an independent governmental organization established under the President to perform the improvement of laws and institutions for the prevention of corruption and the formulation and implementation of anti-corruption policies.[18] KICAC Secretariat, staffed with 205 employees as of 2006,[19] is responsible for presenting anti-corruption policies to the board of the Commission and handling administrative affairs in accordance with the board's decision. It has four bureaus including inspection headquarters, legal affairs management, policy planning, and public relations. As of 2006, its annual budget is approximately 19.6 billion won (equivalent to approximately US$20 million). In comparison, ICAC in Hong Kong had a total staff of 1,286 members and a budget of HK$686.7 million (US$88 million) in 2001; and Singapore's CPIB had a total staff of 80 members and a budget of S$10.7 million (US$6.3 million) in 2001 (Quah, 2004).[20]

In a nutshell, KICAC is a major national anti-corruption authority in South Korea, but some critics indicate that it lacks investigative powers (Quah, 2006).[21] Nonetheless, the presence of such an organization exclusively in charge of anti-corruption measures indicates the South Korean government's will and readiness to tackle corruption issues as the top priority of national development agendas. The role of a newly created agency is usually weak in the beginning of its establishment so it is expected that the function and the role of KICAC will be strengthened over time in the future.

# THE DEVELOPMENT OF MAJOR ANTI-CORRUPTION MEASURES BY KICAC

The launching of KICAC in 2002 was of considerable significance in that it is a national-level anti-corruption agency that plays a crucial role in the government's fight against corruption by implementing a broad range of measures to prevent corruption, provides checks and balances between authorities in power, and, for the first time in the nation's history, introduced the whistle-blower protection and reward system. KICAC is currently carrying out almost comprehensive policy measures for anti-corruption in both prevention and punishment dimensions. Among such programs, notable major anti-corruption measures are: (1) institutional improvement for anti-corruption; (2) handling corruption reports; (3) protecting and rewarding whistle-blowers; (4) assessment of anti-corruption activities; and (5) raising public awareness on the corruption issue through the code of conduct for public officials and anti-corruption training.

## Institutional Improvement for Corruption Prevention

The South Korean central government made systematic measures for institutional improvement, comprised of three tasks (voluntary, special, and common tasks). First, the voluntary task specifies that each government agency should identify and remove corruption factors from its law and regulation. KICAC conducts an extensive examination of the laws and regulations in the public sector. Second, the special task identifies that each government agency should refocus its anti-corruption efforts on the areas that are prone to fraud and corruption. KICAC works to make sure that the specific areas (i.e., taxation, public projects and award of contracts, inspection, public corporations, and transactions with foreign business) receive policy priorities. Third, the common task, whose successful implementation will have a positive spillover effect on society as a whole, is made up of several tasks: revise corruption-causing laws and regulations, enhance transparency in administrative procedures, encourage public involvement, foster a corruption-free environment, and ensure detection and punishment of corruptors.

## Handling of Corruption Reports

KICAC has Inspection Headquarters (IH) with several teams: the Inspection Planning Team, the Code of Conduct Team, and the Corruption Report Center Team with inspection officers. In particular, the Corruption Report Center analyzes and manages the reports of suspected corrupt conduct which are provided by personal visit, the Internet, counseling, telephone, mail, and fax. As of late December 2004, it has obtained 6,014 corruption reports and dealt with 18,673 counseling cases in a number of different ways (KICAC, 2004, p. 46). KICAC received a total of 92 new cases of corruption in 2004, 89 of which were processed. KICAC referred 76 corruption reports among them to the Public Prosecutor's Office, the National Police Agency, or the BAI, according to the type of suspected corrupt conduct (KICAC, 2004, p. 48). The role of KICAC's inspection is somewhat limited at this time, but it is expected to grow over time.

## Protection and Reward

The Anti-corruption Act specifies that the identity of informants should not be disclosed without their consent and that they should not be discriminated against in terms of their public positions as a result of reporting alleged corrupt behavior in good faith. KICAC ensured that the Protection and Reward Division officials deal with a whistle-blower case with the help of the Corruption Report Center and the Inspection Officer. Since its establishment in 2002, KICAC has handled 10 cases which related to the security of public positions. In nine of those cases, it took protective steps by: transferring the informants to other offices, getting them duly reinstated, ensuring personnel exchange, imposing negligence fines, providing job placement service, or calling for disciplinary actions; and KICAC awarded informants 173 million won in total for their reports, which were decisive factors in recovering 2.73 billion won or so (KICAC, 2004, p. 65).

## Assessment of Anti-Corruption Activities

Corruption-causing factors need to be quantified to better evaluate anti-corruption efforts and their outcomes so that KICAC began conducting the "Integrity Assessment" on government agencies and public service organizations to encourage their involvement in anti-corruption efforts and to approach corruption issues scientifically. The "level of integrity" refers to the degree to which public officials perform their duties in a fair and transparent manner and without getting involved in fraud and corruption (KICAC, 2004, p. 7). According to the 2004 Integrity Assessment,[22] the integrity score averages 8.46 on a 10-point scale, up from 7.71 in 2003 and 6.43 in 2002 (KICAC, 2004, p. 77). The level of integrity has been on a steady increase because target organizations worked to implement anti-corruption policies voluntarily.

## Code of Conduct for Public Officials and Public Education

In accordance with the Article 8 of the Anti-Corruption Act, the (CCPO) went into force in 2003 to lay down behavioral guidelines for public officials in their private and public life. Based on the CCPO, central and local administrative agencies put their own codes of conduct in place, which reflect their individual situation. Furthermore, KICAC developed anti-corruption training programs for public officials. Anti-corruption education for public officials include: anti-corruption expert course, training for public servants in charge of civil application and registration, training by non-government institutions, and government agency's in-house training programs. On top of that, KICAC promoted its anti-corruption education, especially about handling of reports, information and complaints by publishing news briefs and placing ads on the Internet, in subways, and in the publications of civil organizations and public corporations.

In a nutshell, typical functions of the independent anti-corruption agency in several Asian countries including Singapore and Hong Kong are investigation, prevention, and training. However, KICAC lacks investigative authorities because of strong opposition of the Prosecutors' Office and the Police. Instead, KICAC collects corruption reports from citizens and requests investigations by the Prosecutors' Office and the Police upon the receipt of corruption reports from citizens. Furthermore, KICAC only deals with corruption in the public sector so that it does not handle corruption in the private sector, while independent anti-corruption agencies in Singapore and Hong Kong deal with corruption in the both public and private sectors.[23] In that regard, KICAC is not regarded as a super-strong anti-corruption agency.

# INTERNATIONAL EVALUATION: CORRUPTION PERCEPTIONS INDEX (CPI) AND GLOBAL CORRUPTION BAROMETER (GCB)

The South Korean government established a basic anti-corruption infrastructure in recent years and developed various anti-corruption policies and programs. Accordingly, it would be interesting to see the evaluation from a professional international organization such as the Transparency International (TI). TI provides useful quantitative diagnostic tools regarding levels of transparency and corruption, both at global and local levels.[24]

## Corruption Perceptions Index (CPI)

The annual TI Corruption Perceptions Index (CPI), first released in 1995, is the best known of TI's tools. It has been widely credited for putting TI and the issue of corruption on the international policy agenda. The TI CPI ranks countries in terms of the degree to which corruption is perceived to exist among public officials and politicians.[25] It is a composite index, a poll of polls, drawing on corruption-related data from expert and business surveys carried out by a variety of independent and reputable institutions. The TI CPI focuses on corruption in the public sector and defines corruption as "the abuse of public office for private gain."[26]

The CPI 2006 ranks 163 countries in terms of perceived levels of corruption, as determined by expert assessments and opinion surveys. CPI Score relates to perceptions of the degree of corruption as seen by business people and country analysts, and ranges between 10 (highly clean) and 0 (highly corrupt). Leading top 10 countries in terms of the TI CPI are as follows: (1) Finland, Iceland, and New Zealand received the same highest score (9.6), followed by Denmark (9.5), Singapore (9.4), Sweden (9.2), Switzerland (9.1), Norway (8.8), Australia (8.7), Netherlands (8.7), Austria (8.6), Luxembourg (8.6), and United Kingdom (8.6).[27] Countries in Northwestern Europe, Northern America, and Oceania received high CPI scores. In general, there might be a possible correlation between corruption and socioeconomic development, but Northwestern European countries have an exceptionally high score. It seems that ethical or cultural legacies brought a high CPI score in Northwestern European countries, but more in-depth further studies might be necessary to explain this phenomenon.

Among Asian countries, Singapore had the highest score (9.4), followed by Hong Kong (8.3), Japan (7.6), Taiwan (5.9), South Korea (5.1), and Malaysia (5.0), as shown in Table 1.[28] It seems that a super-strong anti-corruption agency model the so-called "the Singahong Model" works effectively in both Singapore and Hong Kong. Since Singapore's CPIB was originally established by the British colonial government in 1952, Singapore's anti-corruption policies have been effective.[29] Hong Kong's CPI is also high and such score could be partially interpreted as a result of the performance of Hong Kong's ICAC. South Korea's rank is much lower than Singapore and Hong Kong, but it is improving over time.

South Korea's CPI score is improving over time as shown in Table 2. South Korea's CPI score in 2000 was 4.0, but it was 5.1 in 2006. The rank is fluctuating due to increasing number of participating countries in the surveys. A country's score is a much more important indication of the

***Table 1.*** Rank and Score of the TI CPI 2006 in Selected Asian Countries (Number of Countries: 163).

| Country | CPI Rank | CPI Score[a] |
|---|---|---|
| Singapore | 5 | 9.4 |
| Hong Kong, PRC | 15 | 8.3 |
| Japan | 17 | 7.6 |
| Taiwan | 34 | 5.9 |
| South Korea | 42 | 5.1 |
| Malaysia | 44 | 5.0 |
| Thailand | 63 | 3.6 |
| China | 70 | 3.3 |
| India | 70 | 3.3 |
| Mongolia | 99 | 2.8 |
| Vietnam | 111 | 2.6 |
| Nepal | 121 | 2.5 |
| Philippines | 121 | 2.5 |
| Indonesia | 130 | 2.4 |
| Pakistan | 142 | 2.2 |
| Bangladesh | 156 | 2.0 |
| Myanmar | 160 | 1.9 |

*Source:* Transparency International's homepage for the Corruption Perceptions Index (CPI) at www.transparency.org/policy_research/surveys_indices/cpi/2006
[a]The scores range from 0 (most corrupt) to 10 (least corrupt).

***Table 2.*** Trends of CPI Score and Rank of South Korea, 1997–2006.

| Year | CPI Score | CPI Rank | Size of Sample (Number of Countries) |
|---|---|---|---|
| 1997 | 4.29 | 34 | 52 |
| 1998 | 4.2 | 43 | 85 |
| 1999 | 3.8 | 50 | 99 |
| 2000 | 4.0 | 48 | 90 |
| 2001 | 4.2 | 42 | 91 |
| 2002 | 4.5 | 40 | 102 |
| 2003 | 4.3 | 50 | 133 |
| 2004 | 4.5 | 47 | 146 |
| 2005 | 5.0 | 40 | 159 |
| 2006 | 5.1 | 42 | 163 |

*Source:* Transparency International's homepage for the Corruption Perceptions Index (CPI) at www.transparency.org/policy_research/surveys_indices/cpi

perceived level of corruption in a country. A country's rank can change simply because new countries enter the index or others drop out.[30] The South Korean government is now aiming to increase its CPI score up to 7–8 points in the near future.

### Global Corruption Barometer (GCB)

TI produces several other surveys and indices in addition to the CPI. Among them, the GCB is one of TI's key global tools for measuring corruption in assessing general public attitudes toward, and experience of, corruption around the world. It asks respondents whether they or anyone in their household has had contact during the past 12 months with seven familiar public sector agencies, including the police, health services, education and so forth, and whether they have had to pay bribes in their dealings with them.

The GCB 2006 reflects the findings of a survey of 59,661 people in 62 countries. The GCB 2006 also shows experience of bribery in selected Asian countries. The GCB 2006 asked the following question: "in the past 12 months have you or anyone living in your household paid a bribe in any form." In South Korea, bribing has been substantially reduced in recent years: only two percent of respondents said that they paid bribes, while over 10 percent of respondents in several countries (India, Pakistan, Philippines, and Indonesia) said that they paid bribes in the past year, as shown in Table 3.[31]

**Table 3.** Experience of Bribery in Selected Asian Countries: Bribe-Paying in the Past Year.

| Country | Yes (%) | No (%) |
|---|---|---|
| Singapore | 1 | 99 |
| South Korea | 2 | 98 |
| Taiwan | 2 | 98 |
| Japan | 3 | 97 |
| Malaysia | 3 | 97 |
| Hong Kong | 6 | 94 |
| Thailand | 10 | 90 |
| India | 12 | 88 |
| Pakistan | 15 | 85 |
| Philippines | 16 | 84 |
| Indonesia | 18 | 82 |

*Source:* TI Global Corruption Barometer (2006).

For international comparison taken together, responses from African, Latin American and newly independent states (NIS), countries indicate that frequent bribe-paying is the common social norm – with a few notable exceptions – as is indicated in Table 4. In Asia-Pacific and Southeast Europe, bribe-paying was moderate, while in North America and EU countries including other Western European nations bribes were seldom paid for services. Among Asian countries, Hong Kong's case is interesting to see because it had a good score of CPI, but its GCB score was not good as shown in Table. 4. The level of corruption is a function of the honesty and integrity of both public officials and private individuals; holding such factors constant, however, the size and incidence of bribes are determined by the overall level of benefits available, the discretionary power of officials, the riskiness of corrupt deals, and the relative bargaining power of briber and bribee (Rose-Ackerman, 1997, p. 38).[32]

The GCB also provides data showing the extent to which people believe corruption affects different public sectors and institutions in their country. This public perception of the levels of corruption is a vital indicator of how

*Table 4.* Countries Most Affected by Bribery.

| | | |
|---|---|---|
| Percentage of respondents that have paid a bribe in the last 12 months | More than 40% | Albania, Cameroon, Gabon, Morocco |
| | 16–40% | Bolivia, Congo-Brazzaville, Czech Republic, Dominican Republic, Greece, Indonesia, Kenya, Mexico, Moldova, Nigeria, Paraguay, Peru, Philippines, Romania, Senegal, Ukraine, Venezuela |
| | 6–15% | Argentina, Bulgaria, Chile, Colombia, Croatia, Hong Kong, India, Kosovo, Luxembourg, Macedonia, Pakistan, Panama, Russia, Serbia, Thailand |
| | 5% or less | Austria, Canada, Denmark, Fiji, Finland, France, Germany, Iceland, Israel, Japan, Malaysia, Netherlands, Norway, Poland, Portugal, Singapore, South Africa, South Korea, Spain, Sweden, Switzerland, Taiwan, Turkey, United Kingdom, USA |

*Source:* TI Global Corruption Barometer (2006).

corrupt or clean the average citizen finds a number of key institutions. Such perceptions can influence the public's dealings with these institutions, creating the expectation that graft might be necessary to get necessary services. The results of the GCB 2006 show that political parties and parliament/legislature are perceived to be most affected by corruption as shown in Fig. 1.[33]

In general, political parties were perceived as the most corrupt institutions in society around the world. According to both TI GCB 2005 and 2006, political parties were ranked as the institutions most affected by corruption, followed by parliament/legislature, as shown in Fig. 1. Thus citizens called their political party system into question and for innovation. Like many other countries, citizens in South Korea have serious doubts about the integrity of their political parties and legislature.

Generally speaking, the public office election is highly costly in terms of campaigning, advocating, and promoting a candidate's popularity to win the election. Accordingly, a prospective candidate is likely to receive illegal donations in order to cover campaign expenses. In the past, South Korea had severe problems of corrupt election practices over a long period. In 2004, however, a new step was taken to curb corrupt election practices in the process of the public office election by the revision of the Public Office Election Act. In particular, various articles related to the election campaign, finance, and accounting have been substantially revised to enhance more transparency and integrity.

For example, the revised Public Office Election Act states that a politician should not provide any money, goods, foods, books, tours, and

*Fig. 1.* Sectors and Institutions Most Affected by Corruption. *Source:* TI Global Corruption Barometer (2006).

transportation to constituencies. According to a newly added Article 261 of the Public Office Election Act revised in 2004, if a politician violates the law, he/she must pay "50 times of the original price incurred" to the National Election Commission. Furthermore, if anybody reports such illegal cases to the National Election Commission, he/she can get monetary rewards up to 500,000,000 won (approximately US$532,000) from the National Election Commission and secrecy of the informant's identification is guaranteed.[34] Since then, corrupt practices in the process of the public office election have significantly declined.

Citizens in many developing countries signaled the police as a highly corrupt institution (Sherman, 1978). According to the GCB 2006, respondents in African and Eastern European countries indicated grave concerns about the integrity of the police. Furthermore, concerns about the law and order sector (police, legal system, and judiciary) are not limited to the police, but extend to the legal system and the judicial bodies.

In South Korea, many citizens indicated several vulnerable areas for corruption (KICAC, 2006). Among several public service areas, construction and building-related areas received the highest score on the citizens' perception survey on corrupt public service areas, followed by tax, correction and customs service including the prosecutor's office, defense and military manpower, education, policy, health and hygiene, environment, and procurement, as shown in Table 5.

Corruption prone areas are major targets for administrative reform in South Korea because they are potential high impact agencies for the general public who feel the quality of public service everyday. Currently, the South

*Table 5.* Citizens' Perception on Corrupted Public Service Areas in South Korea.

| Public Service Areas by Function | 2003 | 2004 | 2005 |
|---|---|---|---|
| Construction, building, housing, and land development | 72.6 | 71.3 | 73.9 |
| Tax | 58.1 | 59.4 | 54.0 |
| Prosecutor, correction, and customs service | 57.0 | 46.0 | 52.6 |
| Defense and military manpower | 54.6 | 51.9 | 52.3 |
| Education | 45.1 | 45.1 | 48.9 |
| Police | 51.3 | 54.9 | 48.0 |
| Health and hygiene | 32.2 | 47.3 | 33.4 |
| Environment | 32.0 | 37.9 | 32.7 |
| Procurement | 27.4 | 36.1 | 26.0 |

*Source:* KICAC's homepage at http://www.kicac.go.kr/

Korean government is carrying out administrative reform in six major vulnerable (wet) areas: construction, housing, tax collecting, law enforcement, food-sanitation inspection, and environment regulation. The South Korean government now regards anti-corruption as one of the most important tasks that it has to resolve for successful administrative reform and national development.

## THE ROLE OF CIVIL SOCIETY FOR CURBING CORRUPTION

The government's anti-corruption convictions and an institutional framework by themselves cannot thoroughly eradicate corruption. Only when there is continued assistance from the private sector, such as monitoring and control by civil society, and corporate reforms in governance and ethics, can public policies on anti-corruption work effectively.

In South Korea, the citizens' movement grew spontaneously from the late 1980s. By the 1990s, with the advancement of democracy and local autonomy, civil groups experienced rapid growth both in terms of size and quality. Some of these groups made outstanding achievements indeed. Three major NGOs are briefly reviewed in the following section: Citizens' Coalition for Economic Justice; People's Solidarity for Participatory Democracy; and Transparency International-Korea (TI Korea).

The Citizens' Coalition for Economic Justice (CCEJ),[35] founded in 1989, was formed to realize the Real Name Financial Transactions System in 1993. The most notable activity of the CCEJ is the establishment of the "real name system" for all financial transactions and for the registration of property. Currently, the CCEJ has expanded its membership to 35,000 and became one of the leading non-governmental organizations (NGOs) in South Korea.

The People's Solidarity for Participatory Democracy (PSPD), established in 1994, also developed a movement for *chaebol* (conglomerate) reform, political reform, and eradication of corruption and improper practices.[36] Since its establishment, the PSPD has been serving as a leading watchdog against the abuse of power. It has developed various activities to bring justice and democracy to many areas in our society. The Civil Actions for the 2000 General Election (the CAGE)[37] and the Minority Shareholders' Campaign might be said to be their most noticeable activities.

TI Korea was founded in 1999 through a coalition of civil organizations with the purpose, "To reform the awareness of people, to eliminate widespread corruption in the society, and to contribute to the righteous construction of society through anti-corruption movements."[38] Recently, the Korean Pact on Anti-Corruption and Transparency (K-PACT) was signed by representative figures from the four sectors of the society – public, private, political, and civil society – in a pledge to create a corruption-free and transparent society. The K-PACT seeks to become a sustainable movement for transparency through participation and agreement between the four sectors to overcome corruption and further our society.[39]

These civil groups not only drafted various and practical policy alternatives to resolve corruption and maladministration problems in South Korean society; they also acted as major players in enacting anti-corruption legislation, the Anti-Corruption Act and the Money Laundering Prevention Act. Thus, it is important to innovate, not only public governance, but also a broad scale of governance in South Korean society by nurturing civil society's activities in public affairs.

# POLICY IMPLICATIONS AND CONCLUSIONS

Government-led economic development in the last decade had proliferated various approval and authorization rules and regulations which increased opportunities for public corruption in South Korea. In particular, the growth-oriented economic policy in the past made it a custom that government awarded special privileges to certain companies which, in return for special favors, provided illegal political funds to the politicians who had influence in shaping government policy and operation (OPM, 1999). However, these are not the only causes for corruption. In fact, there are various kinds of causes for corruption. First, administrative and institutional causes are: unrealistic or unnecessary regulations, unclear definitions and operational standards in laws including rules and regulations, complicated and intricate administrative procedures; and low salaries and poor benefits for public officials. Second, social and cultural causes are: collusive connections in the iron triangle,[40] social structure which supports highhanded personal administration and privileges for former government officials, cultural environment encouraging unreasonable and inordinate treatment including cash gifts (commonly given at celebrations to express gratitude and commonly given at ceremonies to express congratulations and condolences). Third, psychological and attitudinal causes are: low level of integrity and ethics in public office, and prevalence of egotism, nepotism, regionalism, and academic cliques in society (OPM, 1999, p. 9). Thus the South Korean government must find a way to deal with each of these causes of corruption.

South Korean governments have tried to eradicate corruption by introducing institutional frameworks in addition to a number of new laws and regulations. Believing that corruption was one of the main causes of the foreign currency crisis in 1997, South Korean people also strongly demanded that the government exert all possible efforts to eliminate corruption in both public and private sectors (OPM, 1999, p. 11).[41] Consequently, President Kim Dae-jung expressed a strong will in combating and eradicating corruption, pursued reforms in rules and regulations, and set up an infrastructure for anti-corruption efforts by establishing the Anti-Corruption Act in 2001 and an independent corruption organization (KICAC) in 2002. President Rho Moo-hyun also promoted administrative and institutional reforms and initiated public awareness programs for anti-corruption, and invested resources more extensively for the improvement of conditions for public officials.

Moreover, the current South Korean government is strengthening international ties and cooperation with international organizations (such as OECD, IBRD, UN, and TI) as well as other foreign countries for the purpose for curbing corruption. In fact, these international organizations provide various kinds of tools and policy ideas for anti-corruption. If a country is interested in anti-corruption, it can borrow useful ideas from major international organizations without "reinventing wheels" for corruption prevention. Therefore, a critical matter for corruption eradication is to have a strong political will to realistically adopt, and seriously implement, anti-corruption policies. In that regard, it seems that, in recent years, the South Korean government has been more serious in adopting and implementing major anti-corruption policy tools from toolboxes of various international organizations than previous governments (UNDP, 1998; World Bank, 1998; OECD, 1999).

However, the government anti-corruption efforts have been largely limited to investigation and punishment of alleged individual offenders. In other words, preventive measures have been weak. Government should place more emphasis on prevention rather than on reactive measures in combating corruption and prioritize on feasibility and effectiveness of anti-corruption programs. Particularly, more specific reform plans must be developed and implemented against corruption in vulnerable areas. To do so, the role of KICAC's investigative powers in particular, should be enhanced in the near future along with adequate staff and funding. As a matter of fact, the Singahong model (super-strong independent agency model of Singapore and Hong Kong) was successful in Singapore and Hong Kong. It has not only rigorous investigative methods but also strong programs of prevention and public education based on high levels of political and public support. KICAC has both prevention and public education functions, but it currently lacks investigative authority.[42]

Since the 1990s, basic anti-corruption infrastructure and practical anti-corruption measures have been installed in government. Thus, it is fair to say that the South Korean government now laid a more or less realistic ethical foundation on which to build a fair and transparent officialdom. As mentioned earlier, South Korea's CPI score is improving over time: South Korea's CPI score in 2000 was 4.0, but it was 5.1 in 2006. According to the GCB 2006, however, political life was emerged as the most affected by corruption in South Korea.[43] More than 70 percent of respondents living in South Korea said that corruption affects political life to a large extent, while 31–50 percent of respondents in Japan and Singapore think that their political lives are affected to a large extent.[44] Accordingly, political dispute, along with corruption in South Korea, is one of the daunting tasks the South Korean government should deal with for further advancement in the near future. Therefore, political leaders should commit themselves in promoting transparency, accountability, integrity, and democratic governance in societies around the world. The political sector is the area most distrusted by South Korean citizens with a high degree of political cynicism. The political sector is one of major target areas for further reforms in South Korea.

Moreover, the battle for national integrity must be waged in all parts of society including government, as well as the private sector and NGOs (Anechiarico & Jacobs, 1996; Stapenhurst & Kpundeh, 1999). Nowadays, NGOs are a core component of civil society and have a duty in holding governments accountable and transparent. In many cases NGOs have been fighting corruption longer than the government or businesses. As the government creates strategies for combating corruption, reformers must seek to incorporate the views and experiences of NGOs from the beginning. NGOs help governments design legislation and programs to implement strategies and make government into a more open, transparent and participatory governance, creating an environment in which fraud and corruption cannot thrive.

Transparent governance implies openness of the governance system through clear processes and procedures, with easy access for citizens to public information. A high level of transparency stimulates ethical awareness in public service through information sharing, which ultimately ensures the accountability of the performance of individuals and organizations handling resources and/or holding public office (Kim, Halligan, Cho, Oh, & Eikenberry, 2005). The word transparency carries with it a powerful array of moral and political associations: honesty, guilelessness, and openness (Best, 2005). Transparency requires that decisions and their enforcement are done in a manner that follows rules and regulations. Transparency and its fruit, administrative health, is the sine-qua-non of good governance and national integrity. The ultimate goal of national integrity is to make corruption into a high risk and low return undertaking. Building national integrity through corruption eradication in South Korea is a top priority to make a country more competitive and trustworthy in the world.

## NOTES

1. Arnold Heidenheimer (2001) provided three classifications of corruption: public-office-centered, market-centered, and public-interest-centered definitions.
2. Transparency International and UNDP (1999) share this kind of definition (see Transparency International's homepage at www.transparency.org/policy_research/surveys_indices/cpi/2006/faq).
3. For more information, visit the BAI's homepage at http://english.bai.go.kr/
4. In 1999, the Prime Minister was Kim Jong-pil and his office had a substantial degree of autonomy of power in comparison with other former prime ministers.
5. For more details, visit the Regulatory Reform Committee (RRC)'s homepage at http://www.rrc.go.kr
6. The Lee Myung-bak Administration (2008-present) restructured the central government on February 29, 2008. Accordingly, the Korea Independent Commission against Corruption (KICAC), the Ombudsman of Korea and the Administrative Appeals Commission were consolidated into the Anti-Corruption and Civil Rights Commission (ACRC) in safeguarding civil rights and anti-corruption. More detailed information can be found at its new website at http://www.acrc.go.kr/eng_index.jsp
7. Based on the CCPO, 324 central and local administrative agencies put their own codes of conduct in place, which reflect their individual situation.
8. For example, the Seoul Metropolitan Government (SMG) has developed a web-based system that allows citizens to monitor corruption-prone applications for permits and approvals. This Online Procedures Enhancement for civil applications (OPEN) system makes it easier to raise questions in the event that any irregularities are detected (http://www.unpan.org/training-open.asp).
9. Reporting corruption cases is one of the most effective ways to bring corruption under control. Under this recognition, the Anti-Corruption Act provides for a system of protection and rewards for whistle-blowers and informants – and even their relatives. It bans disclosing their identity without their consent or putting them at any disadvantage.

10. The new ethics code is different from its predecessors in its achievability and strong binding power.

11. The Kim Administration initiated a bold reform right after the IMF bailout in 1997. The Act on Preventing Bribery of Foreign Public Officials in International Business Transactions was also enacted in 1999.

12. http://www.cpib.gov.sg

13. http://www.bpr.gov.my

14. ICAC has a strength of 1,314 staff as of 2006, with the majority serving on contracts. http://www.icac.org.hk

15. http://www.nccc.thaigov.net

16. http://www.kpk.go.id

17. Outside the Asia-Pacific region, however, the Anti-Corruption Bureau in Tanzania, for example, faced considerable public criticism particularly in the post Julius Nyerere years (TI, 1999, p. 87). Therefore, it is worthy to consider the fact that having an independent anti-corruption agency does not guarantee the success of corruption eradication because an independent anti-corruption agency model is unlikely to be right for every country (Johnston, 1999, p. 225).

18. The board of the Commission consists of nine commissioners, three of whom are appointed by the President as standing members. The rest, six non-standing members, are appointed or designated by the President, three members on the recommendation of the National assembly and three by the Chief Justice of the Supreme Court. All commissioners serve a term of three years. For more details, visit KICAC's homepage at http://www.kicac.go.kr

19. Detailed information can be found at http://www.kicac.go.kr

20. South Korea's per capita expenditure of US$0.44 for anti-corruption is much lower than Hong Kong's US$12.57 per capital expenditure as of 2001. For more information, visit the Asian Development Bank's homepage at adb.org/Documents/Periodicals/GB/GovernanceBrief11.pdf

21. KICAC has an inspection headquarters with inspection officers, but critics say that the authority of inspection officers is limited in comparison with other law enforcement agencies. As a matter of fact, the Prosecutor's Office and the National Policy Agency opposed the establishment of KICAC during the policy development process for establishing an independent anti-corruption agency.

22. Overall integrity is the arithmetical average of the integrity scores in each service area, with the sum of the weights of each assessment area being score 1 (KICAC, 2004, p. 72). Overall Integrity = Weight X (Perceived Integrity+Potential Integrity).

23. KICAC has the Corporate Ethics Team in the Bureau of Public Relations and Cooperation.

24. For more details, see the Transparency International's homepage at www.transparency.org/policy_research/surveys_indices/about

25. Alan Doig, McIvor, and Theobald (2006) warns that quantitative approaches have policy-relevant weaknesses when it comes to assessing causes, patterns and trends of corruption, as well as acknowledging that an over-reliance on scoring or rankings might overlook the fact that democratization and development may be moving targets in terms of progress and direction.

26. The surveys used in compiling the CPI ask questions that relate to the misuse of public power for private benefit, for example bribery of public officials, kickbacks in public procurement, embezzlement of public funds) or questions that probe the strength of anti-corruption policies, thereby encompassing both administrative and political corruption. www.transparency.org/policy_research/surveys_indices/cpi/2006/faq#general1

27. *Ibid.*

28. TI's homepage for the CPI at www.transparency.org/policy_research/surveys_indices/cpi/2006

29. A similar story can be told in Hong Kong, which was under British rule from 1841 to 1997 (Quah, 2004).

30. If comparisons with previous years are made, they should only be based on a country's score, not its rank, as outlined previously. For more details, see TI's homepage at www.transparency.org/policy_research/surveys_indices/cpi/2006/faq

31. www.transparency.org/policy_research/surveys_indices/gcb/2006

32. www.transparency.org/policy_research/surveys_indices/gcb/2006

33. www.transparency.org/policy_research/surveys_indices/gcb/2006

34. For more details, visit the National Election Commission's homepage at http://www.nec.go.kr/english

35. The CCEJ was formed in response to the unjust structure of Korean economic life and it was founded in 1989 by some 500 people representing various walks of life: economics professors and other specialists, lawyers, housewives, students, young adults, and business people. For more details, visit its homepage at http://www.ccej.or.kr/English

36. Founded in 1994 by more than 200 members, the People's Solidarity for Participatory Democracy (PSPD) is a civil organization dedicated to promoting justice and human rights in Korean society through the participation of the people. For more details, visit its homepage at http://eng.peoplepower21.org

37. Nearly five hundreds of NGOs made coalition for the rejection campaign in 2000. For more details, visit the PSPD's homepage at info.peoplepower21.org/action/year.html#

38. For more details, visit its homepage at http://www.ti.or.kr/engindex.htm.

39. The K-PACT is based on TI's principle of coalition-building and a holistic approach and it is a proposal from civil society to form an anti-corruption system through alliances among the public, political, and private sectors.

40. "Iron triangle" is a term used by political scientists to describe the policy-making relationship between the legislature, the bureaucracy, and interest groups.

41. The World Bank provided financial support (US$345,000) for the initiation of the South Korean government's efforts against corruption in 1998 (OPM, 1999, p. 7). It made a notable influence in the development of anti-corruption policies in South Korea.

42. Outside the Asia-Pacific region, however, the Anti-corruption Bureau in Tanzania, for example, faced considerable public criticism particularly in the post Julius Nyerere years (TI, 1999, p. 87). Therefore, it is worthy to consider the fact that having an independent anti-corruption agency does not guarantee the success of corruption eradication because an independent anti-corruption agency model is unlikely to be right for every country (Johnston, 1999, p. 225).

43. The GCB (TI, 2006) has also asked respondents to assess to what extent corruption affects different spheres of life, including personal and family life, the business environment, and political life on a scale of 1 (not at all) to 4 (to a large extent).
44. *Ibid.*

# REFERENCES

Anechiarico, F., & Jacobs, J. (1996). *The pursuit of absolute integrity*. Chicago: University of Chicago Press.
Best, J. (2005). *The limits of transparency: Ambiguity and the history of international finance*. Ithaca, NY: Cornell University Press.
Dininio, P., Kpundeh, S. J., & Leiken, R. (1998). *A handbook on fighting corruption*. Washington, DC: Center for Democracy and Governance, USAID.
Doig, A., McIvor, S., & Theobald, R. (2006). Numbers, nuances and moving targets: Converging the use of corruption indicators and descriptors in assessing state development. *International Review of Administrative Sciences, 72*(2), 239–252.
Heidenheimer, A. (2001). Terms, concepts, and definitions: An introduction. In: A. Heidenheimer & M. Johnston (Eds), *Political corruption: Concepts and contexts* (3rd ed., pp. 8–11). Somerset, NJ: Transaction Publishers.
International Institute for Management Development (IMD). (2006). *The world competitiveness yearbook*. Lausanne, Switzerland: IMD.
Johnston, M. (1999). A brief history of anti-corruption agencies. In: A. Schedler, L. Diamond & M. F. Plattner (Eds), *The self-restraining state: Power and accountability in new democracies* (pp. 220–228). Boulder, CO: Lynne Rienner Publishers.
Kim, P., Halligan, J., Cho, N., Oh, C., & Eikenberry, A. (2005). Toward participatory and transparent governance: Report on the sixth global forum on reinventing government. *Public Administration Review, 65*(6), 646–654.
Klitgaard, R. (1988). *Controlling corruption*. Berkeley: University of California Press.
Kooiman, J. (2003). *Governing as governance*. Thousand Oaks, CA: Sage.
Korea Independent Commission against Corruption (KICAC). (2004). *KICAC annual report*. Seoul: KICAC.
Korea Independent Commission against Corruption (KICAC). (2006). *Public survey result on corruption in Korea*. (Unpublished document but released in its homepage at http://www.kicac.go.kr; accessed on October 20 2006). Seoul, KICAC. On February 29, 2008, KICAC was reorganized as the Anti-Corruption and Civil Rights Commission (ACRC).
[Korea] Office of the Prime Minister (OPM). (1999) (1999). *Korea's anti-corruption programs*. Seoul: OPM.
Organization for Economic Cooperation and Development (OECD). (1999). *Public sector corruption: An international survey of prevention measures*. Paris: OECD.
Quah, J. (1999). Singapore's anti-corruption strategy: Some lessons for South Korea. *Korean Corruption Studies Review, 4*(1), 173–193.
Quah, J. (2003). *Curbing corruption in Asia: A comparative study of six countries*. Singapore: Eastern Universities Press.

Quah, J. (2004). Best practices for curbing corruption in Asia, (Asian Development Bank's newsletter), *The Governance Brief* (GB Issue 11), 1–4.
Quah, J. (2006). Curbing Asian corruption: An impossible dream? *Current History, 105*(690), 176–179.
Rhodes, R. A. W. (1997). *Understanding governance: Policy networks, governance, reflexivity and accountability.* Buckingham, UK: Open University Press.
Rose-Ackerman, S. (1978). *Corruption: A study in political economy.* New York: Academic Press.
Rose-Ackerman, S. (1997). The political economy of corruption. In: A. E. Kimberly (Ed.), *Corruption and the global economy* (pp. 31–60). Washington, DC: Institute for International Economics.
Sherman, L. (1978). *Scandal and reform: Controlling police corruption.* Berkeley, CA: University of California Press.
Stapenhurst, R., & Kpundeh, S. J. (Eds). (1999). *Curbing corruption: Toward a model for building national integrity.* Washington, DC: World Bank.
Transparency International (TI). (1999). *National integrity systems: The TI source book* (3rd ed.). Berlin: Transparency International.
Transparency International (TI). (2006). *Report on the transparency international global corruption barometer 2006.* Berlin, TI. (English report is available at http://www.transparency.org/policy_research/surveys_indices/gcb/2006; accessed on December 3, 2006).
UN/DESA – United Nations Department of Economic and Social Affairs. (2005). *Global E-Government Readiness Report 2005.* UN/DESA, New York.
United Nations Development Program (UNDP). (1998). *Corruption: Integrity improvement initiatives in developing countries.* New York: UNDP.
United Nations Development Program (UNDP). (1999). *Fighting corruption to improve governance.* New York: UNDP.
World Bank. (1994). *Governance: The bank's experience.* Washington, DC: World Bank.
World Bank. (1998). *Anti-corruption knowledge.* Washington, DC: Anticorruption Knowledge Center of the World Bank.

# CORRUPTION AND GOVERNMENT TRUST: A SURVEY OF URBAN AND RURAL INHABITANTS IN THE NORTH AND NORTHEAST OF THAILAND

Suchitra Punyaratabandhu

## ABSTRACT

*The purpose of this chapter is to investigate citizen attitudes toward control of corruption, their trust in government, and the relationship between trust and corruption in order to determine whether these factors are conducive to governance reform. The sample consists of 3,600 respondents surveyed in late 2005 early 2006 in the north and northeast regions of Thailand. The findings indicate that almost three-quarters of the respondents said that petty and routine corruption was unacceptable; only one-third said they trusted or somewhat trusted public officials. Trust and control of corruption attitudes are positively, although weakly, correlated. The findings suggest that citizen attitudes toward corruption and their levels of trust in government are not antithetical to the notion of good governance. The data reveal considerable variation, however. Using partial correlation analysis, education and urban–rural distinctions are identified as key: persons with higher educational attainment and urban inhabitants are more likely to state that petty and routine corruption is unacceptable, and they are less likely to trust public officials, than persons with less education or persons living in rural areas. Gender and age have surprisingly little effect.*

## INTRODUCTION

Corruption, trust, and good governance are generally viewed as closely interrelated. The accepted wisdom holds that corruption results in bias and distortion of the law, and thus runs directly counter to the rule of law dimension of governance, as well as negatively affecting the transparency and accountability dimensions. Corruption may also lead to a reduction of administrative capacity and a rise in the price of administration (Nye, 1989; Bayley, 1989). Trust in government or political trust, on the other hand, has been described as "the sine qua non of good governance ... While good governance breeds trust, trust is a prerequisite for democratic governance in the first place" (Blind, 2006, pp. 16–17). Trust is fostered through transparency and accountability, and vice versa. Trust is corroded by corruption.

A closer examination of the dimensions and key indicators of good governance reveals considerable conceptual overlap among corruption, trust, and good governance. Elimination of corruption frequently appears as part of the definition of good governance. The argument that where there is transparency and accountability there is trust verges in many formulations on the tautological. Interestingly, there is no standard definition of good governance. It is a multidimensional construct, defined differently by different agencies. Some definitions identify four dimensions of governance, others six, yet others eight (http://www.worldbank.org, http://www.adb.org, http://www.unescap.org). Good governance has been defined as consisting of all or some combination of the following: accountability, transparency, participation/voice, rule of law/predictability, regulatory quality, political stability, responsiveness, consensus orientation, equity, and inclusiveness. Controlling corruption and its variants (e.g., "efficiency") are sometimes treated as a separate dimension, although corruption is generally subsumed under rule of law. The dimensions complement and reinforce one another, and there is also overlap among them.

To sort out the conceptual relationships among political (as opposed to social) trust, control of corruption, and good governance is not the focus of this chapter. Rather, the assumption is made that good governance and controlling corruption are correlated, without entering into a debate as to whether corruption is part of the definition of governance or whether it is an outcome of governance. A further assumption is that trust and good governance are mutually reinforcing. Citizen trust is a necessary condition for good governance, while good governance itself leads to citizen trust.

The question arises: what is the relationship between political trust and control of corruption? If good governance is positively associated with both control of corruption and levels of citizen trust, then logically should not citizen trust be positively associated with control of corruption? Contrary to the preceding argument, however, is it possible to posit that a traditional political culture may weaken the relationship between trust and control of corruption? That is to say, citizen trust may co-exist in a traditional political culture together with prevalent corruption. Moreover, the concept of corruption itself is likely to be culturally determined, to the extent that what passes for corrupt practice in a so-called modern culture characterized by Weberian legal-rational norms may be viewed as acceptable and non-corrupt in a more traditional culture.

The alternative hypothesis, that political trust and control of corruption are unrelated or only weakly related, derives from the concept of traditional societies as antithetical to "a logic of governance rooted in the rule of law" (Heinrich, Hill, & Lynn, 2004, p. 10). In the traditional culture, emphasis is placed on hierarchical relationships and patron–client ties (Girling, 1981; Rabibhadana, 1969; Riggs, 1966; Siffin, 1966). Hierarchy in social relations means that those higher up in the hierarchy are ascribed certain authoritative powers and wisdom, and are deferred to by those lower down in the scale. Patron–client linkages imply an exchange relationship: a patron has the duty to protect and promote the welfare of his clients; a client returns the favor by obeying and carrying out the wishes of his patron (Samakarn, 2004). Charoenwongsawad (2004, pp. 30–31) has identified three core values underlying patron–client ties in Thailand: putting the interests of one's own group above all other interests; making reciprocity and mutual interdependence the basis for patron–client relationships (e.g. superior–subordinate, politicians and public officials, public officials and citizens); and placing a high value on gratitude and loyalty ("*katanyu*" which is akin to filial piety, except in this case it extends to piety shown by clients to their patrons), including the return of past kindnesses and favors. Thus, in the traditional culture, public/private distinctions carry little weight. A holder of public office, in his role either as patron or as client, would pay scant attention to norms of transparency or rule of law.

Thailand presents an example of a transitional culture in which, despite a gradual modernization of the polity, many features of the traditional society remain solidly entrenched, especially in rural areas. Indeed, the political economist Anek Laothammathas (1995) has proposed a framework of "Two Thailands" (*"song nakara"*) for the analysis of Thai politics and society. The first Thailand is predominantly rural and agricultural or working class. Its ways are the traditional ways, and its politics is based on patronage. The second Thailand is primarily urban and middle class, with a tendency to espouse Western standards and norms. Politics provides an arena for a clash of the two cultures.

The Thai government has made a public commitment to good governance, to the extent of promulgating a Royal Decree on Good Governance in May 2003. In 2002, the Office of the Public Sector Development Commission was created, with the objective of promoting effective performance of government agencies consistent with public sector development policies and principles of good governance (http://www.opdc.go.th). Prior to this, 1998 saw the creation of King Prajadhipok's Institute, a juristic body under the supervision of Parliament. One of the stated objectives of the Institute is to present "models of good governance in practice to target groups around the country" (http://el.kpi.ac.th/kpien).

Governance reforms in Thailand have been supply side, by and large. Little attention has been paid to the demand side. Are the values and attitudes of Thai citizens conducive to, and supportive of, governance reform? If they are not, then this does not augur well for the success of reforms. Beginning with Almond and Verba's seminal work in the 1960s, socio-cultural approaches have focused on cultural factors as determinants of the success or failure of public policies (Almond & Verba, 1963, 1980; Inglehart, 1977; Eckstein, 1966, 1988; Laitin, 1995). Schedler and Proeller (2007) summarize the thrust of socio-cultural approaches as follows: "(U)nless a society's political institutions are congruent with its underlying political culture, those institutions will be unstable" (p. 190). The question then can be reformulated as, is the concept of good governance congruent with the underlying Thai culture? What is the nature of trust in government, and what are the attitudes toward control of corruption? Are there urban–rural distinctions, and is there regional variation?

This chapter is part of a series that reports on research designed to address some of these questions. In seeking answers to the questions, the research draws attention to the demand side of governance. Specifically the purpose of this chapter is to investigate citizen attitudes toward control of corruption, trust in government, and the relationship between trust and corruption in a transitional culture, using survey data from the north and northeastern regions of Thailand. The data reported here are by region (north/northeast) and by extent of urbanization (urban/rural dichotomy).

## MEASUREMENT AND SCALE CONSTRUCTION

### The Data Set

The data reported here are taken from a larger field survey conducted by the author in eight provinces in the north and northeastern regions of Thailand in late 2005–early 2006. Each region is divided into two strata based on urban/rural distinctions: urban areas are represented by town municipalities; rural areas are represented by villages outside municipal areas. The data are based on a sample of 3,600 respondents: 840 respondents in town municipalities in the north and 840 respondents in the northeast; 960 respondents in rural villages in the north and 960 respondents in the northeast. A multistage stratified sampling design was used. The National Statistical Office of Thailand provided generous assistance in drawing the sample and supplying area maps.

The data collection instrument was a questionnaire consisting of some 70 items. In addition to demographic and socio-economic questions, the first part of the questionnaire also contained items related to access to information and public officials and offices, and levels of satisfaction with public service provision. The second part of the questionnaire was designed to elicit attitudes toward the dimensions of governance, as well as attitudes toward corruption and citizen trust in government. The questionnaire and survey design are described at length in Punyaratabandhu (2006).

### Scale Construction

For this chapter, four scales have been constructed. The first scale measures attitudes toward petty corruption. The second and third scales measure satisfaction with public officials' performance and satisfaction with the government's ability to solve problems, respectively, as proxy measures for rational or utilitarian trust. The fourth scale measures trust in public officials as a proxy for relational trust. Scale construction is described below.

## Political Corruption

The term "corruption" has a wide variety of meanings, as discussed comprehensively by Heidenheimer, Johnston, and LeVine (1989) in their introductory essay to the *Handbook on Political Corruption*. For this study we employ a public-office centered definition of corruption proposed by Bayley:

> Corruption, while being tied particularly to the act of bribery, is a general term covering misuse of authority as a result of considerations of personal gain, *which need not be monetary*. (Bayley, 1989, pp. 936–937, emphasis added)

This concept of corruption extends not only to bribery, but also to nepotism and misappropriation (Nye, 1989, p. 966):

> (Corruption) ... includes such behavior as bribery (use of reward to pervert the judgement of a person in a position of trust); nepotism (bestowal of patronage by reason of ascriptive relationship rather than merit); and misappropriation (illegal appropriation of public resources for private-regarding uses).

Heidenheimer (1989, pp. 158–160) makes a distinction between petty corruption, routine corruption, and aggravated corruption. Petty corruption and routine corruption involve the bending of official rules and use of patronage powers. In return, gifts are given to, and accepted by, officials and patrons. Heidenheimer notes, "(In traditional patron–client settings) ... activities that would be considered 'routine corruption' by official Western standards are standard procedures deeply rooted in more general social standards and obligations" (1989, p. 159). Aggravated corruption, by contrast, is more heinous, and extends to "dirty graft," kickbacks and payoffs.

For this study, a two-item corruption scale was constructed, designed to measure respondents' attitudes toward petty and routine corruption. No attempt was made to measure attitudes toward aggravated corruption, such as officials tolerating organized crime in return for payoffs, because it was assumed that respondents would uniformly express negative attitudes in such cases. Instead, responses were sought to the following Likert-type items: "Do you think it's wrong for government officials to accept 'envelopes' for speeding up services?" and, "If government officials to accept 'envelopes' to turn a blind eye on petty violations of the law, do you think it's wrong?" The Cronbach's alpha for the two-item corruption scale is 0.825.

## Political Trust

The literature on political trust distinguishes between *utilitarian or rational trust*, also known as strategic or calculative trust (Coleman, 1988; Gambetta, 2000; Hardin, 2002), and relational trust, also known as *affective or moralistic trust* (Giddens, 1991; Parsons, 1952; Cooley, 1956). Rational trust has been described as "I trust X to do Y" (Job, 2005), which involves consideration of information or knowledge about X and calculation of whether X will do what I want. Thus political trust from a utilitarian or rational perspective involves trusting the government to perform. Relational trust, on the other hand, "has ethical roots, and is based on belief or faith in the goodness of others ... (as in) 'I trust you'" (Job, 2005, p. 4). With respect to political trust, relational trust takes the form of trust in public officials and trust in government.

## Rational Trust

In this study, satisfaction with performance is used as a proxy measure for rational trust. The rationale is that if a citizen is satisfied with a government's performance, then he or she is likely also to trust the government to perform. Two satisfaction scales were constructed, each designed to tap a different aspect of performance satisfaction. The first scale measured satisfaction with public services, while the second scale measured satisfaction with the government's ability to solve problems of poverty, education, and health.

a) *Satisfaction with public services scale.* This is a composite of four Likert-scale ("satisfied," "somewhat satisfied," "neither satisfied nor dissatisfied," "somewhat dissatisfied," "dissatisfied") items where respondents were asked to rate their satisfaction with their District Office, their local police station, their local health center, and the local branch of the Bank for Agricultural Cooperatives. The Cronbach's alpha for the four-item scale is 0.809.

b) *Satisfaction with the government's ability to solve problems scale.* Respondents were asked to rate their satisfaction with the government's ability to solve problems of poverty, education, and health. A Likert-scale ("satisfied," "somewhat satisfied," "neither satisfied nor dissatisfied," "somewhat dissatisfied," "dissatisfied") was employed. The Cronbach's alpha for the three-item scale is 0.846.

## Relational Trust

Relational trust or affective trust was measured by asking respondents to rate their trust in public officials, including elected officials. Respondents were asked, "How much would you say you trusted the following (public officials): *kamnan* and village headmen; local *tambon* (or municipal, depending on location) councillors; members of parliament; government officials; and the local police?" The first three categories are elected; the last two categories are civil servants. The Cronbach's alpha for the five-item Likert-type scale is 0.871.

# EMPIRICAL RESULTS

## Characteristics of the Sample

Table 1 reports percentages by region and stratum for gender and age. The percentages are the result of the sampling procedure that was employed for this study. The sample consisted of households drawn using a multistage systematic sampling procedure.

One respondent was selected from each household, alternating between head of household, spouse, and other resident family members over the age of 20. As shown in Table 1, women comprise roughly 55.0 percent of the total sample and men 45.0 percent. The average respondent age is 43.76 years in the north and 45.38 years in the northeast. Over 50 percent of respondents are between 36 and 55 years of age.

*Table 1.* Gender and Age, by Region and Stratum (Percentages).

| Demographic Characteristics | Northeast | | North | |
|---|---|---|---|---|
| | Rural villages ($n = 960$) | Town municipalities ($n = 840$) | Rural villages ($n = 960$) | Town municipalities ($n = 840$) |
| *Gender* | | | | |
| Male | 49.1 | 43.5 | 45.4 | 45.2 |
| Female | 50.9 | 56.5 | 54.6 | 54.8 |
| Total | 100.0 | 100.0 | 100.0 | 100.0 |
| *Age* | | | | |
| Less than 25 | 4.2 | 6.9 | 4.5 | 8.9 |
| 26–35 | 16.9 | 18.3 | 15.7 | 27.4 |
| 36–45 | 27.1 | 29.4 | 28.6 | 29.4 |
| 46–55 | 27.0 | 24.8 | 28.5 | 21.8 |
| 56–65 | 19.4 | 15.5 | 15.0 | 9.8 |
| 66 or older | 5.5 | 5.1 | 7.6 | 2.7 |
| Total | 100.0 | 100.0 | 100.0 | 100.0 |

Table 2 reports percentages by region and stratum for education and occupation. As expected, there is a marked divide between urban and rural populations. Respondents residing in towns show far higher levels of educational attainment than respondents living in villages. In town municipalities, only 10.4 percent and 29.8 percent of respondents in the north and northeast, respectively, had less than a sixth grade education. The figures for rural villages are 52.8 and 59.9 percent, respectively. By contrast, 31.8 percent and 21.9 percent of respondents in the north and northeast,

*Table 2.* Education and Occupation, by Region and Stratum (Percentages).

| Educational Attainment and Occupation | Northeast | | North | |
|---|---|---|---|---|
| | Rural villages ($n = 960$) | Town municipalities ($n = 840$) | Rural villages ($n = 960$) | Town municipalities ($n = 840$) |
| *Educational attainment* | | | | |
| Less than 6th grade | 59.9 | 29.8 | 52.8 | 10.4 |
| 6th grade | 21.7 | 11.8 | 18.4 | 11.9 |
| 9th grade | 5.4 | 12.4 | 9.2 | 13.7 |
| 12th grade or vocational certificate | 7.9 | 16.5 | 10.8 | 17.5 |
| Diploma or higher vocational certificate | 1.7 | 7.6 | 2.7 | 14.8 |
| Bachelor's degree or higher | 3.4 | 21.8 | 6.2 | 31.8 |
| Total | 100.0 | 100.0 | 100.0 | 100.0 |
| *Occupation* | | | | |
| Agriculture/Fishing/Animal husbandry | 65.5 | 1.5 | 41.8 | 1.2 |
| Merchant/Self-employed | 11.7 | 40.5 | 15.3 | 38.6 |
| Employee | 11.6 | 19.9 | 24.6 | 24.3 |
| Company employee | 0.4 | 5.2 | 1.0 | 9.8 |
| Government service/State enterprise | 2.6 | 13.0 | 5.3 | 12.8 |
| Student | 1.4 | 2.5 | 2.4 | 4.3 |
| Retired | 0.7 | 3.5 | 1.7 | 1.7 |
| Housewife | 5.5 | 13.3 | 7.5 | 5.2 |
| Other | 0.6 | 0.6 | 0.4 | 2.1 |
| Total | 100.0 | 100.0 | 100.0 | 100.0 |

respectively, held a bachelor's degree or higher, whereas in rural villages the figures drop to 6.2 and 3.4 percent, respectively.

In addition to urban–rural distinctions, regional differences exist. Respondents in the north are better educated than respondents in the northeast. The education gap is more pronounced in urban areas than in rural areas. Whereas there is only seven percentage points difference between persons having less than a sixth grade education in rural villages in the north and northeast, the difference increases to 42 percentage points for persons living in town municipalities. The same pattern holds with respect to tertiary education. In rural villages in the northeast, only 5.1 percent of respondents had the equivalent of two years or more of college, in contrast to 8.9 percent of rural respondents in the north. The contrast is far more pronounced for urban inhabitants: 8.9 percent in the northeast as opposed to 46.6 percent in the north had two years or more of college.

With respect to occupation, agriculture was given as the primary occupation of respondents in the rural villages of the north and northeast (41.8 and 65.5 percent, respectively), followed by working as hired labor or employees (24.6 and 11.6 percent, respectively), self-employment in trade and commerce or engaged in other business activities (15.3 and 11.7 percent, respectively), and being homemakers/housewives (7.5 and 5.5 percent, respectively).

In the town municipalities, only one percent of respondents gave agriculture as their primary occupation. The leading occupation was trade and commerce or other self-owned business (38.6 and 40.5 percent in the north and northeast, respectively), followed by hired labor or employees (24.3 and 19.9 percent, respectively), public sector employees or officials (12.8 and 13.0 percent, respectively), company employees (9.8 and 5.2 percent, respectively), and being homemakers/housewives (5.2 and 13.3 percent, respectively).

*Control of Corruption*

Respondents were asked whether they had ever heard of, or indeed had personally encountered, instances of corruption concerning government officials within the past three years. "Hearing of corruption" was defined broadly as reading about alleged corruption in the news media, or hearing about corruption from radio or television, or hearing about corruption from local neighborhood sources. The data show surprising regional as well as rural–urban variation (Table 3). Respondents in the northern region were far more likely to have heard about cases of corruption than respondents in the northeast. As expected, urban residents were more likely to say they had

**Table 3.** Knowing About Corruption, by Region and Stratum (Percentages).

| Knowing About Corruption | Northeast | | North | |
|---|---|---|---|---|
| | Rural villages ($n = 960$) | Town municipalities ($n = 840$) | Rural villages ($n = 960$) | Town municipalities ($n = 840$) |
| *In the last 3 years, have you ever heard about cases of corruption involving government officials?* | | | | |
| Never | 54.3 | 40.5 | 33.6 | 15.2 |
| Sometimes | 32.9 | 39.4 | 42.9 | 37.1 |
| Often | 12.7 | 20.2 | 23.6 | 47.7 |
| Total | 100.0 | 100.0 | 100.0 | 100.0 |
| | $\chi^2 = 38.230$, df $= 2$, $p = .00$ | | $\chi^2 = 139.387$, df $= 2$, $p = .00$ | |

heard of corruption cases than their rural counterparts. Whereas 54.3 percent of rural respondents and 40.5 percent of urban respondents in the northeast said they had never heard of corruption cases within the past three years, the figures drop to 33.6 percent and 15.2 percent for respondents in urban and rural areas, respectively, in the northern region.

Attitudes toward petty and routine corruption were measured by a scale created by aggregating the responses to two questions: "Do you think it's wrong for government officials to accept 'envelopes' for speeding up services?" and, "If government officials accept 'envelopes' to turn a blind eye on petty violations of the law, do you think it's wrong?" As shown in Table 4, over two-thirds of respondents in the northeast and three-quarters of respondents in the north said they thought petty and routine corruption was unacceptable (as measured by the preceding questions). In the northeast, urban inhabitants were more likely than rural inhabitants to say that corruption was unacceptable (71.9 percent as opposed to 64.1 percent, respectively), whereas in the north, the percentages for rural and urban respondents were equal (75.2 percent and 75.6 percent, respectively).

### Rational or Performance Trust

Rational trust is measured in this study by two composite proxy variables: satisfaction with the government's ability to solve problems of poverty,

Table 4. Attitudes Toward Corruption, by Region and Stratum.

| Corruption | Percent Responding | | | |
|---|---|---|---|---|
| | Northeast | | North | |
| | Rural villages ($n = 960$) | Town municipalities ($n = 840$) | Rural villages ($n = 960$) | Town municipalities ($n = 840$) |
| *Petty and Routine Corruption is* | | | | |
| Acceptable | 12.5 | 5.6 | 6.8 | 9.4 |
| Somewhat acceptable | 2.6 | 5.0 | 2.3 | 1.0 |
| Somewhere in-between | 13.1 | 11.1 | 9.6 | 10.0 |
| Somewhat unacceptable | 7.7 | 6.5 | 6.2 | 4.1 |
| Unacceptable | 64.1 | 71.9 | 75.2 | 75.6 |
| Total | 100.0 | 100.0 | 100.0 | 100.0 |
| | $\chi^2 = 33.957$, df $= 4$, $p = .00$ | | $\chi^2 = 11.587$, df $= 4$, $p = .02$ | |

education, and health; and satisfaction with public services provided by the local District Office, police station, health center, and local branch of the Bank for Agricultural Cooperatives, a state-run enterprise. The rationale for the selected proxies is that satisfaction with present performance is associated with trust that the government will perform in the future.

*Satisfaction with Public Services*
Less than 10 percent of the overall sample expressed dissatisfaction with public services (Table 5). Of those expressing some degree of dissatisfaction, residents of the northeast tended to be more dissatisfied than residents living in the north. In both regions, urban dwellers were significantly more dissatisfied (13.7 percent and 10.4 percent in the northeast and north, respectively) than rural inhabitants (6.5 percent and 5.5 percent in the northeast and north, respectively).

In contrast, a majority of respondents said they were either "satisfied" or "somewhat satisfied" with public services. Residents of the northern region expressed a significantly higher degree of satisfaction than residents of the northeast. Rural inhabitants were significantly more satisfied (74.8 percent and 57.6 percent in the north and northeast, respectively) than urban inhabitants (58.5 percent and 47.8 percent in the north and northeast, respectively).

**Table 5.** Rational/Performance Trust, by Stratum (Percentages).

| Rational/Performance Trust | Northeast | | North | |
|---|---|---|---|---|
| | Rural villages ($n = 960$) | Town municipalities ($n = 840$) | Rural villages ($n = 960$) | Town municipalities ($n = 840$) |
| *Satisfaction with public services* | | | | |
| Dissatisfied | 1.0 | 2.7 | 0.9 | 1.6 |
| Somewhat dissatisfied | 5.5 | 11.0 | 4.6 | 8.8 |
| Neither satisfied nor dissatisfied | 36.0 | 38.5 | 19.8 | 31.1 |
| Somewhat satisfied | 40.3 | 40.5 | 44.6 | 42.8 |
| Satisfied | 17.3 | 7.3 | 30.2 | 15.7 |
| Total | 100.0 | 100.0 | 100.0 | 100.0 |
| | $\chi^2 = 57.169$, df = 4, $p = .00$ | | $\chi^2 = 70.655$, df = 4, $p = .00$ | |
| *Satisfaction with the government's ability to solve problems* | | | | |
| Dissatisfied | 1.7 | 5.2 | 3.6 | 8.7 |
| Somewhat dissatisfied | 3.3 | 12.0 | 7.1 | 19.2 |
| Neither satisfied nor dissatisfied | 31.3 | 43.5 | 27.6 | 39.5 |
| Somewhat satisfied | 33.0 | 29.2 | 37.0 | 24.6 |
| Satisfied | 30.8 | 10.1 | 24.7 | 8.1 |
| Total | 100.0 | 100.0 | 100.0 | 100.0 |
| | $\chi^2 = 173.141$, df = 4, $p = .00$ | | $\chi^2 = 184.360$, df = 4, $p = .00$ | |

*Satisfaction with the Government's Ability to Solve Problems*
With the exception of the rural northeast, satisfaction with the government's ability to solve problems was lower than satisfaction with public services. In both the north and northeastern regions, rural inhabitants expressed a far greater degree of satisfaction (61.7 percent and 63.8 percent in the north and northeast, respectively) than urban inhabitants (32.7 percent and 39.3 percent in the north and northeast, respectively). Note should be taken that whereas 53.1 percent of the total urban sample had previously said they were "satisfied" or "somewhat satisfied" with *public services*, only 36.0 percent said they were "satisfied" or "somewhat satisfied" with the government's *ability to solve problems* – a drop of 17 percentage points. The responses for the rural sample are not very different, however, on these two items: the percentage of rural respondents who said they were "satisfied" or "somewhat satisfied" was 66.2 percent for public services, and 62.8 percent for satisfaction with the government's ability to solve problems.

Although the percentage of respondents expressing dissatisfaction with the government's ability to solve problems was not very high, nevertheless, the percentages were higher than dissatisfaction with public services. Urban inhabitants showed a greater degree of dissatisfaction (27.9 percent and 17.2 percent in the north and northeast, respectively) than rural inhabitants (10.7 percent and 5.0 percent in the north and northeast, respectively).

## Relational Trust

Relational or affective trust was measured by asking respondents to rate their trust in public officials, including elected officials. The degree of trust evidenced by the responses is not particularly high: half of rural respondents (55.8 percent and 48.2 percent in the north and northeast, respectively), but only one-quarter of urban respondents (26.4 percent and 24.1 percent in the north and northeast, respectively) said they "trust" or "somewhat trust" public officials (Table 6). At the opposite end of the spectrum, about 10 percent of rural respondents said they "don't trust" or "somewhat distrust" public officials, in sharp distinction to the approximately 30 percent of urban inhabitants who expressed distrust of public officials. The percentages are similar for the north and northeast regions.

*Table 6.* Relational Trust, by Stratum (Percentages).

| Relational Trust | Northeast | | North | |
|---|---|---|---|---|
| | Rural villages ($n = 960$) | Town municipalities ($n = 840$) | Rural villages ($n = 960$) | Town municipalities ($n = 840$) |
| *Trust in public officials* | | | | |
| Don't trust | 1.8 | 8.0 | 2.0 | 6.1 |
| Somewhat distrust | 9.2 | 21.9 | 8.6 | 22.8 |
| Neither trust nor distrust | 40.9 | 46.1 | 33.5 | 44.7 |
| Somewhat trust | 28.1 | 20.6 | 40.6 | 22.2 |
| Trust | 20.1 | 3.5 | 15.2 | 4.2 |
| Total | 100.0 | 100.0 | 100.0 | 100.0 |
| | $\chi^2 = 198.678$, df $= 4$, $p = .00$ | | $\chi^2 = 194.166$, df $= 4$, $p = .00$ | |

### Correlations between Corruption and Trust Attitudes

One of the objectives of this chapter was to investigate the relationship between trust and corruption attitudes. Table 7 displays Pearson product-moment correlations between corruption attitudes and trust variables. The relationships are statistically significant: corruption attitudes are weakly but *negatively* associated with both rational trust (as measured by satisfaction with public services and satisfaction with the government's ability to solve problems) and with relational trust (trust in public officials) ($r = -.041$, $-.095$, and $-.162$, respectively). Persons who find corruption unacceptable are *less* likely to say they are satisfied with public services or the government's ability to solve problems than persons who are more accepting of corruption. Persons who find corruption unacceptable are also *less* likely to say they trust public officials than persons who are more accepting of corruption.

Rational/performance trust and relational trust variables are positively associated, as is to be expected. Satisfaction with public services is correlated with satisfaction with the government's ability to solve problems ($r = .342$), and both are correlated with trust in public officials ($r = .455$ and $.580$, respectively).

### Predictor Variables of Corruption and Trust Attitudes

What kinds of respondent characteristics are related to corruption and trust attitudes? In this section we examine the relationship between respondent

*Table 7.* Correlations between Corruption and Trust Attitudes.

| Variable | Rational/Performance Trust | | Relational Trust |
| --- | --- | --- | --- |
| | Satisfaction with public services | Satisfaction with the government's ability to solve problems | Trust in public officials |
| Corruption | $-.041^*$ | $-.095^{**}$ | $-.162^{**}$ |
| Satisfaction with public services | | $.342^{**}$ | $.455^{**}$ |
| Satisfaction with the government's ability to solve problems | | | $.580^{**}$ |

*significant at the .05 level.
**significant at the .01 level.

*Table 8.* Predictor Variables of Corruption and Trust Attitudes: Partial Correlation Coefficients.

| Variable | Corruption | Rational/Performance Trust | | Relational Trust |
|---|---|---|---|---|
| | | Satisfaction with public services | Satisfaction with government's ability to solve problems | Trust in public officials |
| Region | .056** | .195** | −.090** | .043** |
| Degree of urbanization | ns | −.096** | −.215** | −.224** |
| Gender | ns | ns | ns | −.038* |
| Age | .037* | .078** | ns | ns |
| Educational attainment | .082** | −.126** | −.152** | −.170** |

*Note:* ns = not significant. Gender (F = 0, M = 1); Region (NE = 0, N = 1); Degree of Urbanization (rural = 0, urban = 1).
*Significant at the .05 level.
**Significant at the .01 level.

characteristics such as gender, age, educational attainment, place of residence (urban/rural), and region of residence (north/northeast) and respondent attitudes toward corruption and their trust in government. Table 8 reports partial correlation coefficients between respondent characteristics as predictor variables and corruption and trust variables as dependent variables. The interpretation of the partial correlation coefficient is that it represents the average change in the dependent variable per unit change in the independent variable, holding all other predictor variables constant.

*Corruption Attitudes*
Of the five predictor variables, only three are statistically significant: age, educational attainment, and region of residence are weakly but positively associated with corruption attitudes (partial $r$ = .037, .082, and .056, respectively). Older persons and persons with higher educational attainment tend to say that petty and routine corruption is unacceptable more than younger persons and persons with less educational attainment. Residents of the northern region tend to find corruption more unacceptable than residents in the northeastern region.

*Rational/Performance Trust: Satisfaction with Public Services*
Four out of five predictor variables are statistically significant: age and region of residence are weakly but positively associated with satisfaction

with public services (partial $r = .078$ and $.195$, respectively); educational attainment and degree of urbanization are weakly but negatively associated with satisfaction with public services (partial $r = -.126$ and $-.096$, respectively). Older persons and northern region residents are more likely to be satisfied with public services than younger persons and residents in the northeastern region. Persons with higher educational attainment and persons living in town municipalities are likely to be *less* satisfied with public services than persons with lower educational attainment and persons living in rural villages.

*Rational/Performance Trust: Satisfaction with the Government's Ability to Solve Problems*
Three out of five predictor variables are statistically significant: educational attainment, degree of urbanization, and region of residence are weakly but negatively associated with satisfaction with the government's ability to solve problems (partial $r = -.152$, $-.215$, and $-.090$, respectively). Persons with more educational attainment, persons living in town municipalities, and residents in the northeastern region are likely to be *less* satisfied with the government's ability to solve problems of poverty, education and health than persons with lower educational attainment, persons living in rural villages, and residents of the northern region.

*Relational Trust: Trust in Public Officials*
Four out of five predictor variables are statistically significant: gender, educational attainment, and degree of urbanization are weakly but negatively associated with trust in public officials (partial $r = -.038$, $-.170$, and $-.224$, respectively); whereas region is weakly but positively associated with trust in public officials (partial $r = .043$). Men, persons with higher educational attainment, and persons living in town municipalities are likely to have *less* trust in public officials than women, persons with lower educational attainment, or persons living in rural villages. Residents of the north region tend to have more trust in public officials than residents in the northeastern region.

# DISCUSSION AND CONCLUSIONS

The purpose of this chapter was to investigate citizen attitudes toward control of corruption, trust in government, and the relationship between trust and corruption in order to ascertain whether these factors were conducive to governance reform. In regard to control of petty and routine corruption, nearly three-quarters of all respondents said such corruption was unacceptable. More than half of all respondents said they were satisfied or somewhat satisfied with performance (a proxy for rational trust), but only one-third said they trusted or somewhat trusted public officials (relational trust). That trust levels are not very high is consistent with data on trust in other developed and developing countries that indicate a secular decline in levels of reported trust in government (see, e.g., Blind, 2006, pp. 9–12).

The correlation between trust factors and control of corruption attitudes was weak but statistically significant. Persons who found corruption unacceptable were *less* likely to express trust in government or its agencies. These findings are thus consistent with the accepted wisdom which holds that citizen trust is positively associated with control of corruption. The findings do not support the perspective of a traditional society based on personalism and patronage, the logic of which implies that trust and corruption attitudes are unrelated. The preliminary findings would suggest that citizen attitudes toward control of corruption and their trust in government in the north and northeast regions of Thailand are not antithetical to the notion of good governance, which requires mutually supportive and cooperative relationships among government, civil society, and the private sector.

Further examination of the data, however, reveals the existence of considerable variation. Using partial correlation analysis, a multivariate procedure that measures the relationship between two variables holding other variables constant, the following conclusions are drawn. First, educational attainment is a key factor. Persons with higher educational attainment are more likely to say that petty and routine corruption is unacceptable than persons with lower educational attainment. Persons with higher educational attainment are at the same time less likely to express trust in government and its agencies than persons with lower educational attainment. A plausible explanation for the effect of education could be that educated persons are more cognizant of social norms and the stigma attached to corruption. Their responses could be interpreted as either reflecting their true opinions or perhaps the responses simply constitute lip service to the concept. An argument might also be made that more educated persons are likely to have greater access to information and are presumably more sophisticated (are more aware of the shortcomings in their elected officials and bureaucrats) than less educated persons. Hence, they are likely to trust government and its agencies less.

Second, gender and age have far less significance than might have been expected. There are no gender differences with respect to attitudes toward corruption or performance trust. Women, however, are somewhat more likely than men to say they have trust in public officials. Older persons are somewhat more likely than younger persons to say that petty and routine corruption are unacceptable. They are also more likely to say they are satisfied with public services. Age is not significantly related to the remaining trust variables, however.

Third, degree of urbanization makes a difference when it comes to trust. Urban inhabitants tend to trust government and its agencies far less than rural inhabitants. It could be the case that because urban residents have far greater exposure to, and interact more frequently with, local officials as well as central government officials than do their rural counterparts, they are more likely to be aware of flaws and/or irregularities in the provision of public services. As reported earlier, urban inhabitants are far more likely to say they have heard about cases of corruption involving government officials than rural inhabitants. It could also be the case that urban inhabitants have higher standards and expectations regarding public officials than rural inhabitants. Most urban residents in the workforce, except for those employed in the informal sector, pay income taxes. Most persons employed in the rural agricultural sector do not pay income taxes. It is reasonable to assume that income taxpayers are more demanding of the services rendered by government and its agencies than those who pay no taxes.

Finally, regional differences exist. Residents of the north are more likely than their northeastern neighbors to find corruption unacceptable. They are also more satisfied with public services and have greater trust in public officials than residents in the northeast. Nevertheless, they are also less satisfied with the government's ability to solve problems than residents in the northeast. What accounts for the regional differences? One conjecture is that the then Prime Minister (Thaksin Shinawatra) was from the north, and his political party had a strong northern base. The government's populist policies generated popular support in the poorer regions of the country, but the strongest support for Thaksin and his government was to be found in the rural areas of the north region.

In conclusion, the survey data indicate that citizen attitudes toward control of corruption and their trust in government in Thailand's north and northeastern regions are congruent with notions of good governance. For governance reforms to generate stakeholder participation and response, however, consideration should be given to the information needs of citizens.

Information should be tailored to education levels and reading skills. Rural areas in particular should be targeted.

## ACKNOWLEDGMENTS

The author wishes to thank: Danny Unger for his comments on an earlier draft of the chapter; Pachitchanat Siripanich for the more technical aspects of sampling; Jaruwan Rittibanlue and Oy Sae-Uey, her research assistants, for their dedication; the School of Public Administration, National Institute of Development Administration, and the NIDA Research Fund whose support made this research possible.

## REFERENCES

Almond, G. A., & Verba, S. (1963). *The civic culture: Political attitudes and democracy in five nations*. Princeton, NJ: Princeton University Press.
Almond, G. A., & Verba, S. (1980). *The civic culture revisited*. London: Sage.
Bayley, D. H. (1989). The effects of corruption in a developing nation. In: A. J. Heidenheimer, M. Johnston & V. T. LeVine (Eds), *Political corruption: A handbook*. New Brunswick, NJ: Transaction Publishers.
Blind, P. K. (2006). Building trust in government in the twenty-first century: review of literature and emerging issues. A paper prepared for the Seventh Global Forum on Reinventing Government and Building Trust in Government, UN/DESA, 26–29 June 2007, Vienna, Austria.
Charoenwongsawad, K. (2004). *Kolamed Ded Corruption (Thai language)*. Bangkok: Success Media.
Coleman, J. (1988). Social capital in the creation of human capital. *American Journal of Sociology, 94*(Suppl.), S95–S120.
Cooley, C. H. (1956). *The two major works of Charles H. Cooley: Human nature and the social order*. Glencoe, Illinois: The Free Press.
Eckstein, H. (1966). *Division and cohesion in democracy*. Princeton, NJ: Princeton University Press.
Eckstein, H. (1988). A culturalist theory of political change. *American Political Science Review, 82*(3), 789–804.
Gambetta, D. (2000). Can we trust trust? In: D. Gambetta (Ed.), *Trust: Making and breaking cooperative relations*. Oxford: Department of Sociology, Oxford University.
Giddens, A. (1991). *Modernity and self-identity: Self and society in the Late Modern Age*. Stanford, California: Stanford University Press.
Girling, J. L. S. (1981). *Thailand: Society and politics*. Ithaca, NY: Cornell University Press.
Hardin, R. (2002). *Trust and trustworthiness*. New York: Russell Sage Foundation.

Heidenheimer, A. J. (1989). Perspectives on the perception of corruption. In: A. J. Heidenheimer, et al. (Eds), *Political corruption: A handbook*. New Brunswick, NJ: Transaction Publishers.
Heidenheimer, A. J., Johnston, M., & LeVine, V. T. (Eds). (1989). *Political corruption: A handbook*. New Brunswick, NJ: Transaction Publishers.
Heinrich, C. J., Hill, C. J., & Lynn, L. E., Jr.. (2004). Governance as an organizing theme for empirical research. In: P. W. Ingraham & L. E. Lynn, Jr. (Eds), *The art of governance*. Washington, DC: Georgetown University Press.
Inglehart, R. (1977). *The silent revolution: Changing values and political styles among Western publics*. Princeton, NJ: Princeton University Press.
Job, J. (2005). How is trust in government created? It begins at home, but ends in the Parliament. *Australian Review of Public Affairs, 6*(1), 1–23.
Laitin, D. D. (1995). The civic culture at 30. *American Political Science Review, 89*(1), 168–173.
Laothammathas, A. (1995). *Song Nakara Prachatipathai (in Thai)*. Bangkok: Matichon Press.
Nye, J. S. (1989). Corruption and political development: A cost-benefit analysis. In: A. J. Heidenheimer, M. Johnston & V. T. LeVine (Eds), *Political corruption: A handbook*. New Brunswick, NJ: Transaction Publishers.
Parsons, T. (1952). *The social system*. London: Tavistock Publications.
Punyaratabandhu, S. (2006). *Citizens and good governance: A survey of north and northeastern Thais*. A research report submitted to the School of Public Administration and the Research Center, National Institute of Development Administration, Bangkok, Thailand (in Thai).
Rabibhadana, A. (1969). *The organization of Thai society in the early Bangkok period* (data paper no. 74). Ithaca, NY: Cornell University Southeast Asia Program.
Riggs, F. W. (1966). *Thailand: The modernization of a bureaucratic polity*. Honolulu: East-West Center.
Samakarn, S. (2004). *Naew Kid Peua Kan Seuksa Panha Sangkom Thai Lae Naew Tarng Kae Kai* (in Thai). NIDA Research Papers, National Institute of Development Administration, Bangkok.
Schedler, K., & Proeller, I. (2007). Public management as a cultural phenomenon: Revitalizing societal culture in international public management research. *International Public Management Review, 8*(1), 186–195. Electronic Journal Available at http://www.ipmr.net
Siffin, W. J. (1966). *The Thai Bureaucracy: Institutional change and development*. Honolulu: East-West Center.

## Internet Sources

http://el.kpi.ac.th/kpien
www.adb.org/Documents/Policies/Governance/ gov200.asp?p = policies
http://www.opdc.go.th
http://www.unescap.org/huset/gg/governance.htm
http://www.worldbank.org/wbi/governance/govdata

# ASSESSING GOVERNMENT EFFORTS TO (RE)BUILD TRUST IN GOVERNMENT: CHALLENGES AND LESSONS LEARNED FROM JAPANESE EXPERIENCES

Masao Kikuchi

## ABSTRACT

*The decline of trust in government has been a critical issue in many parts of the world. Various surveys have indicated that the public cast suspicious eyes on their government and become less trustful of performance of their public sector. The OECD labels trust in government as a fundamental element of the democratic "contract," while its decline may have significant impacts on government activities. Likewise, the UN also refers to trust as the foundation for good governance; therefore, improving trust would help strengthen sound governance in any polity. As these examples demonstrate, trust in government has increasingly become a central concern for government reformers.*

*In Japan, for a long time, bureaucrats have been perceived to be trustful social agents and they have enjoyed more confidence than those of party members. However, a series of scandals involving high-ranking bureaucrats, in addition to several policy failures and severe financial difficulties, have deteriorated the trustful image of Japanese public officials. Confronted with the problem, both central and local governments in Japan have attempted to improve their public perceptions and tried to rebuild trust in government by resorting to various types of administrative reform. However, the identification of reasons for the decline of public trust in government appear an awesome task and hard to come. While some of the reforms have helped contributed rebuilding trust, others have further eroded the level of government confidence.*

*Against these backgrounds, the chapter aims to show the current level of trust in government, specifically in Japan. It tries to assess government efforts of rebuilding trust by discussing different government reforms at both the central and the local levels.*

## INTRODUCTION

The decline of trust in government has been a critical issue in many parts of the world. Many governments and international organizations have started to identify the reasons for the decline, and how to rebuild trust in government with reform measures. The decline of trust in government may affect the efficacy of the policies that the government attempts to perform. Moreover, the declining support for government activities may result in difficulty to recruit the best talent for civil service, increase in tax evasion, and refusal of voluntary deference to the government authorities (Braithwaite & Levi, 1998). As the government is losing its exclusive public domain, well-informed, critical citizens increasingly expect high quality services, streamlined bureaucratic procedures, and to have their views and knowledge taken into account in the public decision-making process (OECD, 2005a). Trust in government is a critical factor determining whether the government and the society can achieve the consensus to have a more open and more collaborative governance structure. In this view, trust in government is an essential prerequisite for designing sound governance (The United Nations, 2006).

There has been a rash of incidents that causes citizens to cast their dubious eyes on the civil service in Japan: continuing media exposure of public officials' scandals involving in sex, money, and even drunken driving scenes. In some cases, there have also been policy failures. Take the National Pension Program for example, where the government fails to adapt to environmental changes such as a declining working population. In some cases, it has even misused deposited money. The government has not succeeded in persuading citizens to pay premiums. On average, more than 30% of all aged citizens under the program do not pay the premium (Social Insurance Agency, 2006). Given the declining citizen's support, the government decided to dismantle the Social Insurance Agency, which is the responsible government agency of the program (scheduled in 2008). As this case indicates, both central and local governments in Japan currently presume the decline of citizen's support as a serious problem. If the government cannot maintain the support from the citizens, it will not able to accomplish the policy target. Thus, it is in a situation of fear of losing constituencies and being dissolved.

Against these backgrounds, this chapter aims to discuss the trust in government and the government's efforts to (re)build trust in Japan. The chapter is divided into four folds. The first part aims to identify the significance of discussing trust in government in public administration discourse. It also attempts to conceptualize "trust in government" which is extremely general term. The second part investigates into the level of trust in government in Japan from historical and Asian perspectives. By doing so, it seeks to capture common and peculiar characteristics. It is followed by the critical qualitative assessment of Japanese government efforts to (re)build trust in government. The chapter concludes by summarizing the reform impacts on trust in government.

## CONCEPTUAL FRAMEWORK

Trust in government is one of the controversial issues in the public administration discourse. The significance of trust in government for sound governance has gained the prominent interest among government reformers (Nye, 1997; Pollitt & Bouckaert, 2000; Kettl, 2000). It refers to citizens feeling confident in their government. If citizens trust government, they will support the government activities and they will willingly accept the authority on the expectation that the government will work for them and will not abuse them (The United Nations, 2006).

Trust has been implicitly known as an important element for the democratic polity. Indeed, trust in government is a fundamental element of the democratic "contract" and its decline may have significant impacts on how people perceive, comply with, and interact with the public bodies that exercise power in their nature (OECD, 2005a, p. 31). Nonetheless, it is not a groundbreaking subject for political science students. Most familiar topic for modern political science field is a trust in political institutions, mainly declining support for political parties (party alienation). Much of the work reveals that the political parties are losing the allegiance of a public that is increasingly non-partisan and skeptical about political parties as institutions (for instance, see Dalton & Wattenberg, 2000). Nevertheless, popularity of the subject of trust has gained with the recent global decline of trust in government and the scholarly attention to "Social Capital" (Putnam, 1994, 2001).[1]

## Significance of Discussing Trust in Government

The common understanding for trust is that it is a normative subject. The trust in government is also distinctive from the political behavior. While political behavior mainly deals with citizen's voting behavior, the issue of trust is of citizen's perception on judging government mainly expressed in attitude survey. It is rather difficult to capture. However, there are certain advantages in discussing trust in government. There can be of three different significances as follows in a broad sense.

The first significance is of potential advantage for the public administration research. For a long time, an analysis in public administration was emphasized much based on the elite model. It involved with politic–administration interface and the main question was how to reflect political voice and control in decision-making and activities of government. As "governance" is being heard more and more in the spheres of government, research attention in public administration gradually shifted from the elite model to the citizen-oriented model, which emphasizes the government to citizen interface. Despite much of work with this "new model" was developed, most of the citizen-oriented model based research seems to depend on fairly optimistic assumption: when the government is reformed more citizen be oriented, the citizen would spontaneously participate in decision-making and delivering services. However, little is known that whether the hypothesis is always appropriate. Trust in government provides us with an essential ground for the forefront of this new model of public administration research. In this regard, assessing and analyzing trust can assist to understand the extent of (good) governance, although more trust does not always contribute to better governance.[2]

Additionally, not only the level of trust, what citizens perceive the government, namely the "components of trust," can contribute to the better understanding of governance reform orientation. In other words, analysis of public trust in government is a good tool to predict how the government reform would it to be. Citizens may mistrust because of low quality and performance of delivered services for instance, or citizens may do so because they feel the government misuses the power and it is corrupted. Analyzing public trust in government has a significant potential to write the prescription for government reformers.

The third, but not least significance of discussing trust is that trust in government itself can be a progress of governance transformation. As it is often advocated by the international assistance organizations, the extent of trust is an extent of good governance reform. In other words, good partnership between government and civil society depends on public trust. Citizens expect public service to serve the public interest with fairness and to manage public resources properly. Fair and reliable public administration inspires public trust and creates a favorable environment for business, thus contributing to well functioning collaboration between the private entities and the government. When public trust in government is low, citizens may be reluctant to participate in governance process. This can weaken the cohesiveness of society and its ability to effectively address common objectives. Trust, thus can be seen as an essential prerequisite for partnerships and good governance. Although high trust does not always lead to good governance, at least the level of trust is a good indicator to show the level of governance reform process better or worse.

## Components of Trust in Government

Many scholarly works argue trust as one of the necessity prerequisites for social activities. Luhmann (1973–1990) proposed that trust is a mean to reduce the complexity in society. Likewise, Williamson (1975) argues that trust reduces the transaction cost. Fukuyama (1995) stated that the trust is one of the critical factors to determine the prosperity in society and his book came up with unorthodox grouping of high trust society (the U.S., Germany, and Japan). Many scholarly works refer trust as different meanings and significances. It is in fact a concept surrounded by conceptual vagueness. Even then, in the discussion of trust in government, it seems appropriate to divide trust into two different components (Klingemann & Fuchs, 1995; Norris, 1999; Hardin, 2000; Bouckaert Van de, Walle, Maddens, & Kampen, 2002; Blind, 2006). One is the performance (operational) trust and the other is the relational (communal) trust[3] (Table 1).

Performance trust deals with the public support for the government performance or how much the citizens are satisfied with the government

*Table 1.* Components of Trust in Government.

|  | Component | Influence Factors | Government Measures | Background |
|---|---|---|---|---|
| Trust | Performance (operational) trust | Quality of government services, "value for money" | Customer friendly, performance management (overlapped with NPM approach) | Business Administration Economics |
|  | Relational (communal) trust | Transparency, corruption, political culture | Open government Anti-corruption measure Information disclosure Participation | Political Science Democratic theories |

*Source:* Derived from Blind (2006).

performance. In theoretical approaches to trust, many scholarly works perceive trust as rational/instrumental reasons in which citizens employ performance related criteria when judging government. Citizens expect government to fully perform its assigned duty and they judge government with evaluations of the government performance (for instance, see Accenture, 2006).

This approach has many affinities with the customer orientation in New Public Management (NPM). The NPM literatures started to approach the public service users as customers and the reform initiatives favor business like government. In their view, government's fatigue in policy performance is identified as a key aspect in explaining citizen's attitude toward public administration. Therefore, more customer-oriented services and performance management (most often by service recipients) improve the service performance and then citizens evaluate it higher. In this respect, performance trust is retrospective which citizens evaluate government after service is rendered. Many efforts can be seen in the actual government reform. One compelling example is the National Performance Review under Clinton Administration in the United States. In this reform "movement," the famous ultimate objective was "Rebuilding Public Trust through Results and Service." In Japan as well, many local governments currently strive to identify the level of "Citizen's Satisfaction" in respective services.[4]

The concept of performance trust unambiguously perceives citizen as government customer. However, this perspective does not connote the "citizen" or participation in democratic term. It is mainly due to performance trust is inspired by the NPM under the heavy influence of business administration and economics. The other component of trust in government is a relational or communal trust which is under more influence of democratic theories in political science (for instance, see Tyler, 1998). Relational trust puts more emphasis on the faith based on the moral philosophy and it is better understood as a matter of ethics rather than as a strategy for maximizing one's utility. In this view, trust in government means whether government is trustful that it does not intend to abuse citizens' rights: or that how close the citizens can feel with the government. In other words, relational trust means how much citizens feel identical to their government. If there is a certain level of relational trust in government, citizens may be more active to give their resources to the government for solving public issues. Whether citizens can recognize government as a "partner" depends on the relational trust. This kind of trust in government is a critical factor for government to transform into participatory government.

The most influential factor for relational trust can be a political efficacy. If citizens feel government activity is well reflected their will and is controllable, they may feel confident with their government. Actual government measures to ensure the relational trust in government would be to increase transparency in government decision-making process, to develop more participation channel, and a measure to get rid of corruption in government (OECD 2000). If citizens feel government is open, willing to accept their opinion in decision-making, and use resources properly, they may trust government as if they trust themselves.

# LEVEL OF TRUST IN GOVERNMENT IN JAPAN AND SOME COMPARISON WITH ASIAN COUNTRIES

*Trust in Government in Japan*

There is a certain complexity to elaborate the trust in government in Japan due to insufficient data. Nonetheless, with its limited data, trust in government in Japan shows some different perspectives. Fig. 1 illustrates the longest time series data on political satisfaction indicator monitored by the Cabinet Office. This indicates the steady decline of public trust in politics and government. Only 20% of the respondents are satisfied with the government. This poll is conducted by the Cabinet Office and thus the downturn from the mid-1990s would be the reflection to the citizen's low evaluation toward the central government. Its trend corresponds with the policy failures and corruption outbreaks in the 1990s. As Pharr (2000,

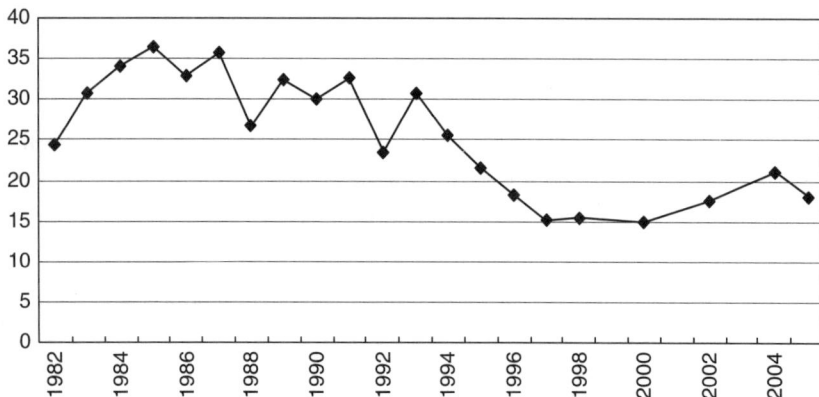

*Fig. 1.* Evolution in Trust in Government in Japan. *Source:* Cabinet Office, Public Opinion Survey on Society and the State (each year). *Note:* Response ratio of "well" and "to some extent" for the question "Does national policy reflect the will of people?" Data on 1999, 2001, and 2003 are not available.

pp. 173–201) pointed out, misconduct reports in media may offer an important key to the understanding declining citizens' confidence in government. The other valid research endorses the citizen's negative view in government. The Central Research Service Report (2004) on "Trust in Social and Public Institutions" revealed that among ten social institutions, bureaucrats marked the least trustful institution and its average trust level is 2.0 in five point scales. In three times research (2000, 2001, and 2004), bureaucrats maintained the lowest trustful institution.[5]

Although these accounts seem to fit the global trend of declining public trust in government (Pharr & Putnam, 2000; Norris, 1999; Klingemann & Fuchs, 1995; Nye, 1997), when the local government is taken into account in the perspective of government, there seems to be a different condition. Fig. 2 shows recent trust level in government institutions (national parliament, central government, and local government) in Japan.

Trust in all institutions slightly increased from 2002 onwards. But the level is still low, especially for the central government and the national parliament. The local government gained more trust than the central level in particular. Though recent and reliable data is unavailable to compare the trust level between central and local level, citizens may trust more in local government than central government. Moreover, this implies that alleged declining trust in government is more entrenched in central government level. It has been argued that the reasons for continuing trust in local

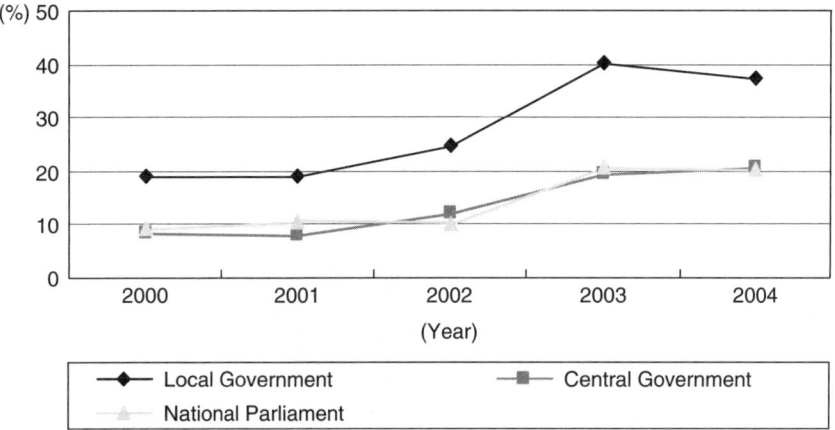

*Fig. 2.* Trust in Government Institutions in Japan (from 2000 to 2004). Data from Yomiuri and Gallop Opinion Survey. *Source:* Yomiuri News Paper each year.

government lie in the role and function of local government. They have been providing the extensive variety of social services much more so than any other countries (Nakamura & Kikuchi, 2006). The conventional way to analyze the importance of local governments in a national system of government is to measure its expenditure size. The size of local public expenditure and the number of local civil service in Japan are about three times larger than that of national level. Local governments are central actors in various social services, including school education, welfare and public health, police and fire services, and the construction of sewerage systems. These wide roles and functions of local governments involve a close relationship with the daily life of citizen. They fulfill a major role in citizen's life. Contrary to the declining role of national bureaucrats and hardly seen their activities, citizens seem to have much a big stake in their local governments. Local governments in Japan have succeeded in developing a sufficiently broad based constituency for themselves (see King, 2000). This account is partly verified by the fact that for most of citizens, civil service means the local civil service, not the national one (Fig. 3).

For ordinary citizens, the image of civil service is just confined to the local civil service; and even for the national civil service, the most frequent contacted national civil service is the mailmen (National Personnel Authority, 2005). For citizens, bureaucrats (literally *Kanryo* in Japanese) recall influential elite (Class 1) public officials at the central government. Japanese citizens may believe that the root cause of problems lie not with the mailmen, but with the

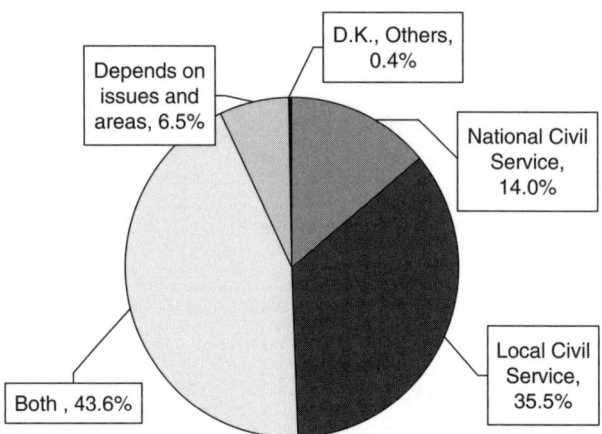

*Fig. 3.* Citizen's Perception of "Civil Service." *Note:* Response Ratio for the Question "Which level of service do you call in your mind with "Civil Service?" Data from National Personnel Authority Policy Monitor Survey (2005).

elite national civil services who are never seen in the daily life. This view may reflect that the bureaucrats had held an extensive power to exercise. But once their image is deteriorated, it could be easy to become disillusioned. Indeed, it is natural for citizens to have more trust in local civil service who serves them in their daily life rather than national bureaucrats whom they never come across. In conjunction with the components of trust in government explained in the previous chapter, local civil service has more relational trust in its proximity; national bureaucrats have negative impacts on performance trust with prolonged policy failures, misconducts, and economic recession (Jennings, 1998; Miller & Listhaug, 1999).[6]

## Trust in Government from Asian Perspectives

This section summarizes trust in government across the countries, especially in Asian regions. Despite common belief that the public trust in government has been on the decline elsewhere, there are large differences among surveyed countries. Fig. 4 shows the cross-national trust level in civil service for 1999–2000 and it does not reveal a clear trend. Trust level is rather low in Japan, Italy, and Germany. On the other hand, South Korea and even the U.S. civil service seem to enjoy high level of trust from the citizen.[7] However, this does not imply that the civil service in South Korea is most

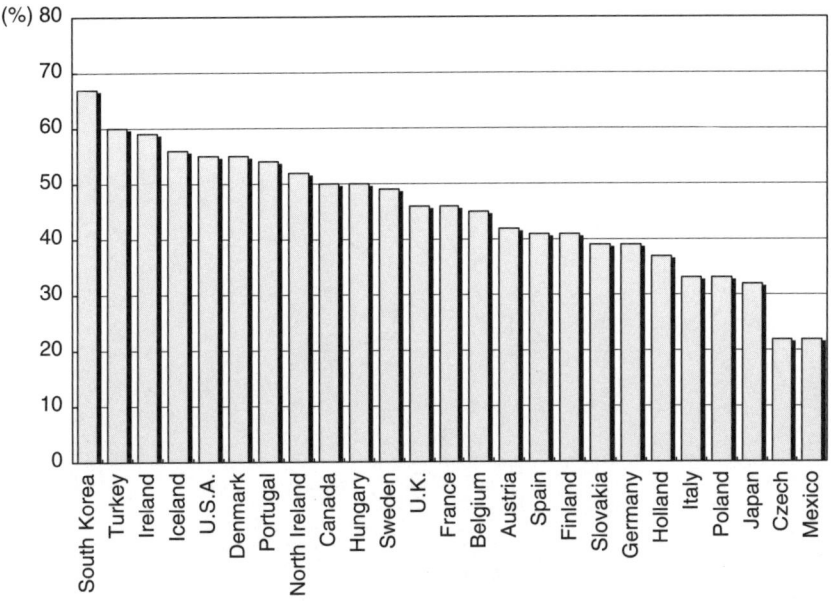

*Fig. 4.* Trust in Civil Service (Data from World Value Survey 1999–2000). *Source:* OECD (2005b).

trustworthy among surveyed countries. Conditions of trust may vary along with each country's "trust culture." For instance, even the level of trust in civil service is high from an international comparison, it may just reflect the "high trust" culture in the country and the trust in civil service could even be the lowest among other government institutions.

In Table 2, there is another perspective, which is the first scientific research on political institutions in Asian countries. Despite being a short, snapshot survey, some salient characteristics can be found. The partisan institutions like political party or parliament are recognized as low trust institutions, while the military is relatively trustful in almost all surveyed countries. Although political and cultural varieties account for the differences must be considered, the data suggest that the government sector (public servant, police, and army) is more trusted than the political sector (parliament, party) in Asia.[8] Also, trust in government in Singapore is significantly higher than in other countries. It corresponds with the Corruption Perception Index by the Transparency International. Here, it does not intend to create a ranking order of the trust level across the countries. The trust level may vary not only with

**Table 2.** Citizen's Trust in Political Institutions in Asian Countries.

| % | Japan | Republic of Korea | Taiwan | Singapore | Malaysia | Indonesia | Thailand | The Philippines |
|---|---|---|---|---|---|---|---|---|
| 80–90 | | | | Police Court Government Public Servant Military Leader | | | Military | |
| 70–80 | | | | Parliament Big business Political Party media | | Public servant | | Media |
| 60–70 | | | | | Government Court Military Leader Public servant | Military Media Government Parliament | Big business Public servant Media | |
| 50–60 | | Military | Public servant | | Police Parliament Media Big business Political party | Police | Court | Military Public servant |
| 40–50 | Military Court Police Public servant | Media | Military Leader Government Big business | | | Leader Political party | Police | Government Court Parliament Police |
| 30–40 | | Police Court Public servant | Police Media Court | | | Court Big business | Leader Parliament | Leader Big business Political party |
| 20–30 | Big business Media Parliament | Government | Political party | | | | Government Political party | |
| 10–20 | Government Political party Leader | Big business | Parliament | | | | | |
| 0–10 | | Leader Political party Parliament | | | | | | |

*Notes*: Survey was conducted on October 2000 at each surveyed country through the Gallup associated opinion poll survey companies. Here the "Government" means "Elected Government."
*Source*: Inoguchi (2004).

the government efforts to ensure it sustains, but it may also be varied along with the political culture embedded in each country. Even then, broadening perspective to international comparison with an overview of empirical data outlining present state and evolutions of trust in government is a good reference to discuss citizen's attitude toward public administration in each country, unless manipulated by political opportunists.

## GOVERNMENT EFFORTS TO (RE)BUILD TRUST

In most nations the government reformers quite explicitly pledged to improve their citizen's trust in government. (Re)building trust in government becomes one of the government reform agenda. This is quite salient among aggressive (former) NPM reformed courtiers (Pollitt & Bouckaert, 2000). In those countries, NPM reforms turned out to entail unexpected consequences; eroding public confidence in government. Theoretically, very fragmented and complex networks create the government hollowing out and they undermine the government capacities to deal with public problems (Kim, 2006). Also, many marketization and devolution processes to both front levels and private suppliers cause concerns about new emerging corruption problems. Moreover, fragmented and complex network of service delivery would result in government insensible and less visible. However, the government position for promoting any reform tends to raise citizen's expectations (Aberbach & Rockman, 2000).

In New Zealand, one of the most aggressive NPM reformers, trust in civil service significantly dropped to around 10% after a series of NPM led reform (State Service Commission, 2000). In the United Kingdom, under Labor Party administration, many initiatives to restore trust in government are underway. The main objective of "Government Modernisation" in the U.K. reform is to restore government capacity, which was once destroyed by NPM inspired reforms and the ultimate goal of the reforms is to restore public trust in government (Committee on Standards in Public Life, 2004; Office of the Deputy Prime Minister, 2005; OECD, 2005a).

### Trust in Government and Reform in Japan

Trust in government is an old and new issue in Japan. Its concept has been found for many years. As early as in 1960s, the government recognized the significance of trust in government. The first Provisional Commission on

Administrative Reform (called *Rincho 1* in Japanese) was set up by law in 1961 and submitted its final recommendation in 1964. The commission was modeled after the Hoover Commission in the U.S. federal government in its authority and structure. The commission member recognized the importance of citizen's support to accomplish its duty in its early session. The commission's activity was expected to encounter severe resistance from the old guard, both from the elected parliament members and the bureaucrats. The commission was afraid of that the bureaucrats would not accept the recommendations and parliament members watered down the reform bill in a legislative process. The commission had to request citizens to support their activity as a final constituency and a reform driving power (Nishio, 1966).[9] The commission utilized public trust in government as a strategic tool to promote reforms. By the same token, the Second Provisional Commission on Administrative Reform (called *Rincho 2* in Japanese) employed the trust in government for a strategic tool to promote privatizations. With the media campaign, they provided many cases on how the Japan National Railway had misused resources in an inappropriate and inefficient manner.

However, the way the government exercise the public trust seems to change after the late 1980s. The collapse of the real estate and stock markets from the speculative bubble economy of the late 1980s left banks with huge portfolios of non-performing loans. It triggered a series of bank crash result in a low growth era referred as "lost decades." For a long time, bureaucrats have been seen as more trustful social agents than the political party members in the government. However, prolonged economic stagnation with these events causes Japanese start to doubt the bureaucrats' capacity to deal with cumulative issues. Japanese commercial banking system was well controlled by the Ministry of Finance with the convoy system and its activity was bounded by strict regulations. Trillions of taxpayer's money was put into banking sector to offset the huge mountain of accumulated bad debts. It turned out how incompetent the government was to adopt the fierce global competition. In addition, high-ranking officials involved in scandals hit the headlines on TV and it accelerated public doubts. Two retired administrative vice ministers, once they sit in the highest position in the civil service carrier, had been arrested for alleged corruption in the late 1990s. Japanese citizens witnessed the dramatic fall of bureaucrats' prestige and clout in the 1990s.

To respond to this severe situation, the government had started to capture the decline of citizen's trust as a serious problem. For the government, trust in government was no longer for supporters to promote reforms. The government had to consider how to restore public trust in government. In 1999, National Public Service Ethics Law (Law No. 129 of 1999) was enacted with the parliament member's initiative and the article one of the law stipulated as:

> The objective of this law is to ensure people's trust for public service, deterring activities that create suspect or distrust against the fairness of performance of duties by introducing necessary measures to contribute to retaining ethics related to the duties of national public service officials, acknowledging that national public service officials are servants of the whole people and their duties are to fulfill public service entrusted by the public.

It was the first legislation which public trust in government was written into the law.

## Major Government Reforms since 1980s at Central Level

There were at least three major reform waves at the central government level: Nakasone Reform (the Second Provisional Commission on Administrative Reform) in the 1980s; Hashimoto Reform (the Administrative Reform Council) in the late 1990s; and Koizumi Reform in the early 21st century. Table 3 summarizes the main reform objectives and contents of the central government reform at each major reform waves. Nakasone Reform was initiated after the Japanese economy was stagnated with oil shock and it was the first attempt to privatize government functions. Three giant government corporations were privatized: Japan Railway; Nippon Telegraph and Telephone Corporation; and Japan Tobacco. The reform was aimed at the fiscal reconstruction with the revision of scope of government responsible sphere. Hashimoto Reform was the most comprehensive reform and its scope was expanded to wide areas: central ministries were streamlined to almost the half in 2001; formal decentralization started in 2000; public information disclosure was legislated in 1999; deregulation was continued in the 1990s; Independent Administrative Agency (IAA), which was Japanese style "Executive Agency," was introduced in 2001; statutory Policy Evaluation System was initiated in 2001; executive leadership in policymaking was strengthened with the establishment of Cabinet Office and political vice ministers and ministers without portfolio. Nonetheless, the main objective of Hashimoto Reform was to improve efficiency of public administration (Yamamoto, 2003; Masujima, 2006). Koizumi Reform was aimed at fiscal reconstruction and structural economic adjustment under the slogan of "From Public Sector to Private Sector"

*Table 3.* Main Reform Objectives and Contents of Central Government Reform since 1980s.

| Main Reform Objectives | Main Reform Contents | | |
|---|---|---|---|
| | 1980s (Nakasone reform) | 1990s (Hashimoto reform) | 2001 ~ (Koizumi reform) |
| Privatization (revision of scope of PA) | JR, NTT, Japan Tobacco | | Japan Highway Corporation, Japan Post |
| Efficiency (NPM) (improve efficiency of PA) | | Deregulation, independent administrative agency | Deregulation, regional deregulation |
| Accountability (strengthening accountability) | | Administrative procedure law, public information disclosure, policy evaluation | |
| Streamlining (revision of scope of PA) | | Streamlining of central ministries, streamlining of number of national civil service, deregulation | (Net) Streamlining of number of civil service both at central and local level |
| Decentralization, central ministries reform (refining national government system) | | Decentralization Central Ministries Streamlining | Fiscal Decentralization Regional Rehabilitation |
| Citizen's participation (ensuring participation) | | Public comments system for regulations change | Special zone for structural reform |

*Note:* Derived from Yamamoto (2003), Masujima (2006) and author's own research.

and "From the State to the Regions": it privatized Japan highway public corporation and Japan Post Office (scheduled in 2007); more drastic streamlining of number of civil service both at the central and the local level; establishment of E-government; more decentralization of fiscal authority; Special Zones for Structural Reform to promote regional regulatory reform. Although Mr. Koizumi was one of the most popular prime ministers for his aggressive attitude of promoting reforms, the reform objective and procedure which his administration employed was not a quite new. The objective and procedure was back to the old Nakasone's style.

## Major Government Reform at Local Level

At the local government level, reforms after the decentralization in 2000 were much more comprehensive and focused more on citizen's participation than central level. After 2000, the extent and significance of local government activities expanded greatly in both substances and kinds. Many local governments, if not all were keen to transform their activities more innovative, productive, and participatory. Table 4 sketches the main reform objectives and contents of the local government reform. Emphasis on strengthening accountability and ensuring participation were more intensive in contrast to reform at the central level. As of 2006, the individual policy evaluations systems were installed in 46 out of 47 prefectural governments and all in designated cities (metropolis), 87% of core cities (population more than 300 thousands), and 90% of special cities (population more than 200 thousands). As for the public comments system, 91.5% of prefectural governments, 71.4% of designated cities, 68.6% of core cities, and 55% of special cities have already installed the system as of 2005. In the same token, as of 2005, almost all local governments (96.6%) have the information disclosure system. All prefectural governments and designated cities have the administrative procedure ordinance to ensure the due process and opportunities for private persons to submit opinions for any administrative actions (data from the Ministry of Internal Affairs and Communications).

*Table 4.* Main Reform Objectives and Contents of Local Government Reform.

| Main Reform Objectives | Main Reform Contents |
|---|---|
| Privatization (revision of scope of PA) | |
| Efficiency (NPM) (improve efficiency of PA) | Outsourcing, administrative evaluations |
| Accountability (strengthening accountability) | Administrative procedure ordinance, public information disclosure, administrative evaluation, public comments system |
| Streamlining (revision of scope of PA) | Streamlining of number of local civil service |
| Capacity Building (strengthening local government capacity) | Municipal merger, Pay per performance, human resource management |
| Citizen' participation (ensuring participation) | Public private partnership with Non Profit Organizations (NPOs) and citizen's group, participatory administrative evaluations |

*Note:* Derived from author's own research.

Above all, with the awareness of critical significance of citizen's participation, many local governments began to adopt the Public Private Partnership (PPP) scheme in every aspect of policy management cycle: intake citizen's opinion in decision-making; outsource the service delivery to Non Profit Organization (NPO) and profit sector; policy evaluations with citizen's participation. In doing so, local governments are likely to change the local governance to participatory, responsive, and partnership governance. As of 2006, more than 30,000 certified NPO play active role in many areas and all prefectural governments. Also, more than 80% of municipalities outsource the services to respective local NPOs (Cabinet Office, 2004). Regarding the outsourcings to private companies, 96% of meal delivery service, 91% of home care services, and 84% of garbage collection are outsourced at the municipal level (as of 2003, data from the Ministry of Internal Affairs and Communications). It is worth to note that these reform measures are not mandatory by laws although they were enhanced to implement by policy guidelines issued from the central government.[10]

*Qualitative Assessment of the Reform Impacts on Trust in Government*

Ensuring trust in government was not explicitly recognized as the main objective in each period of reform both at the central and the local levels. There are still other indirect measures to ensure public trust in government: improving efficiency, strengthening accountability, and ensuring citizen's participation. The issue to clarify is how the each individual reform content influences the components of trust in government even each kind of trust is interrelated to some degree. Table 5 outlines the relative impacts of reforms on each component of trust in government both at central and local levels.

At the central level, performance information from Policy Evaluation System or Independent Administrative Agencies may give a positive impact on performance trust, since the citizens and service recipients can evaluate the services with solid base. In contrast, privatization and streamlining of civil service may create government less competent. Government's responsibility of service delivery became blurred with privatizations. While number of civil service has been on the decline; government responsible sphere has been expanding with the growing number of critical citizens. Deregulation causes troublesome cases. For instance, there has been a big policy debate on the privatization of building inspection authority. Numbers

Table 5. Impacts of Reforms on Each Component of Trust in Government.

|  | Impact | Reforms at Central Level | Reforms at Local Level |
|---|---|---|---|
| Performance Trust | Positive impact | Performance information is provided with policy evaluation system and IAA system | Performance information is provided with administrative evaluation system and citizen's satisfaction survey payer performance makes officials performance oriented |
|  | Negative impact | Privatization and streamlining of civil service make government less competent Deregulation makes government less controllable public information disclosure | Fiscal decentralization makes small and weak municipalities less competent Public information disclosure |
| Relational Trust | Positive impact | Public information disclosure Public comments system Administrative Procedure Law | Public information disclosure Public comments system Administrative procedure ordinances PPP and collaboration with NPOs induces more citizen's participation |
|  | Negative impact | Diversification of quasi-government entities makes government work less visible | Municipal merger weakens citizen's controlability |

of condominiums were turned out to be built and authorized with the poor earthquake proof.

In respect to relational trust, public information disclosure system, public comments system, and administrative procedure law, all these measures have some positive impacts. However, lots of poor performance and management cases were revealed with the information disclosure. This may have a negative impact on performance trust at the same time. On the other hand, with the introduction of Independent Administrative Agencies (IAA), diversification of quasi-government entities causes government less visible. The IAA is a complicated system: its legal status is government, but the status of the staff is private. Also, with establishment of many IAAs, demarcation line between private and public sector becomes quite blurred.

In comparison with the central level, there seems to be more positive impact on trust in government at the local level. Performance information provided by the administrative evaluation furnishes citizens with the solid base information on service. The citizen's satisfaction survey is a part of the efforts to ensure performance trust. Pay per performance system installed in some local governments has forced officials to be more performance oriented than before, and the cases are on the increasing trend. However, fiscal decentralization may have a negative impact for small and weak municipalities without enough tax bases. Public information disclosure system, public comments system, and administrative procedure ordinances have a positive impact on relational trust in the same way as at the central level.

Furthermore, PPP or collaboration with NPOs and citizens has a significant impact on relational trust. This measure may induce the citizens' participation to reflect their view in decision-making and service delivery. Although it is not quite certain these efforts for more participatory, responsive, and partnership local governance become successful, awareness of citizen's participation among local officials has been greatly improved. However, the municipal merger may cause the government to citizen relations far-off and it may weaken the sense of controllability.

In a nutshell, reforms at the central level were much more on performance trust than relational trust dimension. But its positive impacts seem to be rather limited and unsuccessful (see Van de Walle, 2004). There can be many negative impacts on performance trust at the same time. These negative impacts correspond with the side effects of NPM (Dunleavy, 2006; Suleiman, 2005). There are positive impacts on relational trust with the information disclosure efforts toward transparent government. However, these measures seem only confined to be utilized for the exposure of scandals in government. At the local level, there seems to have positive impacts on trust in government. Local governments in Japan are indigenously close to the real public life with extensive list of functions and services. In addition, with more enthusiastic efforts than the central level, many reforms were implemented and there seems to succeed in producing more positive impacts on both kinds of trust: although it is hard to analyze the efforts to ensure the trust level in real term due to insufficient data. Specifically, efforts for PPP or collaboration with NPOs and citizens for participatory, responsive, and partnership governance would have considerable influences on public trust in local governments. Nonetheless, local governments are currently encountering financial difficulties; the citizens would be disenchanted with the fraud of the reform, if the efforts of PPP or collaboration are just resulted in the offloading of local governments' responsibilities to their citizens.

## CONCLUDING REMARKS

It is my tentative conclusion that trust in government in Japan has been eroding mainly due to the deteriorating image of central bureaucracy and the reforms in the central government have contributed little to rebuild trust level, while the reforms of local level have positive impacts on trust level to some degree. Consequently, the influences of reform efforts are confined to the local level more or less. The central bureaucracy was once seen as one of the most trustful social agents with influential powers of the nations. With policy failures to adopt the environmental change (global equal competition, growing awareness of civil society, and the like) and dirty scandals, the trustworthy image has been gradually vanished. The extensive reforms were cyclically implemented within last twenty years or so. There have been indirect measures to ensure public trust in government. Yet, each measure seems not to succeed in improving positive impacts on trust in government.

In contrast, local governments' efforts seem to be comparatively successful to have favorable impacts on trust in government. The wide roles and functions of local governments involve a close relationship with the daily life of citizens. Contrary to the declining role of national bureaucrats and hardly seen their activities, citizens seem to have a much big stake in their local governments. Local governments in Japan have succeeded in developing a sufficiently broad based constituency for themselves. Local governance reforms for more participatory, responsive, and partnership governance strengthened positive impact on trust in local government.

This account is still a plausible assumption and need an empirical scrutiny. Lack of sufficient data causes some difficulties to have a proper understanding of conditions of trust in government and to assess the causality between reform efforts and trust level (Nye, 1997; Suleiman, 2005).[11] Even then, trust in government is a central concern for the government reformers. Without sufficient support from the citizens, the government cannot accomplish the policy target and moreover it will lose constituency and could be dissolved at any times. It is also considerably significant and a necessary prerequisite in the pursuit of sound governance. In that sense, trust in government is imperative for the future role and shape of public administration.

## NOTES

1. When discussing trust, there are broadly two types of "trust" (Hardin, 2000). One is trust among citizen or diffuse trust in society at all. The other is trust in institution. Putnam's work was a catalyst for the issue of trust in government. Nevertheless, his argument of "Social Trust" deals with how the trust among citizens influences the citizen's support for government. On the other hand, "trust" in this chapter deals with the trust in governmental institutions. In the chapter, trust is used as trust in government institutions otherwise specified.

2. As often time government is regarded as "necessary evil" in liberal democracies, certain level of mistrust represents healthy barometer for the democracy. In some countries, trust in government is extremely high whenever surveyed. But this may be because of its authoritarian regime or due to lack of the freedom of political voice.

3. Borrowing from famous Tönnies idea, performance trust can be fallen under the heading of "Gesellschaft" where citizen and government are connected more with common interests. On the other hands, relational trust can be referred as the "Gemeinschaft" where citizen and government are connected more with communal proximity.

4. In author's view, government efforts to improve citizen's satisfaction for services may be a risky challenge. Unlike (or even) in private business, satisfaction cannot reach 100% simply because government services are collective consumption without market principle. Also, government cannot employ individual marketing like CRM (customer relations management) to improve citizen's satisfaction, as "equity" is one of the most important principles for the government activities. Furthermore, asking satisfaction to citizens makes them more dependent on government and it would excavate their hidden demand to government.

5. Number of sample is 1,353 (2000), 1,272 (2001), and 1,483(2004). Ten social and public institutions and average trust level in 2004 are as follows: Self Defense Force (3.3), Judicial Court (3.2), Medical Institutions (2.9), Commercial Banks (2.9), School Teachers (2.8), Police Force (2.8), Big Businesses (2.8), Media (2.8), Parliament Members (2.0), and Bureaucrats (2.0).

6. This view is consistent with the survey of public attitude towards conduct in public life in the United Kingdom. Citizens express higher levels of trust in "frontline" professionals (Committee on Standards in Public Life, 2004). Nevertheless, many cases of misconduct by local public officials are observed in the headlines these days. Most of the cases are understood as the political purge of local public officials union set up by the resistance forces for decentralization process. Local public officials union is the biggest single trade union in Japan and it has more than one million members.

7. Although trust in civil service in South Korea is highest among surveyed country with this data, in the other survey, the situation is different (see Fig. 5). This difference

mainly causes from the sampling, wording questions, and survey timing. Survey on trust in government inventively faces these kinds of "Soft Data Problems."

8. According to Almond and Verba's classical work, the Asian countries are under "parochial" or "subject" political culture type. However, their argument was mainly focused in early period of postwar Japan. Post war development in Asian countries must be considered, although the political culture is the lagged indicator of economic growth.

9. In this sense, the commission was strongly aware of the need for "concrete feasible proposals for reform." But the most of the reform proposals were failed to be implemented and in late years, the recommendations were criticized for not meeting this requirement. However, the commission provided the basic model for pursuit of administrative reform followed in Japan thereafter, especially in Hashimoto's Central Government Reform in 2001 (Masujima, 2006, p. 7).

10. In fact, policy diffusions from the local governments to central government can be observed in many policy areas and management innovations. Central government started the policy evaluation system in 2001 after the Mie prefectural government first implemented individual policy evaluation system in 1996. In information disclosure, one small city in Yamagata prefecture enacted the ordinance as a precedent in 1979, long before the central government enacted the law in 1999.

11. There is at least a significant relationship between the frequency of contacting politicians, government or local public officials and levels of trust in public officials (Institute of Local Government Studies, University of Birmingham, 2006). This account may present the evidence that efforts for participatory government have positive impact on trust in government.

# REFERENCES

Aberbach, J. D, & Rockman, B. A. (2000). *In the web of politics: Three decades of the U.S. federal executive*. Washington, DC: Brookings Institutions Press.
Accenture. (2006). *Building the trust: Leadership in customer service*.
Blind, P. K. (2006). *Building trust in government in the twenty-first century: Review of literature and emerging issues*. UNDESA.
Bouckaert, G., Van de Walle, S., Maddens, B., & Kampen, J. K. (2002). *Identity vs performance: An overview of theories explaining trust in government*. Leuven, Belgium: Public Management Instituut voor de Overheid, Katholike Universiteit Leuven.
Braithwaite, V., & Levi, M. (Eds). (1998). *Trust and governance. Russell Sage Foundation series on trust* (Vol. 1). New York: Russell Sage Foundation.
Cabinet Office, Government of Japan. (2004). *White Paper on National Lifestyle FY 2004*, (In Japanese), Tokyo.
Cabinet Office, Government of Japan. *Public Opinion Survey on Society and the State (each year)* (In Japanese).
Committee on Standards in Public Life, Government of UK. (2004). *Survey on Public Attitudes towards Conduct in Public Life*.
Dalton, R., & Wattenberg, M. P. (2000). *Parties without partisans: Political change in advanced industrial democracies*. New York: Oxford University Press.

Dunleavy, P., Margetts, H., Bastow, S., & Tinkler, J. (2006). New public management is dead – Long live digital-era governance. *Journal of Public Administration Research and Theory, 16*(3), 467–494.
Fukuyama, F. (1995). *Trust: The social virtues and the creation of prosperity.* New York, NY: Free Press.
Hardin, R. (2000). The public trust. In: SJ. Pharr & R. D. Putnam (Eds), *Disaffected democracies: What's troubling the trilateral countries?* (pp. 31–51). Princeton: Princeton University Press.
Inoguchi, T. (2004). *National identity and globalism: A cross national analysis of political cultures* (In Japanese). Tokyo: NTT Publishing.
Institute of Local Government Studies, University of Birmingham. (2006). *Empowerment, trust and local government powers: A report for the ESRC knowledge transfer team.*
Jennings, M. K. (1998). Political trust and the roots of devolution. In: Braithwaite, V. & Margaret, L. (Eds), *Trust and governance. Russell Sage Foundation series on trust* (Vol. 1, pp. 218, 244). New York: Russell Sage Foundation.
Kettl, D. F. (2000). *The global public management revolution.* Washington, DC: The Brookings Institutions.
Kim, P. S. (2006). *Public sector capacity and innovations: Challenges, crisis, and opportunities.* Presentation at the Regional Forum on Reinventing Government in Asia. Seoul, Republic of Korea.
King, A. (2000). Distrust of government: Explaining American exceptionalism. In: SJ. Pharr & R. D. Putnam (Eds), *Disaffected democracies: What's troubling the trilateral countries?* (pp. 74–98). Princeton: Princeton University Press.
Klingemann, H. D., & Fuchs, D. (Eds). (1995). *Citizens and the state.* New York: Oxford University Press.
Luhmann, N. (1973). *Vertauen(Trust).* Japanese edition (1990), translated by Ken Oba and Masamura Toshiyuki.
Masujima, T. (2006). *Administrative reform in Japan: Trends in the latter half of the twentieth century and future directions in the twenty-first century.* Tokyo: Institute of Administrative Management.
Miller, A., & Listhaug, O. (1999). Political performance and institutional trust. In: Norris, P. (Ed.), *Critical citizens: Global support for democratic government* (pp. 204–216). Oxford University Press.
Nakamura, A., & Kikuchi, M. (2006). The declining public trust in government and the changing role of bureaucrats: From a Japanese perspective. Paper prepared at the IPSA Fukuoka Conference, Fukuoka, Japan, RC27(SOG) RC27.18 Bureaucracy and Democracy, July 10, 2006.
National Personnel Authority, Government of Japan. (2005). *The Third National Personnel Authority Policy Monitor Survey* (In Japanese).
Nishio, M. (1966). Significance of public support in the administrative reform process. In: *Annal of the Japan Society for Public Administration Vol. 5* (In Japanese).
Norris, P. (Ed.) (1999). *Critical citizens: Global support for democratic government.* Oxford: Oxford University Press.
Nye, J. S., Zelikow, P. D., & King, D. C. (1997). *Why people don't trust in government.* Cambridge, Massachusetts: Harvard University Press.
OECD. (2000). *Building public trust: Ethics measures in OECD countries.*
OECD. (2005a). *Modernising government the way forward.*

OECD. (2005b). *Main issue for discussion annex: Data on trust in the public sector*. Meeting of the Public Governance Committee at Ministerial Level, 27–28 November, Rotterdam, The Netherlands.
Office of the Deputy Prime Minister, Government of UK. (2005). *Meta-evaluation of the local government modernisation agenda: Progress report on public confidence in local government*.
Pharr, S. J. (2000). Official's misconduct and public distrust: Japan and the trilateral democracies. In: S. J. Pharr & R. D. Putnam (Eds), *Disaffected democracies: What's troubling the trilateral countries?* (pp. 173–201). Princeton: Princeton University Press.
Pharr, S. J., & Putnam, R. D. (Eds). (2000). *Disaffected democracies: What's troubling the trilateral countries?* Princeton: Princeton University Press.
Pollitt, C., & Bouckaert, G. (2000). *Public management reform*. Oxford: Oxford University Press.
Putnam, R. D. (1994). *Making democracy work: Civic traditions in modern Italy*. Princeton: Princeton University Press.
Putnam, R. D. (2001). *Bowling alone: The collapse and revival of American community*. New York: Touchstone Books.
Social Insurance Agency, Government of Japan. (2006). *Status of National Pension Program (FY 2005)* (In Japanese).
State Service Commission, Government of New Zealand. (2000). *Declining government performance? Why citizens don't trust government*. Working paper No. 9 (Authors: Cheryl Barnes & Derek Gill), Wellington.
Suleiman, E. (2005). *Dismantling democratic state*. Princeton: Princeton University Press.
The Central Research Service. (2004). *Research Report on Trust in Social and Public Institutions* (In Japanese).
The United Nations. (2006). *AIDE MEMORIE of the 7th Global forum on Reinventing Government: Building Trust in Government*.
Tyler, T. (1998). Trust and democratic governance. In: Braithwaite, V. & Levi, M. (Eds), *Trust and governance. Russell Sage Foundation series on trust* (Vol. 1, pp. 269, 294). New York: Russell Sage Foundation.
Van De Walle, S. (2004). *Perceptions of administrative performance: The key to trust in government?* Proefschrift tot het verkrijgen van de graad van Doctor in de Sociale Wetenschappen. Nr. 79. Katholieke Universiteit Leuven.
Williamson, O. E. (1975). *Market and hierarchy*. New York: Free Press.
Yamamoto, H. (2003). New public management – Japan's practice, IIPS Policy Paper 293E, Tokyo.

# LINKING ACCOUNTABILITY, CORRUPTION, AND GOVERNMENT EFFECTIVENESS IN ASIA: AN EXAMINATION OF WORLD BANK GOVERNANCE INDICATORS

Gene A. Brewer, Yujin Choi and Richard M. Walker

## ABSTRACT

*This study utilizes World Bank Governance Indicators to investigate government effectiveness in Asia, both regionally and across sub-regions. Several factors seem to influence the level of government effectiveness: accountability and voice, control of corruption, and wealth and income. The presence of a democratic form of government does not seem to be an important factor, but we note that more sensitive measures of democracy might produce more positive results. We then comment on the strengths and weaknesses of the dataset and offer some suggestions for future research.*

---

Comparative Governance Reform in Asia: Democracy, Corruption, and Government Trust
Research in Public Policy Analysis and Management, Volume 17, 227–245
Copyright © 2008 by Emerald Group Publishing Limited
All rights of reproduction in any form reserved
ISSN: 0723-1318/doi:10.1016/S0723-1318(08)17012-8

## INTRODUCTION

In the past 30 years questions about governance capacities and the performance of governments has become internationally prevalent, and performance management has become a central concern in the field of public management (Boyne, Meier, O'Toole, & Walker, 2006; Organisation for Economic Co-operation and Development – OECD, 2005; Pollitt & Bouckaert, 2004). New Public Management (NPM) reforms within OECD nations have accelerated this trend, and currently many public institutions in the world are implementing various reforms to measure and improve their performance. Although growing attention has been given to the question of improving government effectiveness (Boyne, 2003), surprisingly little cross-country research has been carried out using an evidence-based approach (Brewer, 2004; Knack & Keefer, 1995; Van de Walle, 2005). Furthermore, most research about governance and performance has been largely limited to historical case studies, which makes systematic testing and comparison between countries difficult.

In fact, from an international and central government standpoint, large-N studies within a single country (such as U.S. Federal agencies, state health and human service organizations, English local authorities, or Texas school districts) are little more than intensive case studies that supply an incomplete picture of government effectiveness in the country being studied and provide a weak basis for generalizability to other settings or countries. Such studies merely inform us about one part of the public sector in one country, and are typically time-bound. Such "snapshots" do not capture the rapidly changing social, economic, and political environment that frames the public sector, or the dynamism and innovativeness of many public sector organizations. Our point is not to disparage these important studies, for indeed, they have provided path-breaking evidence about government performance and effectiveness, and from a more parochial standpoint, we (Brewer and Walker) have been primary contributors to that growing body of literature. Rather, our main purpose is to highlight the sizable gap that exists in the performance literature on cross-country studies because very few of these studies have been mounted so far. Moreover, the studies described previously may contribute to theory development, but they cannot satisfy the need for more descriptive work on government performance in the Asian region, which is sorely lacking.

To help fill this gap in the literature this chapter empirically investigates the relationship between accountability, corruption, and government effectiveness, focusing on Asian countries. We are interested in Asia because of recent changes. Notably the Asian Financial Crisis fundamentally affected many Asian societies during the late 1990s and led to many countries launching NPM reforms to improve governance in various areas. In addition, corruption levels are a prominent bureaucratic pathology in many Asian countries and have been commented upon for some time (Schaffer, 1986). Furthermore, cross-country studies on governance have mainly focused on OECD and Western countries. This scarcity of research is partly due to the difficulty of assessing information, such as written documents in English (Jones & Kettl, 2003) though a comparative literature is emerging (Wescott & Jones, 2007).

In this chapter we are interested to know if Asia is different from other regions in the world on key measures of governance that include accountability, corruption, and government effectiveness. Our analysis also extends to examining governance capacities within Asia in an attempt to identify some key variables that are likely to influence governance outcomes. Alongside this geographically focused analysis we also explore the impact of societal wealth on progress on accountability, corruption, and government effectiveness.

The present study is organized as follows. The first part summarizes previous cross-country literature regarding government effectiveness. We then introduce the dataset and research method used in this study. The data used are the 2006 update of the World Bank's worldwide governance indicators (Kaufmann, Kraay, & Mastruzzi, 2006). This dataset is particularly robust, for it incorporates various data sources constructed by different organizations. The preliminary nature of this study is evidenced in our findings section where we explore descriptive statistics and use three background variables to explore variations in the accountability, corruption, and government effectiveness indicators. In the conclusion, some future directions for research are discussed.

## LITERATURE REVIEW

In this section, we first review government performance research in cross-country settings. Then we argue that more cross-country studies are needed, particularly in underdeveloped regions. Finally, we explain the need for more studies of Asian countries.

Performance management is currently in vogue in the worldwide public sector, but cross-country research on government performance is relatively rare. Moreover, researchers have employed different indicators for measuring government performance (e.g., effectiveness, bureaucratic quality, efficiency, corruption, and rule of law) due to the lack of agreement regarding the definition of performance. Carvalho, Fernandes, Lambert, and Lapsley (2006) indicate that cross-country comparisons of government effectiveness are impeded by different data collection methods and different definitions of variables (also see, Bouckaert & Van de Walle, 2003; Boyne et al., 2006).

There is a paucity of cross-country research on government performance overall. However, several scholars have conducted empirical studies and assessed the impact of various independent variables on performance across countries. For instance, bureaucratic structure, cultural and social differences including religion or ethnic diversity, openness, administrative reform, bureaucratic structure, and political accountability have been tested as determinants of government performance in the previous studies. La Porta, Lopez-de-Silanes, Shleifer, and Vishny (1999) analyze measures of government performance and their possible determinants in 152 countries. The determinants of government effectiveness are drawn from economic, political, and cultural theories. La Porta et al. (1999) conclude that quality of government is closely related to cultural differences such as religion or ethnic diversity. In contrast, Islam and Montenegro (2002) find that social characteristics, including ethnic diversity, are not associated with institutional quality. Concerning the size of government, the authors suggest that bigger governments are more likely to perform better. However, Afonso, Schuknecht, and Tanzi (2003) and Brunetti and Weder (1999) present evidence supporting the opposite conclusion.

Several studies have shown that bureaucratic structure is a significant factor which influences government performance. Rauch and Evans (2000) conclude that meritocratic recruitment, internal promotion, and career stability lead to increased performance. From a survey in 20 African countries, Court, Kristen, and Weder (1999) find that better bureaucratic performance is associated with more bureaucratic power and autonomy, better career opportunities in the public sector, higher pay of public employees, and minimal shifting between public and private employment.

The relationship between openness and government performance is also analyzed in previous studies. Openness is mainly measured in terms of economic trade between countries. Brunetti and Weder (1999) find that more open countries have better governments. Islam and Montenegro's (2002) study finds the same result. Also, Brewer (2004) conducts an empirical study of the relationship between administrative reform and bureaucratic performance in 25 OECD nations. His study shows that contextual factors (i.e., political risk variables) have a greater effect on bureaucratic performance than the particular type of administrative reforms that have been implemented.

Adsera, Boix, and Payne (2003) consider level of democracy, including civil liberties and free circulation of daily newspapers per person, as indicators of political accountability. They find the positive impact of political accountability on the quality of government using panel models. Similarly, Brewer and Choi (2007) investigated the relationship between democracy and government performance with panel data compiled from 213 countries over the period 1996–2005. Their results showed that democracy was positively and significantly related to government performance. More democratic countries tended to have more effective governments and do a better job of controlling corruption.

To summarize, there are few cross-country studies of government performance, and most of these studies have focused on developed nations. Few studies have examined regional differences, and even fewer have focused on sub-regional trends. The studies mounted thus far have identified some promising variables, but their findings are not wholly consistent. More studies are needed to fill in these gaps and sort out conflicting findings from prior research. Cross-country studies of Asian countries are extremely rare in this line of research. There is an urgent need for scholars to attempt more empirical research on government performance in the Asian region, in part because China and several other countries are among the fastest growing economic powers in the world, and also because the region faces a number of unique challenges.

## DATA AND METHODS

In this chapter we use the World Bank's Governance Indicators to explore accountability, performance, and corruption in Asian countries. The indicators provide data on 213 countries and territories for the period 1996–2005 (the data are biannual from 1996–2002 and annual thereafter). Six dimensions of governance are included in the set of indicators:

- Voice and accountability;
- Political stability and absence of violence;
- Government effectiveness;
- Rule of law;
- Regulatory quality; and
- Control of corruption.

The construction of the indexes is complex, drawing upon data from 25 organizations, many tens of variables and over 30 datasets. Unobserved components models are used to create the indexes, and the resultant measures range from −2.5 to 2.5 with a mean of zero. Our purpose in this chapter is not to critique these data, but to use them to examine variations in voice and accountability, government effectiveness, and control of corruption. Further details of the Worldwide Governance Indicators can be found in the papers by Kaufmann and colleagues at the World Bank (for details, see Kaufmann et al., 2006 or visit www.worldbank.org).

We focus on three indexes: "voice and accountability," "control of corruption," and "government effectiveness." These are selected because they are more related to our interest in public management and policy. Of the others, political stability is more clearly associated with political science while the rule of law is linked to legal studies. Kaufmann et al. (2006, p. 4) describe the measures as follows:

(1) Voice and accountability measures "the extent to which a country's citizens are able to participate in selecting their government, as well as freedom of expression, freedom of association, and free media."
(2) Control of corruption measures "the extent to which public power is exercised for private gain, including both petty and grand forms of corruption, as well as capture of the state by elites and private interests."
(3) Government effectiveness measures "the quality of public services, the quality of the civil services and the degree of its independence from political pressures, the quality of policy formulation and implementation, and the credibility of the government's commitment to such policies."

To ascertain if there were variations in these measures of governance, comparisons between different countries by region, sub-region, democracy, and wealth of nations were undertaken. Countries were categorized into regions based upon United Nations groupings (unstats.un.org/unsd/methods/m49/m49regin.htm). This includes: Asia, Africa, North America, South America, the Caribbean and Central America, Europe, and Oceania. Asian countries are examined in more detail, and the list of countries used for Asian sub-regions and those classified as a democracy, or not, are included in the appendix. We use income level as a measure of the wealth of nations. To classify the countries used in this study, we used the World Bank List of Economies (2006) which includes data for gross national income per capita (in U.S. dollars). Four groups are identified: low income, $875 or less;

lower middle income $876–$3,465; upper middle income $3,466–$10,725; and high income $10,726 or more.

The analysis is undertaken on a cross-sectional panel of 1,369 cases. Descriptive statistics are examined and similarities and differences between groups and measures are made using correlations, $t$-tests, and analysis of variance (ANOVA).

# RESULTS

Our initial task is to inspect the relationships between the three World Bank Governance variables explored in this chapter to determine if there are positive relationships between corruption and effectiveness and accountability and effectiveness. Table 1 provides a correlation matrix that suggests that there are strong relationships between these variables with correlation coefficients ranging from .75 to .94. This suggests that the control of corruption is strongly associated with government effectiveness ($r = .9425$), and that accountability is also associated with government effectiveness, though with a lower correlation ($r = .7744$). These findings imply that government effectiveness is enhanced when corruption is controlled for and societies have voice and accountability channels. These findings are not surprising, but indicate that the measures perform as might be anticipated and give us some confidence to go on to examine these variables in more detail.

To analyze the collected data, we first consider geographical region (Table 2). North America and Europe are ranked first and second across all three domains of governance, respectively. Africa is consistently in the bottom two places based upon these means. Asia's mean score on all three

*Table 1.* Correlation between Select World Bank Governance Indicators.

|  | Voice and Accountability | Government Effectiveness | Control of Corruption |
|---|---|---|---|
| Voice and accountability |  |  |  |
| Government effectiveness | 0.7744 |  |  |
| Control of corruption | 0.7526 | 0.9425 |  |

***Table 2.*** Means of the Select World Bank Governance Indicators by Region.

|  | Variable | Voice and Accountability | Government Effectiveness | Control of Corruption |
|---|---|---|---|---|
| Region | Asia | −.6586994 | −.1139589 | −.2056637 |
|  | Africa | −.6285246 | −.6527322 | −.5947009 |
|  | North America | 1.228333 | 1.704444 | 1.805556 |
|  | South America | .2070455 | −.1645455 | −.21625 |
|  | Caribbean and Central America | .4392814 | .0759756 | .0921519 |
|  | Europe | .821115 | .8216606 | .806803 |
|  | Oceania | .7620619 | −.1151515 | .0616049 |

measures generally ranks at a low position; last for voice and accountability, fifth for control of corruption, and on the mid-point for governance effectiveness. Asia is the only region to display such a range of scores, performing adequately on effectiveness, but more poorly on control of corruption and voice and accountability. Notably, the score for voice and accountability ranks the lowest while the government effectiveness score ranks fourth among seven regions of the world.

If we take a mean of the rankings for all three measures, we find that North America places first, Europe second, and Caribbean and Central America third. Oceania is in the middle placing fourth. Asia is fifth, followed by South America and Africa. To see if these differences are statistically significant, an ANOVA test was run and the results are presented in Table 3. These results reveal that the differences between each region and for each of the three governance variables are statistically significant at the .001 level. Thus the achievements and experiences of these global regions are very different.

In Table 4 we focus more intently on Asia and undertake a $t$-test to compare the means of Asian and non-Asian countries. As shown in Table 4, the mean scores for the two groups of countries are significantly different. For all three measures – voice and accountability, control of corruption, and government effectiveness – the score for Asian countries is lower than the score for non-Asian countries. These results suggest that the performance of Asia is generally quite poor on these measures of governance and that the region's performance is, in broad terms, worse than that of non-Asian societies in general.

The difference between the two groups of countries probably involves more than geographical region because significant cross-country variations

**Table 3.** Analysis of Variance of the Select World Bank Governance Indicators by Region.

| Source of Variance | Sum of Squares (SS) | df | Mean Squares (MS) | F | $p$-Value |
|---|---|---|---|---|---|
| *Voice and accountability* | | | | | |
| Model | 606.8 | 6 | 101.1 | 177.5 | 0.0000 |
| Residual | 776.2 | 1,362 | .6 | | |
| Total | 1,383.0 | 1,368 | 1.0 | | |
| *Government effectiveness* | | | | | |
| Model | 403.5 | 6 | 67.3 | 95.4 | 0.0000 |
| Residual | 948.7 | 1,346 | .7 | | |
| Total | 1,352.2 | 1,352 | 1.0 | | |
| *Control of corruption* | | | | | |
| Model | 377.4 | 6 | 62.9 | 84.8 | 0.0000 |
| Residual | 962.2 | 1,297 | .7 | | |
| Total | 1,339.6 | 1,303 | 1.0 | | |

**Table 4.** Comparing Asian with Non-Asian Countries.

| Group | Observations | Mean | Standard Error | Standard Deviation |
|---|---|---|---|---|
| *Voice and accountability* | | | | |
| Asia | 346 | .66 | .05 | .86 |
| Non-Asia | 1,023 | .19 | .03 | .96 |
| t | | −15.37* | | |
| *Government effectiveness* | | | | |
| Asia | 341 | −.11 | .05 | .89 |
| Non-Asia | 1,012 | .01 | .03 | 1.03 |
| t | | −2.07* | | |
| *Control of corruption* | | | | |
| Asia | 339 | −.21 | .05 | .90 |
| Non-Asia | 965 | .04 | .03 | 1.04 |
| t | | −4.20* | | |

*$p < .05$.

within each region also exist. Thus, income level, another explanatory variable, is employed in the following analysis. Table 5 shows that countries with high income have higher mean scores of accountability, government effectiveness, and control of corruption. If we again rank the mean scores, as

**Table 5.** Means of the Select World Bank Governance Indicators by Income.

|  | Variable | Voice and Accountability | Government Effectiveness | Control of Corruption |
|---|---|---|---|---|
| Income level | Low | −.7845924 | −.8140164 | −.7858592 |
|  | Lower middle | −.3750246 | −.4688557 | −.5259694 |
|  | Upper middle | .4062257 | .1499216 | .0992593 |
|  | High | .847931 | 1.330098 | 1.408562 |

**Table 6.** Analysis of Variance of the Select World Bank Governance Indicators by Income.

| Source of Variance | Sum of Squares (SS) | df | Mean Squares (MS) | F | p-Value |
|---|---|---|---|---|---|
| *Voice and accountability* | | | | | |
| Model | 552.2 | 3 | 184.1 | 303.5 | 0.0000 |
| Residual | 816.2 | 1,346 | .6 | | |
| Total | 1,368.4 | 1,349 | 1.0 | | |
| *Government effectiveness* | | | | | |
| Model | 878.6 | 3 | 292.9 | 846.9 | 0.0000 |
| Residual | 458.5 | 1,326 | .3 | | |
| Total | 1,337.1 | 1,329 | 1.0 | | |
| *Control of corruption* | | | | | |
| Model | 922.1 | 3 | 307.4 | 961.2 | 0.0000 |
| Residual | 410.9 | 1,285 | .3 | | |
| Total | 1,333.0 | 1,288 | 1.0 | | |

we did with region, the results offer very clear and stark evidence on the relationship between governance indicators and country wealth, as measured by income per capita. Each income band retains the same ranking for each governance variable thus: high income countries score first, upper middle second, lower middle third, and low income countries are always last. The evidence in Table 6 confirms that there are significant differences among income groups. The differences are substantial: the lowest $F$-score is 303.5, while for corruption the $F$-score rises to 961.2. This suggests that wealth/income is a powerful explanatory variable of the selected aspects of governance, and more so than the regional aspects examined above (the *F*-scores in Table 3 range from 84.5 to 177.5).

Given the strength of wealth as an explanation of governance capacity, we returned to the earlier correlations reported in Table 1 between the governance variables of interest in this chapter. A partial correlation is used for statistical control, thus we recomputed the correlations in Table 1 while controlling for income. When this is done the correlation coefficients drop from the original values suggesting that income mediates the relationships. The partial correlation coefficient between voice and accountability and government effectiveness is $r = .4806$, a decrease of nearly .3 from the original correlation coefficient, $r = .7744$. When controlling for income, the coefficient between control of corruption and government effectiveness drops by .1 to $r = .8405$ compared to the original correlation, $r = .9425$. Income clearly influences the relationship between our variables.

The remaining analysis focuses on Asia. We present a similar analysis to that reported previously, focusing upon region and income, but also include a dichotomous variable that classifies countries by their democratic status. As shown in Table 7, Eastern Asia (i.e., China, Hong Kong, Macao, Japan, Mongolia, and the Republic of Korea) produces the highest scores on the three measures of interest. By contrast, Central Asia scores lowest on voice and accountability, government effectiveness, and control of corruption. These countries are in the former Soviet block and are transitional economies. Moving up the ranking, Central Asia is followed by Southern Asia, Southeastern Asia, and Western Asia. The differences between these mean scores for each region of Asia were then compared via an ANOVA test. The differences of mean scores among sub-regions of Asia are statistically significant at the .01 level for each governance indicator (Table 8). The biggest difference is found on the control of corruption measure where the *F*-score is 214.2.

*Table 7.* Means of the Select World Bank Governance Indicators by Sub-Region within Asia.

|  | Variable | Voice and Accountability | Government Effectiveness | Control of Corruption |
|---|---|---|---|---|
| Sub-region | Central Asia | −1.324286 | −1.057143 | −1.09 |
|  | Eastern Asia | −.183913 | .386087 | .2676087 |
|  | Southern Asia | −.7985714 | −.3398361 | −.5038983 |
|  | South-Eastern Asia | −.6839474 | −.01 | −.2757895 |
|  | Western Asia | −.5619841 | .0152033 | .0553659 |

Table 9 presents the results of the comparison of means by income. The same pattern of results is found in Asia as was noted in our global analysis. Higher income is clearly associated with higher achievement on these measures of governance. One result of note for the Asian societies included in this analysis are the negative means for all countries on the voice and accountability measure – all of which are below the mean of zero. The results of the ANOVA test on these data again show statistically significant differences between each income group in Asia, with the biggest differences again found on the control of corruption (Table 10).

*Table 8.* Analysis of Variance of the Select World Bank Governance Indicators by Sub-Region within Asia.

| Source of Variance | Sum of Squares (SS) | df | Mean Squares (MS) | F | p-Value |
|---|---|---|---|---|---|
| *Voice and accountability* | | | | | |
| Model | 28.3 | 4 | 7.1 | 10.6 | 0.0000 |
| Residual | 226.9 | 341 | .7 | | |
| Total | 255.2 | 345 | .7 | | |
| *Government effectiveness* | | | | | |
| Model | 48.6 | 4 | 12.2 | 18.6 | 0.0000 |
| Residual | 219.4 | 336 | .7 | | |
| Total | 268.0 | 340 | .8 | | |
| *Control of corruption* | | | | | |
| Model | 51.7 | 4 | 12.9 | 214.2 | 0.0000 |
| Residual | 220.2 | 334 | .7 | | |
| Total | 271.9 | 338 | .8 | | |

*Table 9.* Means of the Select World Bank Governance Indicators by Income within Asia.

| | Variable | Voice and Accountability | Government Effectiveness | Control of Corruption |
|---|---|---|---|---|
| Income level | Low | −1.01319 | −.7214035 | −.7890265 |
| | Lower middle | −.9026786 | −.4737838 | −.6538182 |
| | Upper middle | −.485 | .3033333 | .165 |
| | High | −.0331579 | .9017391 | .9128261 |

*Table 10.* Analysis of Variance of the Select World Bank Governance Indicators by Income within Asia.

| Source of Variance | Sum of Squares (SS) | df | Mean Squares (MS) | F | p-Value |
|---|---|---|---|---|---|
| *Voice and accountability* | | | | | |
| Model | 59.3 | 3 | 19.8 | 34.7 | 0.0000 |
| Residual | 198.6 | 349 | .6 | | |
| Total | 257.9 | 352 | .7 | | |
| *Government effectiveness* | | | | | |
| Model | 156.5 | 3 | 52.2 | 154.96 | 0.0000 |
| Residual | 115.5 | 343 | .3 | | |
| Total | 272.0 | 346 | .8 | | |
| *Control of corruption* | | | | | |
| Model | 179.8 | 3 | 59.9 | 214.2 | 0.0000 |
| Residual | 95.4 | 341 | .3 | | |
| Total | 275.2 | 344 | .8 | | |

Within Asia, income level continues to play a crucial role in explaining relationships among all three measures of governance. Yet after controlling for income, the correlation is still greater than 0 suggesting that there could be a causal link between the two measures. Specifically, the correlations of government effectiveness with accountability and control of corruption are, respectively, moderate (.5286) and strong (.8034) while controlling for income. This is in comparison with the original correlation coefficients (shown in Table 1) which were .7744 and .9425, respectively. All correlation coefficients are significant at the .01 levels providing relatively high confidence.

Last, we run a *t*-test to analyze the influence of democracy on our measures of governance. Asian countries are classified into two groups: countries with a democratic central government (e.g., Japan, South Korea, and Malaysia) and those with other forms of central government (e.g., China, North Korea, and Vietnam). According to the results shown in Table 11, democracy significantly matters for voice and accountability within the Asian region, but not for control of corruption or government effectiveness. This suggests that wealth/income is a stronger predicator of governance capabilities in Asian societies, and a strong predictor elsewhere in the world.

This finding is interesting in light of research by Brewer and Choi (2007), who found a modest positive relationship between democracy and government effectiveness in a study of 213 countries during the period 1995–2006, while

*Table 11.* Comparing Asian Democracies with Non-Democracies.

| Group | Observations | Mean | Standard Error | Standard Deviation |
|---|---|---|---|---|
| *Voice and accountability* | | | | |
| Democratic | 88 | −.39 | .10 | .92 |
| Non-democratic | 67 | −.94 | .12 | .10 |
| t | | 3.50* | | |
| *Government effectiveness* | | | | |
| Democratic | 88 | .01 | .12 | 1.15 |
| Non-democratic | 67 | −10 | .12 | .95 |
| t | | 0.68 | | |
| *Control of corruption* | | | | |
| Democratic | 88 | −.18 | .12 | 1.10 |
| Non-democratic | 67 | −.31 | .11 | .88 |
| t | | 0.85 | | |

*$p < .05$.

controlling for more macro-economic measures of wealth; e.g., inflation, trade, and gross domestic product. The latter variable was by far the strongest predictor in the model. Thus, it appears that economic success – whether at the individual level or on more macro-economic measures – has a strong positive impact on government effectiveness. This finding bodes well for Asian countries that are currently emphasizing economic development and trying to improve their people's standard of living. Future research should try to sort out the impact of democracy, which was not consistent in these two studies.

# CONCLUSION

In this chapter we have examined the relationship between three government performance measures – accountability, corruption, and effectiveness – in a cross-country setting using the World Bank Governance indicators. The results of the analyses point towards four findings, of which the main conclusion is that the wealth of nations is the most likely variable in this study to affect performance on these three measures.

First, we found that both accountability and corruption are significantly correlated with government effectiveness. Countries with higher scores on the accountability and control of corruption index have higher government effectiveness. This might be expected, and it tends to confirm what we know from prior research on government performance. More open and transparent societies are likely to be more effective at delivering public services: no bribes are paid to receive services and government dollars end up in the desired program. Although strong and statistically significant correlations are not sufficient evidence of a causal relationship, they do make causal assertions seem more convincing. In this case, our correlations suggest that an increase in accountability and control of corruption leads to better government effectiveness.

The second finding is that corruption has a corrosive effect on government effectiveness across countries. Government effectiveness is more strongly correlated with control of corruption than with accountability. This finding remains valid within Asian countries. Third, the wealth of nations affects the performance of nations on our three governance variables and reduces the correlation between corruption and government effectiveness, as well as between accountability and government effectiveness. The impact is greater for the correlation between voice and accountability, reducing the coefficient by nearly .3 for all countries in our study, but has a slightly less dramatic impact in Asia where the correlation falls by .25. The relationship between corruption and effectiveness is not mediated to the same extent, but reduces the correlation by nearly .15 in Asia.

Finally, within South and East Asia, countries with democratic governments have statistically significant correlations with voice and accountability at .05 levels of statistical significance. This positive relationship seems reasonable, in part because some sub-indicators of voice and accountability are considered essential elements of democracy; e.g., freedom of association and press, political rights, and civil liberties. On the other hand, the presence of a democratic government within a country does not correlate statistically with corruption or government effectiveness. This interesting finding calls for future research. Although several cross-country studies have considered a "democracy" variable in their analyses (e.g., Brewer & Choi, 2007; Adsera et al., 2003; Islam & Montenegro, 2002; Isham et al., 1997), they do not provide systematic evidence regarding the impact of democracy on government performance (Skelcher, 2006; Treisman, 2000). Despite the common assumption that democracy is detrimental to corruption, empirical results are not consistent with the assumption (Sung, 2004; Trang, 1994).

One implication of these findings is that the variables may be interrelated in ways that have not yet been explored. For example, controlling corruption may increase economic success in a country, which in turn increases government effectiveness. The mechanisms of change also need to be explored and documented more fully. For example, researchers need to explain *how* per capita income increases government effectiveness. Does it merely increase perceptions of effectiveness, or does it act in more substantive ways such as by providing increased funding for government operations or making social problems more tractable?

The World Bank Governance dataset has advantages in that it gives general snapshots on each measure and covers a wide range of countries, but there are several critiques of these measures that need to be taken into account when interpreting our results. The correlations among all indexes are very high. This raises a critical question about the measurement validity of the dataset: What exactly do these indexes measure? High correlations amongst different measures of performance and governance would normally suggest that they are tapping the same topics and concepts, and, as Van de Walle (2006) has noted, it is difficult to grasp what the indicators really mean.

The three World Bank Governance Indicator variables used in our study were created by aggregating several hundred individual variables from different sources. While the aggregation process increases the reliability of indicators, it simultaneously deteriorates their conceptual precision (Knack & Manning, 2000). For example, Svensson (2005) demonstrates that the control of corruption indicator used by the World Bank dataset represents a particularly broad definition of corruption because it aggregates various cross-country sub-indexes which often focus only on specific aspects of corruption. A more technical issue relates to Kaufmann et al.'s treatment of the independence of measurement errors. Kaufmann et al. (2006) assume the measurement errors of sub-indicators made by different sources are not correlated with each other. This assumption can increase the reliability of the indicators, but the possibility remains that the measurement errors are highly correlated because the experts are likely to share perceptions and read the same reports to assess complex concepts. If the assumption of independent measurement errors is disregarded, the advantage of precision from aggregating various sources would be less clear (Svensson, 2005).

More systematic work needs to be undertaken using these indicators to test their robustness over time and also to explore their true explanatory capacity. Researchers should consider unpacking the measures to increase measurement validity. Some sub-indicators may be more useful than others depending on the research questions. Researchers can refine complex, broad concepts by thinning out less useful sub-indicators for their own studies.

Furthermore, the variables used in the present study are not all of the factors that impact government effectiveness. For example, the extent of managerial reforms related to accountability, corruption, and government effectiveness were not included in this study (Knill, 1999; Brewer, 2004). Legal origins also might be related to corruption. For example, La Porta et al. (1999) argue that countries with English legal origins (i.e., former colonies) have less corruption, while countries with French and Socialist legal origins have higher levels of corruption.

Building a new database from the World Bank dataset is encouraged. This effort might have positive effects on the growth of government performance research in cross-country settings. In this study, we have run introductory statistical techniques using small research models with 3–5 variables. With these simple correlation analyses, it is hard to distinguish between independent and dependent variables and plot causal paths. Thus, more fully specified models and multivariate regression analyses need to be utilized in a future study. Though this study is preliminary and suffers a number of limitations, we hope that the results will foster discussion and research on government effectiveness, globally as well as in Asia where more work is urgently needed.

## UNCITED REFERENCES

Isham, Kaufmann, & Pritchett (1997); United Nation.

## REFERENCES

Adsera, A., Boix, C., & Payne, M. (2003). Are you being served? Political accountability and quality of government. *The Journal of Law, Economics, and Organization, 19*(2), 445–466.

Afonso, A., Schuknecht, L., & Tanzi, V. (2003). *Public sector efficiency: An international comparison.* Working Paper. European Central Bank, Frankfurt, Germany.

Bouckaert, G., & Van de Walle, S. (2003). Comparing measures of citizen trust and user satisfaction as indicators of 'good governance': Difficulties in linking trust and satisfaction indicators. *International Review of Administrative Sciences, 69*, 239–343.

Boyne, G. A. (2003). Sources of public service improvement: A critical review and research agenda. *Journal of Public Administration Research and Theory, 13*(3), 367–394.

Boyne, G. A., Meier, K. J., O'Toole, L. J., Jr., & Walker, R. M. (Eds). (2006). *Public service performance: Perspectives on measurement and management.* Cambridge: Cambridge University Press.

Brewer, G., & Choi, Y. (2007). Toward a performing public sector: A cross-country study of democracy's impact on government performance. Paper presented at the Annual

Meeting of the International Research Society for Public Management, April 2–4. Potsdam, Germany.

Brewer, G. A. (2004). Does administrative reform improve bureaucratic performance? A cross-country empirical analysis. *Public Finance and Management*, *4*(3), 399–428.

Brunetti, A., & Weder, B. (1999). More open economies have better governments (electronic version). *Economic Series*, 9905. Retrieved from www.wiwi.uni-sb.de/economics-wp/pdf/wp9905.pdf

Carvalho, J., Fernandes, M., Lambert, V., & Lapsley, I. (2006). Measuring fire service performance: A comparative study. *International Journal of Public Sector Management*, *19*(2), 165–179.

Court, J., Kristen, P., & Weder, B. (1999). *Bureaucratic structure and performance: First Africa survey results*. Working in progress, Tokyo, Japan.

Isham, J., Kaufmann, D., & Pritchett, L. (1997). Civil liberties, democracy, and the performance of government projects. *The World Bank Economic Review*, *11*(2), 219–242.

Islam, R., & Montenegro, C. (2002). *What determines the quality of institutions?* Working Paper. The World Bank, Washington, DC.

Jones, L. R., & Kettl, D. F. (2003). Assessing public management reform in an international context. *International Public Management Review*, *4*(1), 1–19.

Kaufmann, D., Kraay, A., & Mastruzzi, M. (2006). *Governance matters v. aggregate and individual governance indicators for 1996–2005*. World Bank.

Knack, S., & Keefer, P. (1995). Institutions and economic performance: Cross-country tests using alternative institutional measures. *Economics and Politics*, *7*, 207–227.

Knack, S., & Manning, N. (2000). *Towards consensus on governance indicators*. Working Paper. The World Bank, Washington, DC.

Knill, C. (1999). Explaining cross-national variance in administrative reform: Autonomous versus instrumental bureaucracies. *Journal of Public Policy*, *19*(2), 113–139.

La Porta, R., Lopez-de-Silanes, F., Shleifer, A., & Vishny, R. (1999). The quality of government. *The Journal of Law, Economics, and Organization*, *15*(1), 222–279.

OECD. (2005). *Modernising governance: The way forward*. Paris: OECD.

Pollitt, C., & Bouckaert, G. (2004). *Public management reform: A comparative analysis* (2nd ed.). Oxford: Oxford University Press.

Rauch, J. E., & Evans, P. B. (2000). Bureaucratic structure and bureaucratic performance in less developed countries. *Journal of Public Economics*, *75*(1), 49–71.

Schaffer, B. (1986). Access: A theory of corruption and bureaucracy. *Public Administration and Development*, *6*(4), 357–376.

Skelcher, C. (2006). Does democracy matter? A transatlantic research design on democratic performance and special purpose governments. *Journal of Public Administration Research and Theory*, *17*(1), 61–76.

Sung, H.-E. (2004). Democracy and political corruption: A cross-national comparison. *Crime, Law, and Social Change*, *41*, 179–194.

Svensson, J. (2005). Eight questions about corruption. *Journal of Economic Perspectives*, *19*(3), 19–42.

Trang, D. V. (Ed.). (1994). *Corruption & democracy: Political institutions, processes and corruption in transition states in East-Central Europe and in the former Soviet Union*. Budapest, Hungary: Institute for Constitutional and Legislative Policy.

Treisman, D. (2000). *Decentralization and the quality of government*. Working Paper. UCLA, Los Angeles.

United Nation (n.d.). Retrieved from unstats.un.org/unsd/methods/m49/m49regin.htm
Van de Walle, S. (2005). Measuring bureaucratic quality in governance indicators. Paper presented at the EGPA Annual Conferences, Study Group on Productivity and Quality in the Public Sector, Bern, Switzerland.
Van de Walle, S. (2006). The state of the world's bureaucracies. *Journal of Comparative Policy Analysis, 8*(4), 437–448.
Wescott, C. G., & Jones, L. R. (2007). Managing for results and performance in Asia: Assessing reform initiatives in the public sector. *International Public Management Review, 8*(1), 56–102.
World Bank. (2006). World Bank List of Economies (electronic version). Retrieved from www.iscb.org/pdfs/World%20Bank%20Classification%20List%202006.pdf

# APPENDIX. SUB-REGIONS OF ASIA

- Central Asia – Kazakhstan, Kyrgyzstan, Tajikistan, Turkmenistan, and Uzbekistan
- Eastern Asia – China, Hong Kong Special Administrative Region of China, Macao Special Administrative Region of China, Democratic People's Republic of Korea, Japan, Mongolia, and Republic of Korea
- Southern Asia – Afghanistan, Bangladesh, Bhutan, India, Iran, Islamic Republic of Maldives, Nepal, Pakistan, and Sri Lanka
- Southeastern Asia – Brunei Darussalam, Cambodia, Indonesia, Lao People's Democratic Republic, Malaysia, Myanmar, Philippines, Singapore, Thailand, Timor-Leste, and Vietnam
- Western Asia – Armenia, Azerbaijan, Bahrain, Cyprus, Georgia, Iraq, Israel, Jordan, Kuwait, Lebanon, Oman, Qatar, Saudi Arabia, Syrian Arab Republic, Turkey, United Arab Emirates, and Yemen

# FORMS OF GOVERNMENT IN SOUTH AND EAST ASIA

- Democracies include: Japan, South Korea, Malaysia, Taiwan, East Timor, Indonesia, Philippines, and Singapore.
- Non-democracies include: China, North Korea, Macao, Hong Kong, Brunei, Myanmar, Laos, Thailand, Vietnam, and Mongolia.

# ABOUT THE AUTHORS

**Bidhya Bowornwathana** is associate professor at the Department of Public Administration, Faculty of Political Science, Chulalongkorn University, Bangkok, Thailand. His research interests are on governance and administrative reform. His writings appear in journals such as *Governance: An International Journal of Policy and Administration*, *Public Administration and Development*, *Australian Journal of Public Administration*, *Asian Survey*, *Public Administration Quarterly*, *Public Administration: An International Quarterly*, *Asia Pacific Journal of Public Administration*, *Asian Review of Public Administration*, and *Asian Journal of Political Science*. He has written several books in Thai on administrative reform and public administration. He co-edited a book with John P. Burns on Civil Services Systems in Asia (Edward Elgar, 2001). He also has chapters in recent books such as in Christopher Pollitt and Colin Talbot, eds., *Unbundled Government* (Taylor and Francis, 2004), Ron Hodges, ed., *Governance and the Public Sector* (Edward Elgar, 2005), Eric E. Otenyo and Nancy S. Lind, eds., *Comparative Public Administration: The Essential Readings* (Elsevier, 2006), and Kuno Schedler and Isabella Proeller, cds., *Cultural Aspects of Public Management Reform* (Elsevier, 2007). He was Chairman of Department of Pubic Administration, Chulalongkorn University. He has served several times as member and secretary of the national administrative reform commissions appointed by Thai governments.

**Gene A. Brewer** is associate professor of Public Administration and Policy at the University of Georgia School of Public and International Affairs in Athens, Georgia. He specializes in public management research (including public sector reform, governmental performance, and bureaucratic accountability in democratic political systems) and actively visits, lectures, and consults with various universities and governments internationally. His work frequently appears in top public administration and policy journals and other outlets published in the U.S. and worldwide.

**John P. Burns** is chair professor of Politics and Public Administration at the University of Hong Kong. His research interests focus on civil service management, administrative reform, and party–state relations in China, including Hong Kong. His most recent book is *Government Capacity and the Hong Kong Civil Service* (Hong Kong: Oxford University Press, 2004). He has served as a consultant to the Asian Development Bank, the OECD, the World Bank, and the UNDP on governance and public administrative reform issues in China and other Asian countries.

**Anthony B. L. Cheung** is the president and professor of Public Administration at the Hong Kong Institute of Education. Prior to 2008, he was professor of the Department of Public and Social Administration, and associate director of the Governance in Asia Research Centre, City University of Hong Kong. He received his PhD degree in Government from The London School of Economics and Political Science, UK. He has written extensively on privatization, civil service and public sector reforms, government and politics in Hong Kong and China, and Asian administrative reforms. His recent books are *Governance and Public Sector Reform in Asia: Paradigm Shift or Business As Usual?* (RoutledgeCurzon, 2003) and *Public Service Reform in East Asia* (Chinese University Press, 2005). An ex-civil servant (1974–1986) and a former legislator (1995–1997), Professor Cheung is now a Non-Official Member of the Executive Council of the Hong Kong Special Administrative Region. He also sits on several statutory and advisory bodies including: the Consumer Council (as chairman), the Housing Authority (as chairman of the Subsidized Housing Committee), and the Hong Kong Mortgage Corporation board. He was the founding chairman of the policy think tank SynergyNet and sits on the board of directors of the Hong Kong Policy Research Institute.

**Yujin Choi** is a PhD student in the Department of Public Administration at the Maxwell School of Syracuse University. Her research interests are in the collaboration between the government and the nonprofit sector, performance management, and diversity management.

**David S. Jones** is an associate professor, Department of Public Policy and Administration, Faculty of Business, Economics and Policy Studies, University of Brunei. Previously, he held various posts in Singapore and elsewhere. These included Associate Professor, Department of Political Science, National University of Singapore, Adjunct Professor, School of Economics, Singapore Management University, and Local Director (Singapore) of the Masters of Public Administration Programme, Australian National University. Before coming to Singapore in 1982, he jointly worked for the University of Botswana and the Ministry of Overseas Development, UK, and prior to that, he was a professional officer in the Northern Ireland Civil Service. He received his PhD in Political Science from Queen's University of Belfast. His research interests include public policy, development administration, public financial management, and government procurement, in which areas he has published widely. He also specializes in land policy and administration, and has published a book and a number of scholarly articles and essays on land reform in Ireland. Alongside lecturing and research, Dr Jones has frequently undertaken consultancy work in public management, policy evaluation, public budgeting, and human resource management in Brunei, Singapore, and Malaysia.

**Masao Kikuchi** is an Assistant Professor of Public Management at Department of Public Management, School of Business Administration, Meiji University, Tokyo, Japan. Prior to his current position, he was a research associate at School of Political Science and Economics, Meiji University and a research fellow at the Institute of Administrative Management. Dr Kikuchi also serves as a member of Research Committee on Market Testing at Local Governments in Cabinet Office and the Administrative Reform Council at Chiba City. His research interests include comparative governance, performance measurement, budgetary management, trust in government, and comparative local governance. He is a member of Japanese Political Science Association, The Japanese Society of Public Administration, and Japan Association for the Study of Local Government. He holds a PhD in Political Science from Meiji University.

**Pan Suk Kim** is currently Associate Dean and Professor of Public Administration in the Graduate School of Government and Business at Yonsei University in Korea. He had been Secretary to the President for Personnel Policy in the Office of the President of Korea. He served as a member of the Administrative Reform Committee (ARC) and a working member of the Presidential Commission on Government Innovation (PCGI) in the Korean central government. After completing his PhD degree in public administration at the American University in Washington, DC, he was an assistant professor at Old Dominion University in Virginia and Austin Peay State University in Tennessee for several years. He also has considerable international experience, having served on the National Council of the American Society for Public Administration (ASPA) and the Executive Board of the ASPA Section for Professional and

Organizational Development (SPOD). He is currently a member of the UN Committee of Experts on Public Administration (UN/CEPA), Vice President (representing Asia) of the International Research Society for Public Management (IRSPM), and a member of the Executive Committee of the IIAS and the Board of Management of the IASIA. He has been the Editor-in-Chief of the Korean Policy Studies Review, the International Review of Public Administration, and the president of the Korean Association of Personnel Administration. He published several books and over 100 scholarly articles in major domestic and international journals.

**Suchitra Punyaratabandhu** is associate professor in the Graduate School of Public Administration, National Institute of Development Administration (NIDA), Bangkok, Thailand. Previous positions include Dean of the Graduate School of Public Administration, Director of the Research Center, Vice President for Administration, and President of the Faculty Senate, National Institute of Development Administration. She is a member of the Committee for Development Policy (ECOSOC/UN). She has served on various committees and commissions of the Thai government as well as state enterprises. Her teaching fields are organization theory and management, public policy analysis, and program evaluation. She has been involved in numerous consultancies involving evaluation of development assistance programs and reorganization of Thai government agencies. She has contributed articles to journals such as *Asian Survey*, *International Review of Administrative Sciences*, *Regional Development Dialogue*, *Crossroads: An Interdisciplinary Journal of Southeastern Studies*, *Public Administration Review*, and the *Thai Journal of Development Administration*. She has authored and co-authored papers which have appeared in a number of texts on development administration and handbooks. She is the co-editor of *Delivery of Public Services in Asian Countries: Cases in Development Administration*. Her research interests include good governance, municipal and metropolitan administration, and public policy issues of the Bangkok metropolis. She is currently conducting a national survey of citizen attitudes toward good governance in Thailand.

**Jon S. T. Quah** was professor of Political Science at the National University of Singapore (NUS) and co-editor of the *Asian Journal of Political Science* until his retirement from NUS in June 2007. His visiting appointments include: the East-West Center in Honolulu; the Harvard-Yenching Institute and Harvard Institute of International Development; the Institute of

Governmental Studies, University of California at Berkeley; the Stanford Program in International Legal Studies and the Asia-Pacific Research Center at Stanford University; and the National Centre for Development Studies, Australian National University. He has published widely on anti-corruption strategies, civil service reform, and public personnel management in Asian countries. His most recent book is *Curbing Corruption in Asia: A Comparative Study of Six Countries* (Singapore: Eastern Universities Press, 2003). As the lead consultant for the United Nations Development Programme's Mission to Mongolia from September to November 1998, he formulated a National Anti-Corruption Plan for the Government of Mongolia. He prepared a report on "Bureaucratic Corruption in Indonesia: Some Suggestions for Reform" for the World Bank office in Jakarta from March to June 2002. He was invited by the Government of Macau Special Administrative Region to evaluate its public personnel system and he submitted his report on "Public Personnel Administration in Macau SAR: Some Suggestions for Reform" in May 2001. He was commissioned by Transparency International of Berlin in August 2006 to prepare the Regional Overview Report of the National Integrity Systems in nine Asian countries. For more details of Professor Quah's publications and professional activities, see his website at http://www.jonstquah.com.

**Milan Tung-Wen Sun** is professor in the Department of Public Policy and Administration, and also serving as Dean of the Office of Research and Development, National Chi Nan University (Taiwan, ROC). Milan Sun's research interests include intergovernmental relations, local governance, administrative reform, professionalism in public administration, and the applications of Q methodology. Recently, he is also interested on issues of environmental governance, Geographic Information System (GIS), and metropolitan governance. Milan Sun has published *From Authoritarian Government to Democratic Governance: The transformation of public administration theory and practice in Taiwan* (2003, in Chinese), and has co-edited several books in areas of GIS and public administration (2007, in Chinese), intergovernmental relations (2001 and 2004, in Chinese), and Taiwan-Hong Kong relations (1996 and 1997, in Chinese). He has also published several articles on international and regional journals including *International Public Management Review* (2007), *The Journal of Comparative Asian Development* (2002), *Democratization* (with Timothy Ka-Ying Wong, 2000), *Nations and Nationalism* (with Timothy Ka-Ying Wong, 1998), and *International Journal of Public Administration* (with John. J. Gargan, 1997).

**Prijono Tjiptoherijanto** is a professor of Economics at the University of Indonesia in Jakarta, Indonesia. He graduated from the University of Hawaii with specialization in human resources economics. He was the Director for the Demographic Institute of the Faculty of Economics and Deputy Director of the Institute for Economic and Social Research at the University of Indonesia from 1984 to 1988. In 1988 he joined government as the Expert Staff to the Minister of Trade. His recent position in government was the Secretary to the Vice President of the Republic of Indonesia. Now he is conducting research in Malaysia with fellowships from the Nippon Foundation, Tokyo, Japan, on the topic: "Civil Service Reform." He will continue his field research in Thailand and the Philippines. He has been a member of the Committee of Expert on Public Administration (CEPA) of the United Nations, Department for Economic and Social Affairs (UN-DESA) for the period of 2006–2009.

**Richard M. Walker** is professor of Public Policy and Management at the University of Hong Kong (Kadoorie Institute) and Cardiff University (School of City and Regional Planning). Richard's major research focus is an empirical one that focuses on the performance of public organizations, innovation, strategy, management reform, red tape, and environmental management. These topics are examined in Asia, the UK, and the USA. He is co-editor of *Public Services Performance* (2006, Cambridge University Press) and *The New Managerialism and Public Service Professions* (2005, Palgrave). He has published articles in *Journal of Policy Analysis and Management, Journal of Public Administration Research and Theory, Public Administration, Public Administration Review* and *Administration & Society*. He is currently the Principle Investigator on an Economic andSocial Research Council Grant entitled *How Public Management Matters: Strategy, Networking and Public Service Performance* (2006–2010).

**Clay G. Wescott** is director of the Asia-Pacific Governance Institute, and Vice President of the International Public Management Network. He has held senior positions with the Asian Development Bank, UNDP, Development Alternatives, Inc., Price Waterhouse and the Harvard Institute for International Development. Dr. Wescott has degrees in Government from Harvard College (A.B., 1968, Magna cum Laude), and Boston University (PhD, 1980), and is an Editorial Board Member of the *International Public Management Journal*, the *International Public Management Review*, and

*Comparative Technology Transfer and Society.* He has edited two books,[1] and frequently publishes articles and chapters in professional journals and books.

## NOTE

1. For full list of publications, see < www.getcited.org/mbrz/11071824 >